VARṆADHARMA, NIṢKĀMA KARMA AND PRACTICAL MORALITY

Utkal Studies in Philosophy

General Editor
P.K. Mohapatra

Editors
T. Patnaik, S.K. Mohanty
G.P. Das, S.C. Panigrahi

Volume One
ACTION, FREEDOM AND RESPONSIBILITY

Volume Two
GOD, TIME AND EVIL

Volume Three
STUDIES ON THE PURUSARTHAS

Volume Four
REALITY AND MYSTICISM

Volume Five
SOCIAL JUSTICE

Volume Six
FACETS OF HUMANISM

Volume Seven
VARṆADHARMA, NIṢKĀMA KARMA AND PRACTICAL MORALITY

Utkal Studies in Philosophy - VII

General Editor : P.K. Mohapatra

VARṆADHARMA, NIṢKĀMA KARMA AND PRACTICAL MORALITY

A CRITICAL ESSAY ON APPLIED ETHICS

by
Rajendra Prasad

D. K. Printworld (P) Ltd., New Delhi

in association with

Department of Special Assistance in Philosophy
Utkal University, Bhubaneswar

Cataloging in Publication Data — DK

Prasad, Rajendra, 1926 –
Varṇadharma, niṣkāma karma, and practical morality.
(Utkal studies in philosophy ; v. 7).
Includes bibliographical references.

1. Applied ethics. 2. Ethics. 3. Philosophy, Indic. I. Title. II. Series: Utkal studies in philosophy ; v. 7.

ISBN 81-246-0125-9

First Edition Published in India in 1999

Published and printed by:
D.K. Printworld (P) Ltd.
Regd. office : *'Sri Kunj'*, F-52, Bali Nagar
New Delhi - 110 015
Phones : (011) 545-3975, 546-6019; *Fax* : (011) 546-5926
E-mail: dkprint@4mis.com

in association with
Department of Special Assistance in Philosophy
Utkal University
Bhubaneswar (Orissa)

For My Wife
Vidyavati
Without Whom Not Possible

"A time must come when the Indian mind will shake off the darkness that has fallen upon it, cease to think or hold opinions at second and third hand and reassert its right to judge and enquire in a perfect freedom into the meaning of its own Scriptures.

Sri Aurobindo (*c.* 1911)
Michael Danino and Sujata Nahar:
The Invasion That Never Was
(The Mother's Institute of Research, New Delhi, 1996), p. (ii).

"You will not attain to one single truth until you have produced at least fourteen false theories, and perhaps a hundred and fourteen, and that is honourable enough in its fashion; but we can't even produce our errors out of our heeds. You can talk the most mistaken rubbish to me, and if it is your own, I will embrace you. It is almost better to tell your own lies than somebody else's truth; in the first case you are a man, in the second you are no better than a parrot."

Razumikhin to Pulkheria
Alexandrovna in Fyodor
Dostoevsky's *Crime and Punishment* (Oxford), p. 193.

From the General Editor

The present volume is the end product of a project on applied ethics on which Professor Rajendra Prasad worked and lectured at Utkal University as a Visiting Professor under the D.S.A. programme during October-November, 1998. Readers will very well realise that, in this work, Professor Prasad convincingly falsifies the common enough impression that philosophy is concerned with abstract speculations with no or little bearing on practical life. A uniquely creative and critical thinker and a very serious philosopher, the illustrious author breaks away from the conventional way of doing Indian philosophy. Philosophical writing must be critical and reconstructive, says the author, and not reportive, as it often has been in the treatment of the ethical and metaphysical concepts by most Indian thinkers and authors. In this reconstructive role the philosopher must show the effective applicability and use of our ethical distinctions in regulating our life and guiding our actions and solving sensitive moral problems. In morally sensitive situations, like the one Arjuna faced in the conflict between *svadharma* and *sādhāraṇa dharma*, Kṛṣṇa's 'synoptic' solutions make matters much more bewildering rather than helping him (Arjuna) out. With a critical and analytic understanding of the two concepts and of the relative importance of their application in the life of a person, a rational solution can be reached by considering what is the best, morally best, thing to do under the circumstances. "We have to be satisfied with doing what is good enough, or right enough, in that situation", says Prasad, "though [it is] not definitely the best, or absolutely the right, thing to do." And this we do for a morally good reason. If the situation so demands, there is nothing wrong in telling a lie, thereby violating — and this would be a *justified* violation — the moral rule that one must speak the truth. At the same time the author brings home the point that moral theories, like any genuine philosophical theory, must be based on logic. Just as it is impossible to think illogically so also, argues Dr. Prasad, a logically indefensible or incoherent normative theory cannot provide guidance for a morally good life. Only by making our moral theories logically consistent we can apply them to human life for promotion of the good life. The author effectively does this by making illuminatingly reconstructive analysis of the crucial ethical concepts of *varṇadharma* and *niṣkāma karma* which is strikingly original and drastically different.

The Utkal Philosophy Department has not only been enriched by Professor Prasad's heightening intellectual discoures, we have been obligingly privileged by his generous choice of this humble department as the place of his research, even if for a very short time. Our grateful thanks to him for this and for much more.

Utkal University
20 November 1998

P.K. Mohapatra

Preface

THE concrete shape this volume has taken is almost exclusively due to an extremely respectful invitation, early this year, to me from Professor Prafulla Kumar Mohapatra, Coordinator of the U.G.C. Special Assistance Programme in Philosophy, Utkal University, to accept a visiting assignment and deliver a series of lectures in his Department of Philosophy. Because of my stay at Muscat in the early part of 1998, the lectures were delivered in October-November, 1998. The volume contains the materials covered in those lectures with some modification and reorganisation of their content. It was Professor Mohapatra's gentle but insistant persuasion to give the volume in a publishable form at the earliest to him which did not let me delay its completion. My most affectionate thanks to him and good wishes for a still more creative career in philosophy. I am also thankful to his colleagues and post-graduate students for having reacted very constructively to the lectures.

The volume is a work in applied ethics, though the titles of some of the chapters may not bear on their faces any sign of being a piece belonging to this field. Even the classical Indian concepts discussed here have been analysed and assessed from the point of view of their applicability. A normative concept, or theory, to be viable, must be applicable to real social situations. In fact, metaethical distinctions too must be applicable in their own zone, and a few of them are of use even in some morally sensitive situations, as has been shown in the concluding chapter.

Over the problems discussed in the volume I have been thinking for some years, of course, in instalments and in a few cases I have also been making drafts and redrafts. Some of the groundwork was done in the period of my National Fellowship offered by ICPR for which I am thankful to the latter.

The methodology of the entire work is that of conceptual analysis. I have discussed classical Indian views, on the topics covered, in a philosophical, or logical, manner, and taken classical works as human, and not divine, documents, which can be evaluated as any human document can be. I have been critical of classical views and believe that to criticise a view is to show no disrespect to its propounder. It is rather to pay one's philosophical respect to him. I also believe that only after looking critically into classical views we can build on them, or with their help, any new conceptual or normative structure. We have not so far used classical Indian ideas creatively because almost all writers on them have been mostly reportive and not critical or reconstructive.

My primary motivation in examining classical views and concepts in Part I is to ascertain how far they can be used to provide us meaningful guidance in living a morally good life in today's world. It is my conviction that a logically indefensible or incoherent normative theory or concept cannot do that. In Parts II and III I have tried to analyse, and take a stand on, some substantive ethical issues, again, from the point of view of the applicability of the basic ethical concepts relevant to them.

Some of the ideas presented in chapter V appeared earlier in my 'Aurobindo on Reality as Value' (*JICPR*, IX/1, 1991) in which I held a position very different from the one held here. Similarly, some of the ideas of chapter X appeared in my 'Applying Ethics: Modes, Motives and Levels of Commitment' (*Ibid.*, XIV/2, 1997, my General Presidential address to the Seventieth Session of Indian Philosophical Congress). In the present work, too, I have not stuck to the position I held there, and the change in this case is drastic. I am thankful to the editor of *JICPR* for not objecting to my using them in this work.

Before I conclude, I would like to sincerely thank Utkal University authorities, particularly those connected with DSA, and Messers D.K. Printworld, New Delhi for publishing this volume. I also thank my friends Professors K.S. Murty, Daya Krishna, D.P. Chattopadhyaya, P.K. Sen and Bhuvan Chandel for having given me the support which one friend can give to another. My ex-student Prof. Ramesh Chandra and his wife, Dr. Vijayalakshmi, have been of immense help to me not only in academic matters, but also in many other ways to my family. My affectionate blessings for both of them and the dear kids.

Utkal University
15 November 1998

Rajendra Prasad

Contents

From the General Editor vii

Preface ix

Part I
Some Basics of Indian Normative Ethics

1. *Varṇadharma* as Natural and Obligatory: How Maintainable? 3
2. Prescription of *Niṣkāma Karma*: Moral or Non-moral? Teleological or Deontological? 33
3. *Jīvanmukti*: Problems of Normativity and Instantiation 69
4. Dreamless Sleep as Empirical Analogue of *Jīvanmukti*: How Much Appropriate? 103
5. Commonly Presupposed Identity of Reality and Value : Aurobindo's Renovated Characterisation Stated and Examined 121

Part II
Ethics in Practice

6. Inculcating Secularism: the Buddhist Way 137
7. Inculcating a General Dharma : Forgiveness as Moral Cement : Wronging, Rupturing, and Rejoining Social Relationships 151
8. Ethics in Professional Practice : Being a Good Professional, a Morally Good Professional, and a Morally Good Person 204

9. A Problem Area : Business Ethics and the Limits of Applied Ethics 236

Part III
The Background Conceptual Framework

10. Acknowledgement, Application, and Morally Justified Violation of a Moral Principle 261

Bibliography of the Author's Works 290

Part I

Some Basics of Indian Normative Ethics

1

Varṇadharma as Natural and Obligatory
How Maintainable?

THE classical Indian concept of a *varṇadharma* or *varṇadharmatā*, is a basic normative structure of classical Indian ethics in the sense that whatever fits into, or is said to fit into, this structure is a *dharma*, and obligation, of all those who belong to a *varṇa*. *Dharma* connotes and denotes a large number of things all of which are not of the same type. Some of them are rooted in the classical Indian picture of a good life, particularly of a well-balanced social structure, and some others in the then understanding of the existing social reality. Both the groups have inexorable links with a complex of metaphysical, religious, and ritualistic beliefs exercising a powerful hold on the then classical Indian mind. Therefore, almost invariably, accounts of *dharma* contain normative ideas, i.e., ideas pertaining to what ought to be, and what ought to be done, as well as ideas pertaining to what normally is, or is normally done. Putting the two sorts of ideas together is not unnatural because the concept of the normative, as well as that of the normal, have their common parentage in the concept of a norm. This does not entail that they also have the same logic. Concepts originating from the same source, when they survive long in interpersonal communicative use, as is the case with these two, because of the different types of jobs and functions they are required to perform in their life-history, are bound to develop different logical characters. Not only their family resemblance becomes, then, too blurred to be visible, but they also sometimes form their own, virtually independent, families. Anyone, who is sensitive to the logical differences between the ways in which 'normative' and 'normal' function in the present-day philosophical grammar, would find it too common a truth to be emphasised.

The theme of *dharma* has been discussed, or referred to, in technical works of classical Indian philosophy, in some casually or ritualistically, while in some others seriously. But its natural homeland seems to be the world of the Purāṇas, epics, and Smṛtis. Some of them do sometimes mythologise or hypostatise[1] it, but they do provide very good materials for creative philosophising. This I am willing to affirm in spite of Svāmī Dayānanda Sarasvatī's prohibiting us from reading all the Purāṇas except the *Bhāgavata Purāṇa*, which he does not call a Purāṇa, and all the Smṛtis except the *Manusmṛti*, excluding its interpolated parts. His prohibition we have already been violating, since he also prohibits us from reading *Tarkasaṁgraha*, *Jāgadīśī*, *Sāṁkhyatattvakaumudī*, *Yogavāsiṣṭha* etc. Not only the philosophers, but even the grammarians, literaturs, astrologers, etc., did not abide by it, and the Hindi-knowing Indian public still continues adoring the *Rāmacarita-mānasa* of Tulsīdāsa,[2] in spite of his forbidding them to read it.

Because of *dharma*'s having been discussed in so many works and in so many contexts, several views about it are available and the term has come to acquire more than one meaning. I shall not be concerned with even all of the most important views about it, nor shall discuss all of the most important meanings of it. However, I shall like to make a special mention of one meaning of it with which I shall not be concerned here, but which has become very prominent, or, according to some, notorious, in present-day India, particularly after its having become politically independent. What I have in

1. Vyāsa's *The Bhāgavata Purāṇa* (Gita Press, pp. 66-8), shows *dharma* as a lotus-white bull struggling to walk at the dawn of *kaliyuga* on only one leg, since the other three legs have got broken because of the merciless beating given to them by a *śūdra*. The leg which it still has is truth (*satya*) and the three it has lost are penance (*tapa*), purity (*pavitratā*) and compassion (*dayā*).

The Mahābhārata, Vol. 5, Śāntiparva (Gita Press, p. 4577) describes *dharma* as having married Śrīdevī who has come out of the golden lotus which, for a very short while, emerged on the forehead of Visnu. Artha, according to it, is the child of Śrīdevī by Dharma.

2. *Satyārthaprakāśa* (Sarbadesika Aryapratinidhi Sabha, New Delhi) p. 61. The list of works he prohibits to read is quite long.

mind is the use of *dharma* to mean religion.

In almost all of modern Indian languages the word *dharma* has been introduced, or had been in use since long, and it is taken to be synonymous, in popular usage, with religion. There are, of course, some classical scholars, or lovers of classical Indian terminology, who still claim that it does not mean religion. Their argument is that in classical Sanskrit usage it does not mean, and, therefore, it should not be used to mean even in vernaculars, what the English word 'religion' means. This argument is untenable because not only its premise is false, but its conclusion also does not follow from the premise. The premise is false because religion also is one of the various things which *dharma* means in classical Indology.[3] The conclusion does not follow because, even if it does not mean religion in classical usage, it can mean it in modern usage as per the modern linguistic explanation of the ways words acquire new meanings or uses. Moreover, it can acquire this new meaning even if its etymology does not permit, because the growth or development of the meanings of a word are, again as modern linguistics has conclusively shown, very meagrely controlled by its etymology. And, modern linguistics, in these respects, has the full motherly backing of classical Sanskrit linguistics, the laws of which cannot be called irrelevant to explaining the semantics of *dharma*.[4] It is important to emphasise these elementary things because they are very crucial to explaining some

3. In Vol. 6 of the *Mahābhārata*, there is a long section called 'Vaiṣṇavadharma Parva' from pp. 6307-82, in which Kṛṣṇa explains to Yudhiṣṭhira the importance of *dharma* meaning religion. He propounds a religion of his own and calls it *vaiṣṇava dharma*, and gives detailed instructions about what a follower of it ought and ought not to do. There also exist a large number of other places in the *Mahābhārata* where *dharma* is used to mean religion, and so is the case with several of the Purāṇas. *The Bhāgavata Purāṇa* abounds in such uses of *dharma*. Rather, it uses *dharma* more often to mean religion than to mean anything else. It is not an accident that it is considered to be one of the most important religious texts of the Hindus, even more important than the *Gītā*. Listening to the recitation of the *Bhāgavata* for seven consecutive days (*saptāhaśravaṇa*) is called Seven days' *yajña* (*saptāhayajña*). If it is done with all the required rituals, it would surely fulfil, the claim goes, the wish of the listener to fulfil which the *yajña* is performed.

4. *Dharma* is derived from the root *dhṛ* and therefore it is said to etymologically mean that which upholds and sustains the human world. But this meaning it can be said to have even if it is said to mean religion. A sincerely religious person would definitely say that religion upholds and sustains the world.

of the confusions and unclarities involved in recent discussions of secularism which are causing some serious problems, almost a deadlock, in current Indian social and political practice.[5]

In another sense of it, *dharma* means the essential property, or properties, of a thing on account of which it is what it is. It comes very close to the Vaiśeṣika category of *guṇa*. In this sense of *dharma*, the *dharma* of a scorpion is to sting. As a folktale goes, a *sādhu* while crossing a river, out of compassion, keeps on his palm a sinking scorpion and thereby saves her life. After getting out of the river, he tries to put her on dry land. But before leaving his palm, she gives him a severe sting in the palm she has so far been resting on. When the saviour of her life asks her what wrong has he done to her, she smiles and replies: "You have done no wrong, but only a great good, to me. But it is my *dharma* to sting." This is the ethically neutral, or non-normative, sense of *dharma*. I shall not be concerned with it here, as I shall not be concerned with its religious sense. I shall be concerned with its normative or ethical sense, but not with all aspects or ramifications of it. For example, I shall not discuss its place as a *puruṣārtha* in the *trivarga* or *caturvarga*, the three-membered, or four-membered, set of human values, nor with its relationship with other *puruṣārtha*s. This topic, as well as that of its being a means to *mokṣa*, or an independent end, I have discussed in some earlier works of mine.[6] Therefore, I do not want to bore myself by repeating what I have already said on these issues.

I have chosen to limit my discussion to *dharma* as *varṇadharma* the concept of which is a very specific, and also very neat, crystalisation, or systematisation, of *dharma* as a basic normative ethical structure, or code, available in the classical theory of society as *varṇa-vyavasthā* (a system or organisation of classes or castes of the then Indian people).

I shall refer to the concept of *āśrama-dharmatā* (i.e., that of

5. For an elaboration and analysis of some of the issues involved in the Indian concern with secularism see chapter VI of this book.

6. See my *Karma, Causation, and Retributive Morality* (ICPR, New Delhi), Chapters 13, 14, & 15, and my "The Theory of Puruṣārthas: A Proforma of Human Values", *Studies on the Purusarthas* ed. by P.K. Mohapatra (DSA in Philosophy, Utkal University, Bhubaneswar, 1994).

being a *dharma* of any one of the four stages of an individual's life), or to some aspect or aspects of the general theory of *dharma*, only when required to clarify some issue or issues arising out of my concern with *varṇadharmatā*. Even in dealing with the latter I shall primarily attend to some of those aspects or implications of it which create some serious logical or theoretical, or normative or practical, problems. Such an endeavour would obviously be critical, but I would also not hesitate to take an ethical stand, or to be reconstructive in offering an analysis or interpretation, when the logic of my endeavour requires me to. I do not think philosophical neutrality is always an inviolable virtue.

The theory of *varṇāśrama-dharma*, putting it a little too precisely, is one about the duties of the four classes, or castes, of people into which the classical Hindu society was then divided and about those of the four stages of an individual's life into which the latter was divided. This four-fold division of the society into the four *varṇa*s called *brāhmaṇa*, *kṣatriya*, *vaiśya* and *śūdra*, and of the individual's life into four *āśrama*s called *brahmacarya*, *gārhasthya*, *vānprastha* and *saṁnyāsa*, was taken to be complete and exhaustive. According to the theory, a set of duties, or *dharma*s, called *varṇadharma*s, are prescribed for everyone as a member of the *varṇa* he belongs to, i.e., as a *brāhmaṇa*, a *kṣatriya*, a *vaiśya*, or a *śūdra*. In a similar way, some specific duties are prescribed for each *āśrama* of the life of an individual belonging to each one of the first three *varṇa*s. The *āśrama*-wise assignment of duties does not seem to have been done for the *śūdra*, and there are indications in the tradition that all the four *āśrama*s or stages were not normally available to him.

Manu says[7] that the *brāhmaṇa*, *kṣatriya* and *vaiśya* are twice-born (*dvija*) because the first time they are biologically born and the

7. ब्राह्मणा: क्षत्रियो वैश्यस्त्रयो वर्णा द्विजातय: ।
चतुर्थ एकजातिस्तु शूद्रो नास्ति तु पंचम: ।। ४ ।।

The Manusmṛti, chapter 10 (Vaidika Dharma-Śāstra Prakasan, New Delhi), p. 188:4

The three *varṇas* — *brāhmaṇa*, *kṣatriya*, and *vaiśya* (because of their having-undergone the culturisation ceremonies, *saṁskāras*) — are twice-born and the fourth *varṇa*, *śūdra* (not having undergone those *saṁskāras*), is only once-born. There is no fifth *varṇa*.

second time culturally when they undergo, in the school, under the teacher's direction, such cultural ceremonies (*saṁskāra*s) as being given the sacred thread (*yajñopavīta*), etc. The second birth is metaphorical, and it may be called initiation into the process of culturisation. The *śūdra*, on the other hand, is not allowed to undergo such ceremonies, and therefore, he is born only once, i.e., only biologically, and never culturally, born (*ekajanmā*). Since these ceremonies were held in the school under the *guru*'s direction, the implication is that the *śūdra* was not allowed to be admitted in any school, i.e., not allowed to be formally educated. To be taught the Vedas was an important constituent of one's formal education or culturisation. Therefore, it is reasonable to assume that the *śūdra* was not allowed to be taught the Vedas because he was not allowed to be taught. His only duty is said to be his service to the other three *varṇa*s all his life. This means that his life consisted of only one *āśrama*, the *āśrama* of life-long service which is not even remotely comparable to anyone of the four *āśrama*s of the life of a member of anyone of the other three *varṇa*s. He was not allowed to own any property and his cost of living was to be met by his master, the person he served. It was the latter's duty to meet all his needs, for example, his clothing needs by giving him his old, torn, clothes which had become unusable for him, etc.[8] Therefore, he had only one obligation, namely, the obligation to serve his master, and no other, not even one to look after himself.

I shall not give any detailed account, or even a list, of *varṇadharma*s, the *dharma*s every *varṇa* is required to fulfil, because I am more interested in discussing *varṇadharmatā* as a basic ethical or normative structure. My treatment is not intended to be exhaustively, or even primarily, historical, narrative, or

8. अधार्याणि विशीर्णानि वसनानि द्विजातिभीः ।।
शूद्रयैव प्रदेयानि तस्य धर्मधनं हि तत् । 33-34 [said by Bhīṣma to Yudhiṣṭhira]

The Mahābhārata, Vol. 5, Śāntiparva, p. 4580:29, 30, 32, 33-4. Old and torn cloths, which have become unwearable for a twice-born, should be given by him only to the *śūdra* serving him because morally they are the property of that *śūdra*.

(There is mention of some other used articles, in the first line, not quoted here, of 32, which may be given by the master *dvijāti* to the *śūdra* in his service. They are umbrellas, turbans, cosmetics, shoes, fans, etc. — R.P.)

exegetical. But I shall give the details which are necessary for, or relevant to, providing the contextual ground, or background, of the points, conceptual, critical, or reconstructive, I shall make in the course of the discussion. Moreover, details about the *varṇadharma*s are readily available at so many places.[9]

About the origin of the four *varṇa*s, I shall mention two accounts which are generally referred to in philosophical or sociological discussions about classical Indian morals.[10]

(1) One account is that of ancient Indian historians. According to it the *varṇa*, or caste-system, was the result of division of labour. As per the needs of the society and in accordance with the capabilities of its members, different sorts of functions were assigned to different types of people, with the possiblity of a change in the assignments with a change in the capabilities of individuals. The system had nothing, say the historians, to do with the birth-conditions of individuals. But when did this system begin, how long did it continue, what was the actual *modus operandi* of the assignment of duties, how frequent was the change from the existing *varṇa* of an individual to another consequent upon a relevant change in his capabilities, etc., are still questions which cannot be answered even with a tolerable amount of accuracy. And, it is also true that quite early in the history of India the *varṇa* system became birth-determined. That is, the caste of an individual got determined by the caste of his parents, in most cases, of his father, no matter what sort of capabilities or aptitudes he had.[11]

9. The following may be consulted:

The Gītā, XVIII.41-8, the *Bhāgavata Purāṇa*, Gita Press, Seventh Skandha, chapters. 11-15, pp. 422-35, The *Manusmṛti*, IX.317-36, X.1.131. The *Gītā* is a part of the *Mahābhārata*, occurring in the Bhīṣmaparva. But the *Mahābhārata* refers to *varṇadharma*s in so many other sections of it as well. For example, in the Śāntiparva, chapters 60-3 give a lot of information about them. Vālmīki's *Rāmāyaṇa* and Tulsīdās's *Rām-carita-mānasa* also refer to them here and there.

10. There is also available a third account according to which the first division of the society was into *Ārya*s who were of white complexion and *Anārya*s or *śūdra*s who were of black complexion. But it is not clear how the white *Ārya*s were again divided into three *varṇa*s of *brāhmaṇa*s, *kṣatriya*s, and *vaiśya*s.

11. For some interesting details, see the *Manusmṛti*, X.5-62.

It is this system which is in existence today, with the difference that the number of castes has become many times more than the classical four. But the birth-factor, as the sole determinant of one's caste, still has its unalterable authority. That is why an illiterate *brāhmaṇa*, if born in a *caturvedī* family, calls himself a *caturvedī* (knower of the four vedas), even if he has no idea about what kind of a thing a Veda is. On the other hand, a non-*brāhmaṇa* scholar of all the Vedas, and many other classical works besides, cannot call himself even an *ekavedī* (knower of only one Veda).

(2) The second is the theological account which can also be called the theory of the divine origin of the castes. According to it the four *varṇa*s emerged from, or were created by, god himself. The *Bhāgavata* version,[12] as directly narrated by Kṛṣṇa himself to Uddhava, and reported by Śukadeva to king Parīkṣita, is that from the mouth of the *virāṭa puruṣa*, who is none other the Kṛṣṇa himself, emerged the *brāhmaṇa*, from his arms the *kṣatriya*, from his thighs the *vaiśya* and from his feet the *śūdra*, having their importance that descending order. There is also a mention here of a class of people called the *antyaja*, the last born, who perhaps were taken to be the lowest among the *śūdra*s. They were considered even by Kṛṣṇa to be the lowest because, according to him, it was in their nature to be impure (*apavitra*), to lie, to steal, not to care for god and the otherworld, to quarrel for no reason, and to remain subjugated by sex, anger, and lust. He does not attribute such a lowly nature to any other *varṇa*.

A similar version is found in the *Gītā*, chapter IV.13, in which Kṛṣṇa avers that the four *varṇa*s have been created by him in accordance with their *guṇa*s and *karma*s. He makes no mention of the *antyaja*. A little later, in chapter XVIII.41-9, he mentions the *dharma*s, or duties, assigned by him to them. Arjuna is the direct recipient of this account from Kṛṣṇa in the battle-field of Kurukṣetra, purportedly recorded and reported by Vyāsa. The *Bhāgavata* and *Gītā* versions are not very different from each other. Śaṅkara, while

12. *The Bhāgavata Purāṇa*, Skandha 11, chapter 17, pp. 908-9.

commenting on IV.13 of the *Gītā* in his commentary on the *Gītā*, refers to the *Bhāgavata* version as that of the Śruti and supportive of the *Gītā*'s.[13]

The theory of *varṇadharmatā*, particularly the *Gītā* version of it, still seems to have a great hold on the Indian mind, perhaps more on the mind of the literati than on that of the laity. It definitely has a great hold on the mind of quite a few of modern Indian philosophers. This fact is one of my reasons for choosing it for discussion in this chapter.

Among the commentators on the *Gītā*, neither the classical ones like Śaṅkara, Rāmānuja, or Śrīdhara Svāmī, nor the modern ones like Bāl Gāṅgādhar Tilak, or Śrī Aurobindo, question the divine origin of the *varṇas*, or the divine assignment of their *dharmas*. It is surprising that even Tilak and Aurobindo do not do that in spite of their knowing the history of ancient India well.

Although many modern philosophers, Indian as well as non-Indian, have discussed this theory, they do not seem to have highlighted those aspects of it which need to be highlighted in a *philosophical* treatment of it. It has been claimed by many to be an almost perfect theory of man's duties. Tilak and Aurobindo consider it as almost paradigmatic of an ethical theory, or rather of a general theory of human values.[14] Most of the recent writers on it do not seem to lag behind them in their admiration for it. But it seems to me that, if some of the aspects, or claims, of it, which will be discussed here, are studied in a non-partisan, critically philosophical, manner, serious objections can be raised, on both theoretical and practical grounds, against calling it a viable ethical, or normative theory. This is my second reason for choosing it for a close examination.

The creation of the four *varṇas* has been done by Kṛṣṇa, according to Kṛṣṇa himself, by means of the classification of their *guṇas* (*guṇavibhāgaśaḥ*) and of their *karmas* or duties (*karmavibhāgaśaḥ*). In the being of every individual there exist the

13. Śaṅkara: *The Gītā-Bhāṣya*, (Gita Press), pp. 112-13.

14. Bāl Gaṅgādhar Tilak, *Śrīmadbhāgavadgītā-Rahasya*, chapter 15; Śrī Aurobindo, *Essays on the Gītā*, 2nd series, Part II, chapter 20.

three *guṇas*, *sattva*, *rajas*, and *tamas*, though the relation of dominance or subjugation, among the three differs from one individual to another. As per Śaṅkara's elaboration,[15] a *brāhmaṇa* is he in whom *sattva* is predominant. In a *kṣatriya rajas* is predominant and *sattva* is secondary. In a *vaiśya*, *rajas* predominates and *tamas* occupies the secondary position. A *śūdra*, on the other has, is one in whom *tamas* predominates, and *rajas* is secondary. The implication of leaving some *guṇa*, or, *guṇas*, unmentioned in each case, it seems to me, is not that they are totally absent, but that they are present only minimally. For example, in *brāhmaṇas rajas* and *tamas*, in *kṣatriyas tamas*, in *vaiśyas sattva*, and in *śūdras sattva*, can be said to have only a minimal existence. The three *guṇas* are the consituents of *prakṛti*, the primal matter, and nothing worldly can remain devoid of any one of them.

The nature (*svabhāva*) of an individual, belonging to any *varṇa,* is determined by his *guṇa* complex. Thus the nature, or natural property, of a *brāhmaṇa* who is *sattva*-dominated, is tranquillity (*śānti*), that of a *kṣatriya*, who is *rajas*-dominated with *sattva* subordinated to his *rājasika* nature or lordliness (*aīśvarya*), that of a *vaiśya*, who is *rajas*-dominated with *tamas* subordinated to his *rājasika* nature, industriousness (*ceṣṭā*), and that of a *śūdra*, who is *tamas*-dominated with *rajas* subordinated to his *tāmasika* nature, dullness (*mūḍhatā*). The duties of the individuals of each *varṇa* are determined in accordance with their nature. For example, those of a *brāhmaṇa*, or of the *brāhmaṇa* caste, are control of internal organs (*śam*), control of external organs (*dam*), purity (*śauca*), knowledge (*jñāna*), wisdom (*vijñāna*), etc., those of a *kṣatriya* heroism (*śaurya*), boldness (*teja*), not running away from a battle (*yuddhe apalāyanam*) etc.; these of a *vaiśya* farming (*kṛṣi*), trade (*vāṇijyaṁ*), etc., and that of a *śūdra* to do anything which is of the nature of a service to anyone belonging to the other three *varṇas* (*paricaryātmakaṁ*). Each one of the *varṇadharmas*, or duties assigned to the members of each one of the four *varṇas*, is said to be natural because it is born out of his nature (*svabhāvajam*),[16] i.e., assigned to him on account of his having the nature he actually has.

15. Śaṅkara, *The Gītā-Bhāṣya*, (Gita Press), pp. 112-13.
16. *The Gītā-Bhāṣya*, pp. 434-7.

Every *varṇadharma* of an individual of every *varṇa* is thus bound to be in concordance with, suitable to, or fitting, his nature. It means that if something is a duty for an individual, it is something he is naturally capable of and disposed to doing, i.e., something which is natural for him to do. This point is emphasised by Kṛṣṇa by repeating, in each one of the three *ślokas* stating the duties of each one of the *varṇas*, the word *svabhāvajam* (XVIII.42-4). Since natural propensities and capabilities differ in individuals belonging to different *varṇas* different sets of duties have been assigned to individuals of different *varṇas*.

There is no mention anywhere, not only in the *Gītā* but even in any other work I have looked into, of a *varṇadharma* one is not naturally disposed to do, or is naturally disposed not to do, but can be taught, trained, or conditioned, to do, and be required to do, on the ground that it is worth doing in spite of its not being a natural thing for him, or his *varṇa*, to do. The question 'Can morality be taught?', or 'Cannot one be trained to inculcate a virtue he, as per his present natural propensities and predispositions, is not disposed to inculcate?', does not seem to have been raised in the *varṇadhārmika* tradition, though an affirmative answer, particularly to the latter question, is a presupposition of any worthwhile effort to raise the cultural status of a culturally undeveloped, underdeveloped, or maldeveloped, people, or sector of society.

We can say, then, that a *varṇadharma*, or a duty, of an individual is natural for him to do because it has been assigned to him by god on account of his having the nature he has. Thus, duty is, for the *Gītā*, nature-born. But is it the only thing which is nature-born? May not a non-duty also be nature-born? If this is possible, of the nature-born things some would, and some others would not, be duties. We cannot then say of an action, simply from knowing that it is nature-born, that it is a duty. When it is possible that both a duty and a non-duty are nature-born, nature-bornness (*svabhāvajatā*) cannot be the duty-making property of any action, i.e., the criterion of an action's being a duty, because the duty-making property of an action cannot be present in another action which is a non-duty. The same property, which is present in two actions, cannot make one action a duty and the other a non-duty.

From this it also follows that its presence in any action cannot make it a duty. Therefore, there has to be another property of actions, a property other than their nature-bornness, or *svabhāvajatā*, which is present in duties and only in duties, on the basis of which we may call one action a duty and another, in which it is absent, a non-duty. Kṛṣṇa does not mention any such property. And if he does, he would thereby be giving up his original claim that all duties, or *varṇa-dhārmika karma*s, of all the *varṇa*s are *svabhāvaja*, i.e., solely determined by the natural qualities, and by nothing else, of the individuals belonging to them.

But Kṛṣṇa does not seem to admit that a non-duty, a non-*varṇa-dhārmika* action, could also be nature-born, or natural. Perhaps this is why the problem posed above does not occur to him. But it is not an unreal problem because the empirical possibility of an *adharma* having roots in an individual's nature cannot be denied outright. On the other hand, if the *varṇadharma* theory denies it, and affirms that only *dharma* and nothing else is nature-born, or natural, then everything natural would become a *dharma*, a duty. This would be a moral untruth because it is a fact, and was a fact even in ancient India, that some of the things which some individuals sometimes naturally do (did) are (were) obviously wrong, or, *adhārmika*. That some individuals sometimes naturally forbear doing some of their *dharma*s is also a classical, as well as a contemporary, truth.

In one sense of 'do', we do only that which we naturally, willingly, or freely, do. It is such actions for which we are held responsible. When we have been forced, or coerced, to do something, we feel like saying that we did not really do it, but were made, or caused, to do it. Normally we do not blame a man for having done something wrong when he has been forced by someone else to do it. That is, one can be said to have really done an *adharma* only if he has done it naturally, i.e., done it being naturally disposed to have done it. But if every natural action is called, or made, a *varṇadharma* of the doer, then all natural actions, i.e., actions which can be called right or wrong, would become right or *varṇa-dhārmika*. The distinction between right and wrong, *varṇa-dhārmika* and *varṇa-adhārmika*, actions would then vanish because it can, conceptually speaking, exist only between any two actions which have been done in a natural, uncoerced, manner. This means that it cannot be maintained either (a) that all *varṇadharma*s are nature-born but all nature-born actions are not *varṇa-dhārmika*, or (b) that all *varṇadharma*s are nature-born and all nautre-born actions are *varṇa-dhārmika*. If we assert (a), we shall have to give up the *varṇa-dharma* theory's claim that an action's *svabhāvajatā* is the criterion of its *varṇadharmatā*. If we assert (b), we obliterate the distinction between right and wrong, or *varṇa-dhārmika* and non-*varṇa-dhārmika*, actions. This is a conceptual, or theoretical, deadlock the *varṇadharma* theory lands itself in because of its basic premise, or claim, that all *varṇadharma*s are *svabhāvaja*. It seems to me that it cannot emancipate itself from the deadlock unless it introduces some radical change in its conceptual and/or normative structure.

For the *varṇa-dhārmika* theory *svabāvajatā* of an action is a necessary condition of its being a *varṇadharma*. That is, if *X* is a *varṇadharma*, it necessarily is *svabhāvaja*. The theory is silent about whether or not *svabhavajatā* is also a sufficient condition of *varṇadharmatā*. But the way it emphasises the importance of the *svabhavajatā* of an action in its *varṇadharmatā*, it gives the impression that it alone is required, or is sufficient, according to the theory, to make an action a *varṇadharma*. This is obvious particularly in its giving an overriding role to a *svadharma*, a role which makes it inviolable. Therefore, it can be said that, though the theory does not openly say that *svabhāvajatā* is both a necessary and a sufficient condition of *varṇadharmatā*, in practice it does treat the former as if it were both. The logical consequence of all this would be, as has been already shown, that all *varṇadharma*s are *svabhāvaja*, which the theory maintains, and all *svabhāvaja* actions are *varṇa-dhārmika*, i.e., duties, which no theory can maintain, since it would abolish the distinction between duties and non-duties. But let us not worry about this unpleasant episode in the life of the theory, and proceed to examine the role it assigns to *svadharma* in the *varṇa-dhārmika* world to play.

The *varṇadharma* of an individual *A* is his *svadharma*, his own *dharma*, *because* it is determined or regulated by his own nature (*svabhāva-niyata-karma*). It has to be different from the *varnadharma*, or *svadharma*, of *B* belonging to another *varṇa* because the latter would be determined by *B*'s nature which would be different from *A*'s nature. Obviously, then, *B*'s *svadharma* would be, for *A*, a *paradharma*, another man's *dharma*, or, more accurately, another *varṇa*-man's *dharma*. Kṛṣṇa says twice that one's own defective duty, or defectively performed duty, is more meritorious than a non-defectively performed, or well-performed, duty of another man (*Gītā*, III.35, XVIII.47). He goes to the length of saying that even meeting death while performing one's own duty (*svadharma*) is better, and another man's duty (*paradharma*) is full of fear, or is fear-yielding (*bhayāvaḥ*). He who performs his *svadharma*, a duty determined, or regulated, by his own nature, incurs no sin. Śaṅkara elaborates it by adding that, just as to a worm born in venom, venom does no harm, in a similar way a man who does an action determined by his nature incurs no sin.[17]

Kṛṣṇa exhorts Arjuna never to give up his *svadharma* which is his *sahaja* or *sahajanya*, i.e., a duty since his birth, a duty he is born with, even if it suffers from some defect. Everything which is initiated, or begun (*sarvārambhāḥ*), i.e., every action contains some defect, just as every fire is covered with some smoke (*Gītā*, XIII.48). Therefore, another man's *dharma* would also be defective, and in addition, fear-producing. Then why not do only one's own *dharma* (*svadharma* or *sahaja-dharma*) which causes no sin? The sum and substance of all this is that one's own *dharma*, *svadharma* or *varṇadharma*, i.e., the *dharma* that is natural to him, ought to be always done and another man's *dharma*, because it is not natural to him, ought not to be even attempted. That is, one should do the *dharma* which is natural, and only that which is natural, to him. Since it is not admitted by the theory that the natural may sometimes be non-*dhārmika*, it seems to make the natural and the *varṇa-dhārmika*, or obligatory, co-extensive: What is natural is obligatory and what is obligatory is natural. As I have already pointed out, in such a theoretical framework or structure, we would have only two options: Either to accept that, according to the *varṇa-dhārmika* theory, what one is naturally disposed to do is always morally right (or never morally wrong), which is an untruth, or to conclude that, if it could sometimes be right and sometimes wrong,

17. Śrī Aurobindo, *Essays on the Gītā*, p. 497; Śaṅkara, *Gītā Bhāṣya*., p. 433.

then, the theory fails to give any criterion to distinguish between the right and the wrong.

Whether or not the theory makes the natural and the obligatory co-extensive, there is another problem, and not an easy one, with making the naturalness (*svabhāvajanyatā*) of an action the determiner of its being a duty or *dharma* (*dharmatā*). One can easily smell the entry of the naturalist fallacy in the theory at this point. A defender of the theory cannot nonchalantly attribute it to his faulty perception. Why the natural be made the determiner of *dharmatā* is a very important question and there is no answer to it in the *varṇa-dhārmika* tradition. The great emphasis which the classical Indian tradition puts on self-control, inner and outer, and on self-purification, implies that it does not consider man's nature morally impeccable, incorruptible, unerring, or needing no improvement. The possibility of its being morally corrupt, or occasionally fallible, is thus not denied. Therefore, 'Why is naturalness, or nature-born-ness, to be called the determiner of *varnadharmatā*, or *dharmatā*?' is bound to be an open question, no matter whether the propounder of the *varṇa-dhārmika* theory is a venerable *ṛṣi*, or even a divine being.

The question raised above would not be an open question if human nature itself is conceived as duty-centric, i.e., taken to be imbued with the power to throw up, or determine, the duties of human beings. Butler says that conscience, which is an organ of human nature, is so constituted that it decides what is right and what is not. Therefore, in his ethical theory, it is not an open question to ask why what conscience declares to be right is right. Similarly, one may say that, according to Kṛṣṇa, or classical Indian tradition, the nature of an individual has its built-in potentiality to determine his *varṇadharmas*. If this is the case, then it too would not be an open question to ask why what human nature determines to be a *varṇadharma* is a *varṇadharma*. But nowhere Kṛṣṇa calls human nature duty-centric. Rather, he considers it very liable to be corrupted and befogged by desires, passions, indiscrimination, etc. He considers even Arjuna's disinclination to fight a sign of his confused, misguided, nature. Even the general Indian tradition considers human nature to be easily corruptible, and therefore emphasises on its purification by self-control, penance, instruction from a learned teacher, etc. Therefore, it would not be fair to say that, for Kṛṣṇa. or classical Indian tradition, human nature is intrinsically equipped with the ability to always unerringly determine duties.

Moreover, even if it is admitted that sometimes it throws up some norms, or duties, it cannot be denied that it also throws up sometimes some non-duties, or things which ought not to be done. If Vidura's nature throws up his duty of extremely earnestly requesting the assembly of great men to stop Duḥśāsana from trying to derobe Draupadī, Bhīṣma's nature throws up his duty to remain a silent spectator, which is obviously morally wrong. And, this is what their nature does when both Vidura and Bhīṣma are highly learned, cultured, individuals, well-equipped with the knowledge of what is morally right and what is not. Therefore, at the most it can be said that, even according to classical Indian ethos, of the things which a man's nature brings before him as his duties, some of them really are his duties, while some others are not. The latter may even be contrary to his real duties. This brings us back to our earlier conclusion that, therefore, being natural, being nature-determined, or being nature-born, cannot be the criterion of an action's being a duty, because all of such actions are not morally right, and consequently they cannot be anybody's duties. It is obvious, then, that to call any *X* a *varṇadharma because* it is *svabhāvaja* (nature-born, or nature-determined), or *on the ground* that it is *svabhāvaja*, would remain vulnerable to the open-question argument.

There is another problem with the *varṇa-dhārmika* theory's use of the concept of naturalness. Kṛṣṇa warns Arjuna that he is so bound (*nibaddha*) by his duty born from his nature that he cannot go against it. Rather, because of his indiscretion, though he says he won't fight, he would fight being necessitated by his own nature (*Gītā*, XVIII.60). This means that there is natural necessitation, i.e., necessitation by the agent's nature to do a duty because of its having been born out of his nature (*svabhāvaja*). This would make an agent do what he does not want to do due to indiscrimination (*mohāt*). But if this is so, it becomes inexplicable why one fails to do a *varṇadharma* of his. And, the problem of akrasia becomes still more inexplicable. Even Kṛṣṇa cannot deny, already having in his clear vision, Duryodhana, on the other side of the battleline, that one is not always necessitated by his nature to do what, according to Kṛṣṇa, is his (natural) duty, and that one is also sometimes akratic by not doing, or in not being inclined to do, what he acknowledges to be a *varṇadharma* of his. The oft-quoted confession of Duryodhana, that he knows what *dharma* and *adharma* are, but he has neither the inclination to do the former, nor the disinclination to do the latter (*jānāmi dharmam na ca me pravṛttiḥ, jānāmyadharmam na ca me nivṛttiḥ*: Vidyāraṇya Svāmī : *Pancadaśī*, 192 : 176), very well illustrates that one is not only not always necessitated but not even inclined to do what he knows he ought to do.

That the admission of necessitation by nature to do a nature-born duty amounts to denying the agent's freedom, and therefore his praisworthiness for having done a duty, is too obvious to be doubted. Denying freedom to him would also entail that there is no need to agrue with him that he ought to do his duty *D*, say, to try to persuade Arjuna that he ought to fight the battle, because he would necessarily do it being bound (*nibaddha*) by his nature to do it. This would entail the disutility of all moral instructions, or persuasions, even of the type which Kṛṣṇa gives to Arjuna in the *Gītā*. Kṛṣṇa forgets that his own declaration to Arjuna that he would necessarily do his duty of fighting, in spite of his apparent disinclination, would entail that there was no need of his spending so much of his time in giving to Arjuna the arguments, he takes great pains to give in the *Gītā*, to make Arjuna willing to fight.

The way Kṛṣṇa emphasises the inviolability of a *svadharma*, which is nothing other than a *varṇadharma*, even if it leads to the doer's death, gives the impression that a *svadharma* (or *varnadharma*) is an absolute duty and the injunction to do it a categorical imperative amounting to 'Do your *svadharma* (or *varṇadharma*) come what may.' But in the last chapter of the *Gītā* (XVIII.48) he offers a reason for not giving it up even if it is defective. The reason, as it has already been mentioned in another context, is that, since every action contains some defect, doing a *paradharma* would also be defective. In addition, it would be fear-yielding, while doing *svadharma* would not be. Rather, the latter would have the extra advantage over the former in being exempt from causing or yielding any sin. Therefore, taking into account the pros and cons of doing one or the other, doing *svadharma* is more advantageous than doing *paradharma*.

The above reasoning is obviously utilitarian or consequentialist. It justifies preferring *svadharma* to *paradharma* on the ground of its being consequentially better. In their constitution both are equal, because both are defective. But their consequences are not of the same value. The consequences of doing *paradharma* being fraught with fear and those of *svadharma* being free from fear, and, in addition, from any sin, *svadharma* is better than *paradharma*. Therefore, Kṛṣṇa concludes, doing *svadharma* is preferable to, or more meritorious than, doing *paradharma*.

I would only mention, and discuss, the two obvious gaps in the above reasoning: Kṛṣṇa nowhere explains (a) why a *svadharma*, for example, that of Arjuna to fight the battle involving killing his elders, does not cause any sin, and (b) why even a consequence, like the destruction of the doer in doing a *svadharma*, is better in merit than, or preferable to, a consequence, like the feeling of fear, emanating from doing, or from, an attempt to do, a *paradharma*.

To rate doing one's *svadharma* higher than doing a *paradharma* on a consequentialist ground would entail that *svadharma* is a conditional, and not a categorical, duty, because it would then be a duty not because of its being what it in itself is, but because of its consequences. Kṛṣṇa's and the general classical Indian, position is that doing *svadharma* would always, unexceptionally, be more advantageous than doing *paradharma*. The Indian tradition seems to be making it something like a synthetic *a priori*. But even then, if its having the consequences it has, no matter contingently or unfailingly, is considered to be the reason for doing it, it would remain a conditional duty.

Calling any *svadharma*, or *varṇadharma*, a categorical imperative would be unfair to the spirit of the general classical Indian theory of values. It would be because it would amount to ignoring another aspect or principle of the latter, namely, the principle that, when there is a conflict between a *svadharma*, or *varṇadharma*, and a *sādhāraṇa dharma*, i.e., a *dharma* obligatory for every individual, irrespective of his *varṇa* and *āśrama*, the *sādhāraṇa dharma* should override the former. This would mean that doing a *svadharma*, or *varṇadharma*, is not an absolute or categorical duty. It is relative, or conditional, to its concordance with the set of *dharma*s called *sādhāraṇa dharma*s.

It is the primacy of this principle which Rāma points out to Lakṣmaṇa when the latter proposes to fight with their father, king Daśaratha, and to get Rāma enthroned, when the king, on account of his prior promise to Kaikeyī, his youngest wife, agrees to the enthronement of Bharata, and to Rāma's being exiled for fourteen years. Lakṣmaṇa's argument is that, because they are *kṣatriya*s, it is his (and Rāma's) *svadharma* to fight a righteous battle which the fight with the king, or Bharata, would be, as Rāma's claim to the throne is unquestionable. Even the crying Kauśalyā, Rāma's mother, does not see anything totally wrong in Lakṣmaṇa's stand. But Rāma rejects his proposal on the ground that his and Lakṣmaṇa's *sādhāraṇa dharma*, as sons, is to obey their father and this *dharma* is superior to, and therefore should override, their *svadharma*s, or *varṇadharma*s, as *kṣatriya*s (Vālmīki: *Rāmāyaṇa*, *Ayodhyākāṇḍa*, canto 21).

But if a *varṇadharma* is not a categorical, or absolute, duty, can't we say that a *sādhāraṇa dharma* is ? It seems to me obvious that we cannot. Even a *sādhāraṇa dharma* cannot be called a categorical *dharma* because Kṛṣṇa and the general classical Indian tradition allow its violation in certain conditions. It is admitted that there could be a situation in which violating a *dharma*, or doing an *adharma*, is more meritorious, more *dhāmika* than acting in accordance with it. For example, truthfulness is a *sādhāraṇa dharma*. No *dharma*, says Kṛṣṇa, is higher than it. And, so says Bhīṣma at several places in Śāntiparva of the *Mahābhārata*. But, Kṛṣṇa reminds us, it is extremely different to know how well-meaning people really make permissible, or commendable, violations of it in their behaviour. When the effect of telling a lie is as felicific as that of telling a truth ordinarily is, or where the effect of telling a truth is as evil as that of telling a lie ordinarily is, then truth is not to be told. Rather, it would be appropriate to tell the untruth that is called for. He says that in some situations, for example, when a marriage ceremony is being performed, when one is having a sexual relationship with a woman, when somebody's life is in danger, when all that one has is being snatched away from him, and when a *brāhmaṇa*'s welfare is in question, if the need be, one may tell a lie. In all these five situations lying, he asserts, causes no sin.[18]

He cites the example of the saint Kauśika who takes a vow to always tell the truth and only the truth, and is therefore called the truthful speaker (*satyavādī*). One day it so happens that some people, to protect themselves from some murderous dacoits, hide themselves in the forest in which the saint is having his hut. The dacoits too, chasing them, enter the forest and ask the truthful saint where are they hidding. Not realising that telling the truth is not always superior to telling a lie, he tells them the truth about the part of the forest they had hidden themselves in. The dacoits, then, find them out, and kill all of them. The *satyavādī* saint Kauśika, because of his having told the truth, incurs a great sin and is made to suffer the agonies of the hell. His fault is that he does not know the subtle nature of *dharma*. To know the subtle nature of *dharma* is, thus, to know when to follow a *sādhāraṇa dharma* and when to make an exception to it.

When exceptions to, or violations of, a *dharma*, are, in any condition, considered commendable, or even permissible, it ceases to be an absolute, or unconditional, *dharma*, or duty, and the injunction or imperative to do it ceases to be a categorical imperative. This has been shown above to be true of the *sādhāraṇa dharma* of truthfulness. But what is true of it is true of almost all the other *sādhāraṇa dharmas*. Non-stealing too is an important *sādhāraṇa dharma*. But in a famine, when the great *brahmarṣi* Viśvāmitra does not find anything to eat to keep himself and his family alive, his trying to steal the thigh of freshly killed dog from a butcher's house is considered permissible. The tradition justifies it on the ground that his is the condition of an emergency, an unusually calamitous situation, in which anything could be morally allowed, even the most glaring violation of a *dharma*, to save one's life. There has thus emerged the concept of an *āpad-dharma*, of a duty in an emergent, calamitous, situation, which may be a blatant violation of a *sādhāraṇa dharma* which is ordinarily taken to be valid for everyone and in all conditions. Even Kauśika's situation could be

18. *The Mahābhārata*, Vol. 4, Karṇaparva, p. 3987:31-3.

called an unusual one in which lying would have been more appropriate than telling the truth because the latter led to the killing of some innocent people.

Many ethical systems or theories consider some duties, or, principles, violable in some conditions. But whoever considers the violations of a duty *D* permissible in the situation *S* would say that *S* is, or has to be, in some sense unusual. What makes the violation permissible is invariably some prizable consequence *C* of the violation which is not likely to be achieved in *S* unless *D* is violated. The contribution of *S* is that it makes it extremely unlikely, or, impossible for the agent to produce *C* without violating *D*. In both the cases of Kauśika and Viśvāmitra saving an innocent life is considered extremely prizable and unachievable by a normal observance of the duty or *dharma* concerned in each one of the two cases. Kauśika chooses to fulfil, and not to break, his vow of always telling the truth and therefore fails to save the lives of the innocent people who were hidding themselves in the thickest part of the forest. Viśvāmitra chooses to violate the principle of non-stealing and thereby to save himself and other members of his family from dying of starvation. What I mean to point out is that the theory which considers the violation of a duty in any sort of condition permissible is bound to be, or very likely to be, consequentialist. The classical Indian theory of *dharma* not only considers some violations of *dharma*s permissible but also commendable.

It is obvious, thus, that the classical Indian theory of *dharma*, i.e., of *sādhāraṇa dharma* and *varṇadharma*, and therefore of *svadharma* because it is a *varṇadharma*, is consequentialist. For a consequentialist theory no duty can, in principle, be categorical, or absolute. For it, an action would be a duty if and only if it produces, or is likely to produce, a certain consequence. That an action produces, or is likely to produce, a certain consequence is an empirical matter, and therefore it cannot be said that it would necessarily do that. This means that there cannot be any absoluteness, necessity, or unconditionality, about its being always a duty.

According to a consequentialist theory, an action which is forbidden, an *adharma*, done in a normal, not unusual, situation, may also sometimes be considered commendable, a *dharma*, if its consequences are extraordinarily good. This is true according to the Indian theory as well, which strengthens my conclusion that it is consequentialist. Bhīṣma admires an owl for doing something extremely commendable by breaking in the night thousands of eggs laid by a poisonous she-snake. Normally breaking eggs, and thereby killing the would-be living creatures which would have come out of those eggs, would be considered morally wrong. In this case, however, had the poisonous snakes come out of those eggs, they would have caused the death of so many people. By not letting this possibility become real by breaking the eggs the owl saved their lives. Since this is a great moral good, the *adharma* done by the owl is as good as a *dharma*, or better than the normally considered *dharma*, or *sādhāraṇa dharma*, of non-killing (*ahiṁsā*).[19]

It is a logically interesting fact, though not noticed by interpreters of Indian value-theory, that the very concept of a *svabhāvaja varṇadharma* rules out the possibility of its being categorical. To say that righteous fighting is a *varṇadharma* for a *kṣatriya* because it is *svabhāvaja* to him, i.e., because it is in his nature to fight, is to say that it is his *varṇadharma* not because of its being what it in itself is, i.e., because of its being righteous fighting. Rather, it is his *varṇadharma* because of a factor external to righteous fighting, i.e., because of a *kṣatriya*'s having a certain kind of nature. It is not a *varṇadharma* of a vaiśya because he does not have that kind of nature. Anything could be a categorical duty only if the ground of its being a duty lies in itself and not in anything external to it. Therefore, no *varṇadharma* can be called categorical because the ground of its being a *dharma* is said to be located in something external to it, namely, the nature of the person or persons whose *varṇadharma* it is said to be. All *varṇadharmas* are *svabhāvaja* and no *svabhāvaja varṇadharma* could be categorical. Therefore, no *varṇadharma* could be categorical.

Let us analyse a bit further the concept of *svabhāvajatā* and see what is involved in calling a duty, or anything, *svabhāvaja*. Speaking conceptually, a duty is not an effect, an event, or a thing, which happens, or comes into being, because of something else which may be called its cause. This is so because it refers to something which

19. *The Mahābhārata,* p. 4705:8.

ought to be done, or ought to be brought into being, and not to what has been done, is being done, or, is going to be done, nor to what was, is, or is going to be brought into being. It is because of this conceptual truth about duties that we do not talk about cause of duties. Instead of talking about their causes, we talk about grounds of, or reasons for, them. The fulfilment of a duty too is not treated as an event, or as an ordinary event, because it involves the notion of agency, the notion of the agent's having done the action, doing which meant doing his duty, in a free manner. If we can explain it as a purely causal behaviour, without any reference to his freedom of will, or free agency, we would not give to him the credit of having done a duty.

If a man, under the influence of alcohol mixed, without his knowledge, in the cold drink given to him by the police, tells the court the truth that he has hidden the entire looted money in his barn, we would not give him the moral honour of having fulfilled his duty, expressed in his oath taken in the court, to tell the truth and nothing but the truth. Speaking in a precise way, we would say that his blurting out the truth was an effect, or an event, caused by the influence of the alcohol, and not the fulfilment of any duty. It is because of this conceptual, or deontic, truth about a duty, or an obligation, that a moral law pertaining to duties, or obligations, is not considered to be a causal law, or that, to put the matter slightly differently, duties, or obligations, are not treated as inmates of the causal world.

Therefore, though grammatically *svabhāvaja* means 'born out of nature', the link between *svabhāva* and *dharma*, or, duty, in calling a duty *svabhāvaja*, must not mean a causal link. Duties cannot be the effects of one's nature because they are not the effects of anything. Śaṅkara, Śrīdharasvāmī, and Aurobindo,[20] all interpret *svabhāvaja*, *svabhāvajanya*, and *svabhāvaniyata* in a literal sense, i.e., to mean 'born out of, or regulated by, nature'. Even if '*svabhāva*', is taken to mean the Sāṁkhya *prakṛti*, i.e., matter, it would not make things better. Duties would then become material effects of material *prakṛti* which they cannot be. Therefore, to protect the

20. Śaṅkara, *Gītā Bhāṣya*, p. 434; Śreedharasvāmī, *Commentary on the Gītā* (R.K. Mission, Madras), p. 506, Śrī Aurobindo, *Essays on the Gītā*, pp. 492-3.

duty-character (*kartavyatā*) of a *svabhāvaja karma*, it must not be taken to mean a *karma* born out of, resulting from, or caused by, *svabhāva*, as a *pittaja jvara* (bile-born fever) means *jvara* (fever) born out of, resulting from, or caused by, an imbalance of *pitta* (bile). All this has to be done to safeguard the categorial difference between a duty and an effect.

The best way, it seems to me, is to interpret '*svabhāvaja* duty' to mean a duty which is *in concordance with* the nature of the agent concerned, i.e., a duty in the determination of which the agent's nature has been taken into account and which has been found compatible with his nature. Two questions would then arise: (a) What does taking an individual's nature into account mean, or amount to ?, and (b) What is the agency which does, or should do, this taking into account (of an individual's nature to determine his duties)?

(a) To determine any *A*'s dutes we have to take his nature into account, because only by doing that we shall know what he can and what he cannot do, i.e., shall have an idea of his capabilities. But this knowledge would help us only in deciding what cannot be his duty because what he cannot do cannot be assigned to him as a duty of his. Our knowledge of what he can would help us to delimit the zone of his duties in the sense that only that can be called his duty which he can do. But beyond this our knowledge of his nature would not take us. It cannot help us to determine what exactly he should be required to do. Among the various things he can do, something may be fit to be called a duty, i.e., prescribable, something else may be worth doing but not so important as to be prescribed as a duty, a third something may be so bad that he should be forbidden from doing it, and there may be a fourth kind of thing which may be ethically neutral, neither commendable nor condemnable, and therefore doing or not doing it may be left to his own choice or convenience. To segregate one as a duty from the rest of the three kinds of doables, we shall need a criterion of duty, or rightness, etc., in addition to a knowledge of his nature. We cannot get the criterion from our knowledge of his nature alone, and therefore not from our knowledge of what is *svabhāvaja* to him, i.e., in concordance with his nature.

Svabhāvajatā of an action, therefore, cannot itself be the criterion of calling it a *dharma* or duty. To know that fighting is *svabhāvaja* for a *kṣatriya* is not the same as knowing that it is his duty. This means that one's duties have to be determined, or assigned, by himself or by someone else, on some ground other than the *svabhāvajatā* of actions. Therefore, let us see who, according to the classical theory, or Kṛṣṇa's theory, assigns duties to different *varṇa*s and how does the notion of *svabhāvajatā* figure in the exercise of assignment.

(b) Kṛṣṇa says[21] that he has done the assignments in accordance with the nature of individuals. He has created the four *varṇa*s by classifying individuals into four groups in terms of their *guṇa*s, i.e., nature, and assigned them their duties in concordance with their nature. Tilak interprets Kṛṣṇa to mean that he first created the four *varṇa*s, and the four-fold caste-system (*cāturvarṇya-vyavasthā*) assigned different sets of duties to different *varṇa*s.[22] Classical interpreters take Kṛṣṇa to mean that even the assignment of duties was done by him. They seem to be right because the identity of a *varṇa* is determined by its *dharma*s or duties. Therefore, it is not possible that there are first *varṇa*s, and then the *varṇa-vyavasthā* assigns to them their duties. Without their duties they would not be the *varṇa*s they are. Therefore, he who creates the *varṇa*s must also assign to them their duties in the very same act of creating the *varṇa*s, because to create a *varṇa* is to create a *varṇa* with its distinctive *varṇadharma*s.

Whichever way we go, Tilak's way, or the classical interpreters' way, it is obvious that the assignment of the *varṇadharma*s of any individual *A* has been done, according to the classical Indian scheme, by an external agency, societal or divine. Such a duty, i.e., a *varṇadharma*, which is not self-assigned, but assigned by an external agency, cannot be categorical because, as already explained, the justification, or reason, of its being a duty does not lie in the concept of it but in something external to it. *A*'s honouring it, revering it, is conditional to his honouring, or revering, the external agency, no matter whether it is a divine person, or a social system.

21. *The Gītā*, XVIII.45, 46.

22. Bāl Gaṅgādhar Tilak, *Śrīmadbhagavadgītā-Rahasya*, p. 842

Even the ethics of *divine* determination of duties, like any other ethics of external determination, cannot yield a categorical duty. Moreover, when we concede that a duty assigned by a divine agency is categorical, a question very similar to that of the *Euthyphro* would immediately pop up: Does the divine agency assign it because it is already a categorical duty, or is it a categorical duty because the divine agency assigns it ? The very fact that such a question can be raised shows that to call a duty god-assigned is not necessarily to call it a categorical duty.

Doing one's *svadharma*, one's *svabhāvaja varṇadharma*, is further recommended on the ground that by doing it its agent attains his *sansiddhi*, which may be called his highest objective, perfection, self-fulfilment, or salvation. It thus is, once again, straightforwardly admitted to be an instrumental, and therefore a non-categorical, duty. The idea of its instrumentality is further developed by saying that it is not the plain performance of one's *svadharma*, but doing it thinking it is a way of worshipping god, who has created everything and is present in everything, which brings about the attainment of the doer's salvation.[23] That is, if a *brāhmaṇa* can attain his *sansiddhi* by studying and teaching the Vedas etc., a *kṣatriya* by fighting a righteous war, etc., and a *vaiśya* by doing commerce, etc., a *śūdra* can attain it by only serving his master, assuming that each one thereby also worships god.

Salvation being a state of perfection, a *śūdra*'s salvation cannot be inferior to a *brāhmaṇa*'s. Both must have the same value. But if each one gets his salvation by worshipping the same god by his *svadharma*, a *śūdra*'s *svadharma* must also have the same value as that of a *brāhmaṇa*, because only means of equal value can lead to the attainment of the same end, or completely similar ends. This line of thinking may be used to tell a *śūdra*, or an outsider to the *varṇa-vyavasthā*, that a *brāhmaṇa* and a *śūdra* have in the *varṇa* theory the same, equal, status. But it would convince neither a mentally alert *śūdra*, nor a neutral outsider. The work of the *śūdra*, without denying its importance, is not of the same value as, or rather is of a much lower value than, any work assigned to a member of anyone of the other three *varṇa*s. And, a *śūdra* was, in

23. *The Gītā*, XVIII.45, 46.

actual practice, treated as a much lower kind of human being than anyone of any other caste.

That his social devaluation was of the extremest kind, even in Śaṅkara's times, is illustrated by Śaṅkara himself by the way he comments, in his commentary on VIII.41 of the *Gītā*. While giving his principle on which he has classified people into four *varṇa*s, in the first line of 41, Kṛṣṇa puts the words '*brāhmaṇa*', '*kṣatriya*' and '*vaiśya*', as per their grammatical suitability, together as one compound: *brāhmaṇakṣatriyaviśām*. Quite separately from it, but in the same line, he puts the word for the *śūdras śūdrānām*. The line then runs as *brāhmaṇaksatriyaviśām śūdrāṇām ca paraṁtapa* and the second line as *karmāṇi pravibhaktāni svabhāva-prabhavairguṇaih* (*brāmaṇaṣatriyaviśām śūdrāṇām ca paraṁtapa* । *karmāṇi pravibhaktāni svabhāva-prabhavairguṇaiḥ* ॥). The meaning of 41 is quite simple: O scorcher of your enemies, the duties of *brāhmaṇa*s, *kṣatriya*s and *vaiśya*s, as well as those of the *śūdra*s, have been already classified according to the *guṇa*s, dispositions, born from their nature.

According to a lay neutral reader, putting the word *śūdrāṇām* separate from the compound *brāhmaṇakṣatriyaviśām* is merely a grammatical accident, or the result of metrical, or poetic, suitability, having no deeper meaning or implication. But Śaṅkara's interpretation is that the word *śūdrāṇām* has been kept separate from the compound *brāhmaṇakṣatriyaviśām* because the *śūdra*, not being a *dvija* (twice-born), is not allowed to read the Vedas.[24] What is suggested by him is this: Since the *śūdra*, being of a lower status than the *brāhmaṇa*, *kṣatriya* and *vaiśya*, is not fit to be in their company, the word '*śūdra*' is also of a lower status than each one of the words '*brāhmaṇa*', '*kṣatriya*' and '*vaiśya*', and the compound of the three, and therefore not fit to be in the company of anyone of the three words, or in that of their compound. It seems Śaṅkara treats the word '*śūdra*' also as a *śūdra*, or treats the *śūdra* as so lowly a creature that even the word denoting it, if put together with the words denoting the three higher *varṇa*s, would defile the higher *varṇa*s. A glaring confusion between the use and mention of words seems to have been made here by the great logician Śaṅkara. One

24. Śaṅkara, *The Gītā Bhāṣya*, pp. 434-5.

may like to protect his respect for Śaṅkara's logical acumen by attributing it to his great moral prejudice against the *śūdra*. Then Śaṅkara's moral insenstivity would be glaring. But neither logical, nor moral, insensitivity is a trivial deficiency.

One may like to absolve Śaṅkara from both of the deficiencies by saying that he only gives the real meaning, or intention, of Kṛṣṇa's words. But that would amount to attributing to Kṛṣṇa himself either one or both of the failings mentioned above: the logical failing of non-distinguishing between the use and mention of a word, and the moral failing of treating the *śūdra*, his own creature, to be so lowly a being. This would mean a tragedy, almost a calamity, for a respector of the *Gītā*. He may then find it extremely difficult to accept any of the *Gītā* ideas reverentially when their originator himself is found to suffer from such failings.

Kṛṣṇa represents those in the classical Indian tradition who are in favour of ordering social reality on the basis of *varṇa-dharma*. The social reality so ordered is what is called the *cāturvarṇa-vyavasthā* (the four-fold caste system). Since *varṇadharma*, including *varṇāśrama dharma*, is its cement, if *varṇadharma* declines, it too would decline, which Kṛṣṇa would not like to happen. Therefore, he would not like *varṇadharma* to decline anytime. When he declares that whenever *dharma* declines, or *adharma* prospers, he manifests himself in order to protect the virtuous, i.e., the *dharma*-fulfilling, to destroy the vicious, i.e., the *dharma*-flouting, people and to restore *dharma*, or *dharma*-based social order, he obviously means by *dharma varṇadharma* including *varṇāśrama dharma*.[25]

Because of the problems discussed above, it was not easy to apply the *varṇadharma* theory, in a consistent manner, even in classical times. Merely formal adherence to it created in some cases glaring immoralities. Ekalavya could not be admitted in Droṇa's school, though he had the nature or competence of a *kṣatriya*, because he was a tribal *śūdra* by birth. Karṇa was not given the status of a *kṣatriya*, though he was one if any Pāṇḍava was one, because it was not publicly known that he was of the same status

25. Śaṅkara, *The Gītā Bhāṣya*, p. 109, *The Gītā*, IV.7, 8.

by birth as was Arjuna. And, this happened when he had quite obviously the nature of a *kṣatriya*. Sambūka had to be killed by Rāma because he was performing *tapa*, a *paradharma* for him. It seems to me that contradictions arose in the implementation of the theory, as shown in this chapter, because of its limiting one's *varṇadharmas* to what he was naturally disposed to do and determining his nature in an *a priori* manner. What one can naturally do cannot be determined at birth, and what is his nature cannot *a priorily* be determined, once for ever, because his nature may change. What is natural for him to do is an empirical matter and can be asserted only in a probabilistic manner on the basis of his behaviour, etc.

Even the result of strictly applying the theory would not have been, from the moral point of view, optimistic in every case. For example, it would have been really tragic for the entire world, and not only for India, if using the *a priorily* made distinction between *svadharma* and *paradharma*, a Kṛṣṇa had convinced the *kṣatriya* prince Gautam to abstaiṇ from becoming a recluse on the ground that doing that would be adopting a fear-producing *paradharma* and to rule over his kingdom because doing that was his *svadharma*, he having been a *kṣatriya* prince. A similar tragedy would have occurred if Mahāvīra, the founder of Jainism, would have been persuaded to do his *svadharma*, since he too was a kṣatriya.

The theory of *varṇadharmatā* is intended to be a normative ethical theory. A normative ethical theory is viable only if it is consistently applicable in all cases which are relevant to it, and the consequences of its strict application are always morally optimistic, or at least never morally untoward. But the *varṇa-dharmatā* theory does not satisfy these criteria. It seems to me that too much emphasis on the naturalness (*svabhāvajatā*) of *varṇadharmas*, determining naturalness in terms of an *a priori* conception of human nature, assignment of *varṇadharmas* by an external agency no matter divine, etc., are some of the main factors responsible for its having this fate.

There is, however, another feature of the prescription for doing a *varṇadharma*, or as a matter of that, for doing anything whatsoever. It is to the effect that it should be done with absolutely no desire for its consequences, or for anything whatsoever. It should be done only because it is one's *varṇadharma*, and when it is so done, it would be non-rebirth causing or liberating. One may say that this feature of the prescription makes it categorical, and it is in this feature of it that the real excellence of doing one's *varṇadharma* resides, and that Kṛṣṇa and others refer to its felicific consequences only to make the prescription persuasive or appealing, though the value of doing a *varṇadharma* does not depend on its felicific consequences.

The doctrine of doing one's *varṇadharma* desirelessly (i.e., with *niṣkāmatā*) is a constituent of the theory of *varṇadharmatā*. But it would not make doing a *varṇadharma* a categorical duty. Even then it would be a duty not because of its being what it is, but because of the doer's desirelessness in doing it. And his desirelessness is a feature of his psyche, or character, not one of the *varṇadharma* concerned, and therefore external to the latter. The ground of a categorical duty has to be intrinsic to it. Making it reside in desirelessness itself is recommended because of its being a means to terminating the doer's liability to be reborn after death, i.e., to his salvation (*mokṣa*). Therefore, even with this feature of it the theory of *varṇa-dharmatā* remains consequentialist. That is why doing a *varṇadharma* would not be obligatory for him who does not believe in the possibility of a desireless action, or in the causal power of desireless action to terminate the possiblity of rebirth, or in rebirth, or does not want to terminate the possibility of his rebirth, etc., etc.

All this is natural when one has to choose doing something because it is a means to something else. In addition, the principle of doing something desirelessly has got its own problems which are in no way softer than those of the theory of *varṇadharmatā*. But the concept of desireless action is very central to classical Indian ethics. It can be called another basic normative structure of it because anything, no matter what it itself is, if it is done desirelessly, it is considered to be superior to the same thing done desirefully. Therefore, it needs an idependent discussion. I shall take it up in the next chapter and trace its emergence, or development, *via* Kṛṣṇa's responses to Arjuna's arguments against fighting the Mahābhārata war.

2

Prescription of Niṣkāma Karma

Moral or Non-Moral ?

Teleological or Deontological ?

THE concept of *niṣkāmatā* (desirelessness), or *niṣkāma-karma* (desireless action), as has been said in the last chapter, is another basic normative structure of classical Indian ethics. Any action which fits into this structure, i.e., is desireless, has the highest value which an action can have. This is so because it would then be a means to *mokṣa* (salvation). A desireless action is claimed to have no moral effect, good or bad, to experience which its doer would have to be reborn after his death. A *niṣkāma*, and only a *niṣkāma*, action is instrumental to the attainment of *mokṣa* because it alone makes its doer non-liable to be reborn. The *niṣkāmatā* (desirelessness) of an action, of a *dharma* (duty), or even of an *adharma* (a forbidden action), thus works as a prophylactic insofar as it destroys its potentiality to be rebirth-causing or bondage-causing.

One of the main reasons for Kṛṣṇa's adumbrating this doctrine to Arjuna is to convince him that he would incur no moral vice or discredit if he fights the battle in a *niṣkāma* manner, even if in the course of fighting he kills some of his relatives or elders which would ordinarily be considered morally wrong. Therefore, I would state and examine the doctrine in that context. Both Arjuna's arguments, expressing his moral objections to fighting a familial war, or any war and Kṛṣṇa's responses to meet them, cover a number of very interesting ethical issues. At least the major ones, if not all of them, would be discussed here, and the discussion would he analytical and evaluative, free from the *ṛṣi* bias.

It is well known to students of Indology that just before the commencement of the *Mahābhārata* war Arjuna puts forth before Kṛṣṇa some arguments against fighting the war. They seem so convincing to him that he loses his will to fight, lays down his arms, leaves the combatant's place in the chariot, and takes a seat in its rear part. Kṛṣṇa tries to counter his arguments with his own and to remove what, according to him, are his misunderstandings and false notions. Judged by its result, his attempt is successful and persuasive because it makes Arjuna convinced that he ought to fight the war, and he really fights it as bravely and committedly as is expected of him. But to convert a disagreeing partner in argumentation to one's side by giving a counter-argument does not entail that the latter has enough of probative force to prove that its own conclusion is true, or that the conclusion of the argument it counters is false. I hope the reasoning and analysis presented in this essay would show that this is in fact the case with Kṛṣṇa's counter-arguments and arguments. He is neither able to refute any of Arjuna's arguments against fighting nor to give an irrefutable one of his own in favour of it. What is instrumental in procuring Arjuna's willingness to fight is not his water-tight logic, but exhortative language and personal influence on him.

Such a view about Kṛṣṇa, or even about Arjuna, I admit, would be extremely hard for an orthodox scholar of Indology, or Indian Philosophy, to digest. But I have some optimism that, by the time he completes reading the essay, he would have overcome a large part of his initial resistence to it. The relevant dialogue between Kṛṣṇa and Arjuna is contained in the classic called the *Bhagavad Gītā*, or simply, the *Gītā*. Almost all those who have read, or written on, it believe that the dialogue actually took place, and was recorded by the great *ṛṣi* (*maharṣi*) Vyāsa who included it in the epic, the *Mahābhārata*, in its Bhīṣma Parva. They consider Kṛṣṇa's confutation of Arjuna's arguments conclusive, and the substantive ideas or views which the former elaborated in course of it unfaultable in their own right. That Kṛṣṇa's replies to Arjuna's objections to fighting, and his positive reasons for fighting, satisfy Arjuna is taken to be a clear proof of their being really, or objectively, satisfying. It is not realised that a reply which satisfies the objector need not be really satisfactory in the sense of being logically sound or adequate.

Most of the writers on the *Gītā* are philosophers, or religious thinkers. It is not surprising that the latter write not to logically assess, but to elaborate and extol, in a reverential manner, the views presented in it. This is so because they believe that Kṛṣṇa is an incarnation of Viṣṇu. Even the philosophers have not done anything very different, in spite of the fact that they give to the book the honour of being a philosophical classic. In their case, too, the reason for this is the same. The *Gītā* is a philosophical as well as a religious classic, which it could be even without being taken to be a dialogue between man (Arjuna) and an incarnation of god (Kṛṣṇa). But one who treats the ideas contained in it as having been directly given by god, or a god-incarnate, to a man, and recorded by a *maharṣi* who too is taken to be infallible, would naturally not be critical about any one of them.

A good number of modern Indian scholars of classical Indian philosophy approach a classical philosophical text, even a highly technical one, with what I have elsewhere called the *ṛṣi* bias. They consider its author a *ṛṣi* who is not just a scholar of great repute but a seer of unfalsifiable truths. He is believed to have acquired superhuman, spiritual, or divine, insights, not only into the nature of the problems he discusses but also into that of many others. There is nothing wrong in venerating a classical, or any, great thinker. But their veneration has become infected with the *ṛṣi* bias, the bias that the *ṛṣi* can never be wrong, and therefore what he says is to be studied, understood, interpreted, etc., but not to be criticised, or commented on. If someone claims to have discovered an inconsistency, an untruth, or an invalid argument, in a classical text, howsoever meticulous and insightful a scholar he may be, they presume that there is something wrong with his own understanding, education, philosophical feeding, way of approaching classical Indian philosophy, etc. If he is well-grounded in some modes of modern Western philosophising, he is likely to be accused of not being sympathetic to the Indian *ṛṣi*'s style of thinking, or of not having studied the text concerned in its proper context.

That the *ṛṣi* bias could be a great hindrance to creative philosophising is obvious. It is largely because of its hold on the minds of most of those modern Indians who work in the area of classical Indian Philosophy that their writings are almost exclusively exegetical or reproductive. It is also because of its hold that in oral discussions these scholars take pride in being able to reproduce verbatim long Sanskrit quotations from some text or texts; whether or not they have taken their message to their heart, they must have learnt them by heart. Sanskrit is not a spoken language in the country to any mentionable extent. In any gathering the number of those who can understand a Sanskrit quotation without the help of translation is bound to be negligible. Therefore, long Sanskrit quotations are not likely to contribute to making philosophical progress in a discussion. They may, of course, overawe some of those who cannot play that game. Most of the scholars who play it seem not to distinguish between rote learning and ratiocinative learning, between substantiating that this, and not that, is the position maintained in a text and highlighting the philosophical point of the latter by examining its pros and cons given in the text, or reconstructable out of the materials available in it.

Discussing any theme occurring in the *Gītā* is extremely prone to provide an opportunity for the *ṛṣi* bias to play its role in its full vigour. Very few people talk about the classic without the *ṛṣi* bias. That is why there is almost an absolute dearth of critical literature on any one of the issues discussed in it. Since its content is taken to have been taught to Arjuna by Kṛṣṇa, the completest human incarnation of Viṣṇu, and recorded by the great *ṛṣi* Vyāsa, it cannot be said to contain an untruth about any matter of fact, any unsound principle of action, or any real confusion or ambiguity in expression. If it contains any one of these defects, or a defect of any sort whatsoever, it would mean either that Kṛṣṇa is not an incarnation of Viṣṇu, because an incarnation cannot say or do anything which suffers from any defect, or that Vyāsa is an incompetent recorder and therefore not a *ṛṣi* because a *ṛṣi* cannot record incorrectly any message from a god-incarnate, or rather from any source whatsover. None of these possibilities would be acceptable to an orthodox scholar of classical Indian philosophy.

To approach the *Gītā* in this way would mean that if one finds any defect, conceptual or substantive, in a view held by it, it must be because of his own defective understanding of the latter. To see what it really is, or what exactly does the alleged defective element mean, he has to read and re-read the book and try to understand the text in its proper context. And, he has only to understand and follow its teachings: he cannot criticise them because, *exhypothesi*, they cannot contain anything erroneous or undesirable.

Without wasting any time in crossing my sword with those who take the *Gītā* to be a divine document, I shall take it as a human work, as I would in the case of any book whatsover. It does contain a number of valuable ideas on more than one theme. But I would limit myself to discussing Arjuna's arguments against fighting the war and Kṛṣṇa's responses to them with a view to ascertain how far they really succeed in showing that the former are unsound, or otiose, as the received scholarship claims them to do. Arjuna's arguments express his moral objections to fighting the war; through them he intends to make the point that it is morally wrong for him to fight. Kṛṣṇa tries to convince him that it is not only not wrong but his duty to fight. Arjuna is satisfied with his reasoning[1] and the way he fights gives the impression that Kṛṣṇa, not only drives his chariot but also his moral conscience, because he does whatever Kṛṣṇa advises him to do. But, as has already been said, and would be shown in the sequel, his reasoning's being satisfying to Arjuna is neither a necessary, nor a sufficient, condition of its being logically sound.

Arjuna is not a naive, impulsive, youth. Rather he is a well-educated, well-brought-up, cultured, decent, *kṣatriya* prince, well-acquainted with his family's traditions, rites, and duties, as well as with general social norms, mores, and morals, prevalent in those times. His relationship with Kṛṣṇa is very close. They are cousins, and very good friends too. They love and trust each other. Arjuna's love for Kṛṣṇa is as good as adoration. In Pāṇḍavas' bad days Arjuna has very often been in favour of settling the scores with Duryodhana by fighting the matter out in a full-scale war, and has accordingly prepared and equipped himself, as his brothers have.

On inspecting the two armies, Duryodhana's and his own, arrayed against each other on the battle-field, Arjuna notices that a large number of his relatives, young and old, are present in the former. This is as expected because the battle to be fought is one between the two components of the same Kaurava family. He

1. *The Gītā*, XI.1, XVIII.73.

realises now more clearly that if he fights, he would have to kill men belonging, or related, directly, or indirectly, to his family. Therefore, he feels overwhelmed with grief and sorrow. His will to fight, then, naturally gets weakened. As the *Gītā* portrays him at this juncture, he is emotionally very greatly disturbed. He expresses to Kṛṣṇa his unwillingness to fight because of his having, what seem to him, some good moral reasons against fighting. On account of his emotionally disturbed state of mind, we cannot expect him to present his reasons in a logically well-arranged, cut and dry, manner. However, I would state them formally in as neat a way as the subject-matter permits, so that we may be able to properly judge what sort of reasons they are and how well, or ill, Kṛṣṇa's responses to them counter them. Therefore, I would pay more attention to what they are intended to be than to their linguistic expression or place in the book.

Arjuna's reasons do make him tend to think that it is morally wrong to fight the battle. But it is not completely clear to him what exactly he should do. Therefore, while expressing his unwillingness to fight, he also requests Kṛṣṇa to tell him what should he do. But before discussing his reasons and Kṛṣṇa's counter-reasons, it is important to remember that his reasons are not born out of his self-difidence or cowardice. They are not even purely personal, prudential, or strategic, considerations. He is not akratic and therefore it cannot be said that he is putting forth considerations against fighting as self-deceptive measures to conceal his weakness of the will. Therefore, his reasons, or considerations, against fighting, deserve to be seriously and open-mindedly examined. They do also because they are the reasons of a valiant fighter occurring to him at the time when everybody in his own, as well as in the enemy's camp, expects him to be full of verve and determination.

In my presentation of his arguments, their constituents, in some cases, may not be placed in the same order in which they occur in the book. All of these arguments would have the same conclusion, namely, that to fight the battle is morally wrong. This has to be the case because Arjuna's sole purpose in offering all of his reasons to Kṛṣṇa is to establish the latter. In formalising his arguments some reconstruction has been done but without distorting, or altering, what he intends to convey by means of them. The same thing has been done with Kr̥ṣṇa's counter-arguments and arguments.

Arjuna's arguments can be formally put as follows:

(A) To fight the battle is to fight to kill relatives (*svajanām*) (arrayed on Duryodhana's side).

The relatives (arrayed on Duryodhana's side) are no doubt wicked people (*ātatāyinaḥ*).

But to fight to kill relatives, even if wicked, is morally wrong. Therefore, to fight the battle is morally wrong.[2]

(B) To fight the battle is to fight to kill relatives. I (Arjuna) know(s) that to fight to kill relatives is morally wrong but Duryodhana does not know it. To do what one knows to be morally wrong is morally wrong. Therefore, for me (Arjuna) to fight the battle is morally wrong.[3]

(C) To fight the battle is to fight to kill adorable elders like the grandfather Bhīṣma and the teacher Droṇa.

It is morally better to live on alms than to kill adorable elders, and even after killing them I (Arjuna) would get only blood-soaked material goods to enjoy (which is again morally wrong).

Therefore, to fight the battle is morally wrong.[4]

(D) To fight the battle is to cause the destruction of the Kaurava family (*kulakṣaya*).

To cause *kulakṣaya* is to cause the destruction of the Kaurava ethos (*kuladharma*) (as there would be none left to perform the Kaurava family's rites and duties).

To cause the destruction of *kuladharma* is morally wrong. Therefore, to fight the battle is morally wrong[5].

Arjuna's arguments are moral arguments because they raise moral objections to fighting a civil war. They are also moral in a conceptual

2. *The Gītā*, I.26, 31, 34, 36, 37.
3. *Ibid.*, I.38, 39, 45.
4. *Ibid.*, II.4, 5.
5. *Ibid.*, I.40-4.

sense because they are universalisable, or general, reasons which can be offered by anybody involved in a familial or civil war in which he has to get a wrong righted and the means to be used is large-scale violence. Arjuna has to get a wrong righted in the sense that he has to recover his family's share of the kingdom wrongly usurped by Duryodhana. After the failure of all peaceful methods to get back the share, Pāṇḍavas and their friends, after a serious examination of all the pros and cons, have come to the conclusion that waging a war with Duryodhana is the only way left open to them. It is the moral tone of Arjuna's objections which makes them eternal objections which would occur to any morally sensitive person, who is landed in a situation in which he is to be an agent of violence, mental or physical, and which he would like to be cleared satisfactorily before he decides to play the role the situation requires him to. They need to be answered, therefore, in terms of categories applicable to, or valid in, the general framework of a moral conflict arising, or likely to arise, in the mind of a morally sensitive fighter who has to paly a leading role in a battle with his kith and kin, or with people he is socially related to in some very intimate way. Answering them in terms of those which are peculiar to a particularistic framework, say that of the four castes and the four *puruṣārthas* (*cāturvarṇa-cāturvarga*), as Kṛṣṇa tries to do, may not be appropriate. He answers them in terms of the categories of caste, caste-ethics (*dharma*, *svadharma* or *varṇadharma*), rebirth, bondage, salvation, etc., which are peculiar to the above framework. Anyone who does not accept this framework and therefore its categories may not find Kṛṣṇa's answers satisfactory. The latter would look archaic when this framework has been replaced by another, as it has happened everywhere in today's world, including the country of Kṛṣṇa's birth. What I mean to say is that a more comprehensive ethical theory could have emerged out of the attempt to counter Arjuna's arguments had Kṛṣṇa taken them in their right spirit. Although I would be sailing against the main current of the prevailing interpretation of the *Gītā*, I would like to say that the all-time philosophical importance of the *Gītā* is due more to Arjuna's arguments against fighting the Mahābhārata war than to Kṛṣṇa's counter-arguments, or arguments, in its favour.

Kṛṣṇa assumes a theory about the role and destiny of man,

about what he ought to do and be, which is nothing other than the theory of *cāturvarṇa* and *cāturvarga*, the theory of four classes or castes of human beings and four types of values they seek and ought to seek in a world governed by the law of *karma*. He thinks that the issues which Arjuna has raised can be properly understood and handled by being placed in the conceptual framework of this theory and adequately answered in terms of some of the categories belonging to it. But Arjuna's objections to familial war or violence can arise in other frameworks as well. They are not peculiar to, or generated by, some internal intricacies or demands of the *cāturvarṇa* framework, discussed in chapter 1. He knows that he is a *kṣatriya*, that his, a *kṣatriya*'s, duty (*varṇadharma*) is to fight a righteous battle, and the battle in question is righteous because it is to be fought for recovering his family's rightful share of the Kaurava kingdom. His objections are those of, using a modern terminology, a liberal, free-thinking, young man, whose linkage with his existing societal, or social, framework, the *cāturvarṇa-cāturvarga* one, has been very greatly shaken or loosened by his moral conflict, making him think like one who is not rigidly hooked to any watertight societal, or social, framework. They are moral, not procedural, objections, not even those which have been generated by his belonging to a specific group or class of people. They bother more the morally sensitive person in him than the *kṣatriya* in him. It is because of his reverential relationship with Kṛṣṇa that the great archer, who can use, with equal dexterity, both of his hands in shooting his arrows, is not able to use his reason freely and forcefully in arguing with him. Whatever independence he has shown in putting forth his arguments to him thins down, or evaporates, on being told by him, in a highly persuasive way, sometimes openly, sometimes in between the lines, that he is the supreme creator of the universe, present before him in a human form.

Kṛṣṇa adopts a synoptic, and not an analytical, method to counter Arjuna's arguments. He also uses, in between the argumentative exercises, a lot of selectively chosen emotive, exhortative, expressions, sometimes pulling him down, sometimes pushing him up, with the objective to make him ready to fight the battle. I will not comment on this part of his animadversions, though their role in readying Arjuna for the fight may not be negligible.

I call Kṛṣṇa's method synoptic in the sense that he tries to make all of Arjuna's arguments otiose, or ineffective, in one sweep, by drawing his attention to some such of the constitutive beliefs or truths of the *cāturvarṇa* theory which are considered in the *cāturvarṇa* tradition to be axiomatic or unquestionable. His method is not analytical in the sense that he does not try to refute Arjuna's arguments, one by one, by claiming that from some defect, or defects, each one of them suffers.

By invoking the concept of *varṇadharmatā*, the duty of the *kṣatriya varṇa* (*kṣātradharma*), which we have analysed in chapter I, and treating it as absolutely binding on a *kṣatriya*, he tells Arjuna that, since he is a *kṣatriya*, it is his specific duty, *kṣātradharma* or *svadharma*, to fight a righteous battle (*dharmayuddha*) and that this battle is a *dharmayuddha* because it is to be fought to recover from Duryodhana his kingdom the latter has wrongfully grabbed. Since this *dharma* Kṛṣṇa takes to be unexceptionable, it entails that in no condition Arjuna can decline to fight without incurring the vice of being dutyless (*adharma*). Only a lucky *kṣatriya*, Kṛṣṇa says, gets such an opportunity of fighting a *dharmayuddha* which is like an open door to heaven. He calls it his highest duty (*śreyaḥ*), a duty which a *kṣatriya* cannot drop or question.

To make his argument logically coercive as well as psychologically persuasive to Arjuna, Kṛṣṇa presents it in the form of a dilemma with the conclusion that he ought to fight:

(E) You would choose either not to fight, or to fight. If you choose not to fight, then you would get infamy of running away from the battlefield, which would be worse than death for a respectable, valiant, *kṣatriya* as you are.

If you choose to fight, you would either lose or win. If you lose, i.e., get killed in the battlefield, you would go straight to heaven. If you win, you would enjoy ruling over the world as its conquerer.

Therefore, you ought to choose to fight.[6]

But there are some other possibilities which do not occur to

6. *The Gītā*, II.31-33.

Kṛṣṇa. For example, if Arjuna does not fight, it is possible that he is applauded as a great apostle of peace and non-violence. Secondly, if he fights and loses, it could also be that he is not killed while fighting but caputred alive and then sent to a prison by Duryodhana. Even Kṛṣṇa knows that entering Duryodhana's prison would not be less tortuous than entering Yamarāja's hell. Lastly, if he wins, the world conquered by him might not be worth living in because of the after-effects of the battle, as is Arjuna afraid of, and which really happened. The colour of the conquered world is very different from that of the one which existed before the war. The conquered world was all red with the bloodshed on the battleground during the fighting. It did not even have the people — because they were all killed in the war — to whom Arjuna would have liked to show the celebrations held on the occasion of his eldest brother's coronation.

Arjuna's objection to fighting owes its origin to a consideration to the effect that fighting would mean doing knowingly such morally wrong things as killing relatives, elders, destroying *kuladharma*, etc. This is a consideration belonging to the area of general morality (*sāmānya dharma*) which, as has been shown in chapter 1, if the need be, can supersede, or, override, even according to classical Indian ethical thought, a consideration belonging to caste-ethics (*varṇadharma*). But the latter cannot supersede, or overrride, the former. It is too naive to think that Arjuna does not know that his, a *kṣatriya*'s, *svadharma*, or *varṇadharma*, is to fight a righteous battle. He feels unwilling to fight because he finds that, if he fights, he would be contravening what seems to him a *sāmānya dharma*. Therefore, an appeal to a *varṇadharma* of his cannot, in all fairness to his objection to fighting as well as to the logic of morals, be made to show to him that here is a reason for overriding his objection. His problem simply is that, if he fulfils his *varṇadharma*, he would be contravening *sāmānya dharma*.

To illustrate the point made above, in a general way, not restricted to the *varṇāśrama* framework, suppose *A* argues with *B* that

(F) He (*A*) ought not to tell *C*, when *C* asks him where is *D*, that *D* is in room no. 4 of the building,

Because, *B* would then kill the innocent *D*.

And, anything which would lead to the killing of an innocent person ought not to be done.

Suppose further that *B* counters his argument by means of the following which has a conclusion contrary to that of *A*'s:

(G) You (*A*) ought to tell *C*, when asked where is *D*, that *D* is in room no. 4 of the building,

Because, telling it would be telling a truth and you know that it is

And, one who knows a truth ought to tell it when he is asked to.

Here both *A* and *B* are arguing on the same level, i.e., the level of general morality. *A*'s argument uses, to support his conclusion, the general moral principle 'Anything which would lead to the killing of an innocent person ought not to be done', which applies to all and not only to a particular class of people. So does *B*'s which proves a contrary conclusion by using another general moral principle 'One who knows a truth ought to tell it when he is asked to'. Which one of the two arguments is broader than, and therefore, supersessive of, the other, would depend on which one of the two principles is broader. But even when we would consider one of them supersessive of the other, and reject the other it is taken to supersede, it would not mean a change of level, i.e., a change from the level of general morality to that of class morality, or *vice versa*.

But suppose *B*'s counter-argument is the following:

(H) You ought to tell *C*, when asked where is *D*, that *D* is in room no. 4 of the building,

Because you are the receptionist of the building, and, a receptionist ought to supply, when asked to, the information who is in which room of the building.

Argument (H) is not on the level of general morality, but on that of class morality. Its moral principle 'A receptionist ought to . . .' applies not to all but only to a particular class of people, i.e., to that of receptionists. It is a principle of lesser generality than that of argument (F) as well as of argument (G). Therefore, (H) cannot supersede (F) or (G), but any one of them can supersede it. For example, *A* can say that as a receptionist he ought to, but as a human being, as a member of the moral community, he ought not to reveal the whereabouts of *D* to avoid the killing of an innocent person which *D* is.

Had Kṛṣṇa said to Arjuna that it is not wrong to kill a relative who has done a grave injustice to him, or to kill an elder who has taken the side of injustice, or to destroy a family (*kula*) pursuing the course of injustice, etc., he would have tried to counter one consideration from the side of *sāmānya-dharma* by a counter-consideration from the same side. He would have then tried to meet Arjuna's objection on his own ground. But he, instead, tries to meet an objection from the side of *sāmānya-dharma* by one from the side of *varṇadharma*. Arjuna does not respond to him by pointing out this lapse on his part. But that does not make his stand valid. Arjuna's objection to fighting still remains unrefuted.

Kṛṣṇa's reason for according a high place to *varṇadharma*, or *varṇāśrama dharma* is the fact, as claimed by him, that he, i.e., god, himself has created the four *varṇa*s and assigned to each one of the four their *varṇadharma*s.[7]

When castes are divinely determined, caste divisions become inviolable and unalterable. In a like manner, when caste duties are divinely determined, they too become inviolable and rigidly restricted to their respective castes. In principle, all caste duties become equally sacred.

A social order of this type is bound to be rigid and prohibitive of inter-caste mixing or mobility. It is also necessary that every member of it performs his caste duties and abstains from performing any duty of any other caste. It is to preserve this kind of social order that Kṛṣṇa requires even an enlightened person, a *sthitaprajña*, to continue doing his caste, and other, duties, though he has ceased to have any duty,[8] and not to remain idle, because then others may follow his example and stop doing their duties,[9] thereby leading to the decay of the social order, or causing social disorder.

7. *The Gītā*, II.37.
8. *Ibid.*, III.17.
9. *Ibid.*, III.20.

The *loka* or society is the whole, the orderly organisation, consisting of the four castes. In a social order of this type, a *śūdra* cannot complain that his duties are of a lower type and that therefore his social status is lowly. He cannot, therefore, ask for a social change which enables him to enjoy a better status than that of a servant or slave of the other three castes. It is obvious that such a conception of the social order is inimical not only to social progress but also to the protection of the values of social equity and justice. Fortunately, it has lost its attraction even in the country in which Kṛṣṇa convinced Arjuna to its being inviolable.

It may be urged that the appeal to his *kṣātradharma*, or *varṇadharma*, is not the only means Kṛṣṇa adopts to refute Arjuna's arguments. He also refutes them by means of considerations, or reasons, which are *sāmānya*, or general, and not inexorably hooked to *varṇadhārmic* ethics. For example, he points out that they all involve Arjuna's belief that, if he fights, he would have to kill some relatives and elders. But this belief is false. It is this false belief which fills his heart with grief and sorrow, and generates another belief that moral discredit or sin would accrue to him from his killing them, or from his share in getting them killed. In all of his arguments the possibility of killing them, or of getting them killed, figures as a deterrent to his fighting the battle, Kṛṣṇa tries to remove the deterrant by telling him that either no killing ever takes place, or if it does, it is not worth grieving over. And, as far as the question of moral discredit accruing from killing is concerned, there is a remedy, namely, that of *niṣkāmatā* (desirelessness), which, if used, would make any action whatsoever morally non-effectual or barren, i.e., unproductive of any moral effect, be it moral discredit, or moral credit.

It is something like this that Kṛṣṇa tries to do next. Let us see how he does it and with what amount of success.

Kṛṣṇa's argument against the propriety of grieving over killing in a battle, or over any killing anywhere, is built upon a tactful play on the distinction between the self and the body. Kṛṣṇa assumes the classical Indian theory of the self. According to it, the self is disembodied, non-agent, indestructible, not subject to birth, growth, and death, etc. The body, on the other hand, is material, temporal, destructible, an agent, and its existence has a fixed duration in time. Mind is an organ of the body and not of the self. The living, empirical, individual, called *jīva*, is an embodied self and his death means the separation, or freeing, of the self from the body. The self cannot die and the body cannot avoid dying, i.e., coming to an end at its appointed time. It is this metaphysics which Kṛṣṇa uses to convince Arjuna of the futility of grieving over what he calls killings in a battle. Kṛṣṇa's arguments, or counter-arguments, can be formally put as follows:

(I) Anyone, you, or a relative, an elder, etc., of yours, is an embodied self, i.e., is both a body and self linked in a certain way.

The self is indestructible.

Therefore, the self cannot be killed.

The self is a non-agent.

Therefore, the self cannot be a killer.

Therefore, it is futile to grieve over a self's being killed as well as to feel guilty for one's self being a killer of someone.

(J) The body of every individual is destructible and predetermined to die at a particular point of time. If an individual is killed in the battle, only his body is killed.

The killing of the body, which is its death, takes place as a predetermined event which has to take place when it actually takes place (*aparihārya*)

Therefore, since it has to take place when it does, there is no point in grieving over it.

The combined conclusion of (I) and (J) is: It is futile for anyone, and therefore for Arjuna, to grieve over killing the self, or the body, of any individual, a relative, an elder, etc., who is nothing but an embodied self, or self in embodiment and it is equally futile for anyone, and therefore for Arjuna, to feel guilty for killing anybody because the body's life is predetermined to come to an end, i.e., to die, at the time when, and the way in which, it is killed.[10] If Arjuna accepts this conclusion, it would follow that, if he kills someone, say,

10. *The Gītā*, II.12, 13, 16-28.

Karṇa, in the battle, when he is unarmed and engaged in lifting up the wheels of his chariot half-sunk in the earth, he kills him in this way because it has been predetermined that Karṇa would meet his death in this way. Even though killing a combatant in this way is against the ethics of the war, Arjuna is not responsible, and therefore not guilty, for having done it.

The arguments (I) and (J) are built on a number of confusions. The self, as assumed by them, cannot be killed, nor can it kill anyone. It is both a non-object and a non-agent. It cannot be hurt, broken, burnt, destroyed, etc., because nothing can be done to it, nor can it do anything to anyone. But these things are done to and by the individual, the *jīva*. The *jīva* can kill and be killed. It is not only a self, or only a body, but an embodied self. Killing it means killing it, i.e., severing the link between the body and the self in the body. We can as well call it destroying the embodiment of the self. Of course, then only the body is destroyed, or killed, according to the metaphysics assumed. If we cannot speak of the killing of a self, or of its being a killer, we cannot speak of killing of body, or of its being killed as well. There is nothing like a living self-less body. The killer, or the killed, is always an individual, the self-in-a-body. Arjuna's objection is to killing individuals like Bhīṣma, Droṇa, etc., and not to killing any (body-less) self, or (self-less) body.

Secondly, when an individual is killed, it obviously dies. Still, getting it killed and its dying are not the same thing; killing an individual is not even identical with its accidental death. Killing it is an intentional action done by the killer, but its dying is not. Therefore, an intentional killer, a soldier in a battle, who intentionally kills an opponent, is responsible for killing him, or for his death caused by his act of killing him. It is a very sloppy argument to say that, since the relatives and elders are predetermined to die at time *t*, Arjuna's act of killing them, or causing their death, at time *t* in the battle, is not blameworthy, or that he would not be guilty of any wrongdoing for killing them.

Kṛṣṇa's argument is that the self cannot be killed, and since the body has to inevitably die, killing it is the same as the inevitable taking place. Therefore, it is pointless to feel sorry, or guilty for killing anyone, as well as to blame anyone for having killed anyone.

If this argument is taken seriously, we cannot call any killing morally wrong. Therefore, we cannot call any killer punishable. This implication of Kṛṣṇa's arguments (I) and (J) is a *reductioad absurdum* proofofthe invalidity, or untenability, of the metaphysics he has assumed, or used, in formulating them.

It is very unlikely that Arjuna is unaware of this metaphysics. When he abhors killing, he does not seem to mean killing a self, or a self-less body, but an individual. An individual is killable, and killing it is, or could be, morally wrong, in addition to having some morally undesirable consequences, like causing pain to the killed while killing him, suffering to his dependents, etc. But Kṛṣṇa tries to prove to Arjuna that he would incur no sin in killing anyone in the battle because it is predetermined when and how one would die. That is, if he is killed by Arjuna's arrow, it would mean that it has been predetermined that he would meet his death in this way. It would also mean that it is predetermined that Arjuna would shoot his arrow making him its target and thereby would kill him.

In such a world in which whatever happens it happens in a predetermined way, no killing, not even killing a respected person, would be morally wrong because nobody does anything as a free agent and therefore is not responsible for the killing he does; he does it because he has been predetermined to do it. But then nothing would, in this world, be right either, and for the same reason. It may appear that it would be a morally neutral world, but it would really be a morally bad world because it would lack the great moral value which free agency, or freedom of action, is.

A traditional interpreter of the Kṛṣṇaite way of thinking may like to give a rejoinder that, even if an individual can be killed and killing anybody is a moral wrong, Kṛṣṇa has shown to Arjuna that there is a way to fight or kill without incurring any moral discredit or blame: It consists in adopting the attitude of *niṣkāmatā* (desirelessness), which means giving up all desires, or more specifically, all desires for the fruits or consequences of one's actions. Therefore, he asks Arjuna to fight the battle with no desire for victory or fear of defeat. Rather, he should fight without desire for any kind of consequence resulting from the fight. If his fight is desireless in this sense (*niṣkāma*), then whatever he does, whomsoever he kills, or gets killed by helping some other combatant, not only no sin, but nothing at all, neither any moral discredit, or credit, would accrue to him. If he does whatever he does desirelessly, then, he would be freed from the bondage of birth-death-rebirth. It is only to bear the consequences of one's actions that one is reborn after death, and when his actions yield no consequence he has to bear, he would naturally get released from bondage. Bondage means having been caught up in the chain of birth-death-rebirth, and release, or salvation, the freedom from it.[11]

This in fact is Kṛṣṇa's claim to Arjuna. If he fights with no desire, or no desire for some specific consequence, or consequences, of the battle, he would get his salvation (*mokṣa*), no matter whether he wins, is killed on the battlefield, or is made a prisoner of war. According to the gospel of *niṣkāma karma*, whatever be one's profession, or sphere of activities, if he does, whatever he does, desirelessly, he would be freed from bondage and get salvation. Modern interpreters of the *Gītā* consider it unassailable and the most precious gift of it to the human race. They do not suspect it to contain any built-in conceptual problem, nor its actual adoption in life, difficult no doubt, to involve any insurmountble practical problem. They seem to do that largely because of their *ṛṣi* bias, or because they do not seriously consider the possibility of their own ever leading a life in accordance with it. It is natural, or convenient, to ignore, or unsee, the cracks in the roof of a building one has no intention to live in.

Arjuna is aksed by Kṛṣṇa to fight because it is his duty as a *kṣatriya*, and to fight with no desire at all for what the fighting may result in, because then no moral discredit (or even credit) would accrue to him. But it is not only his duties which he is to perform desirelessly. Rather, he is asked to do desirelessly whatever he does.[12] Anything, whether a duty, or a non-duty, if done desirefully, would cause his bondage. Every desireful action, whether moral, immoral, or neither, causes bondage. A desireless action, like a desireful one, would have its natural, causal, effects. But, unlike the latter, it would have no bondage-producing, or binding, effect.

11. *The Gītā*, II.38, 40, 47, 48, 50, 51.
12. *Ibid.*, II.55, 56, 71.

An arrow shot by Arjuna, on hitting an opponent, would kill him, no matter whether it has been shot with no desire, or with the desire of killing him. The question why a desireless action does not have any bondage-producing effect, while retaining its natural causal power, has not even been raised by Arjuna, or Kṛṣṇa, in the *Gītā*, nor by anybody else in classical or modern Indian thought, what to speak of its having been answered satisfactorily, or even half-satisfactorily.

It is said that a desireless action is like a roasted seed which does not germinate, meaning that what roasting does to a seed, i.e., destroys its potentiality to germinate, desirelessness does to an action. It destroys the potentality of the action to produce any moral credit or discredit to bear which the doer would otherwise have been required to be reborn. But this is an analogy, and not an explanation. The claim about the seed belongs to the empirical world. One can make an experiment and verify whether or not it is valid. But the claim about desirelessness does not belong to the empirical world. Nobody can make an experiment to verify its veracity. Nor can anybody say authentically that such and such a person, who did whatever he did desirelessly, has not been reborn. The gospel of *niṣmāka karma*, therefore, has to be taken as an article of faith, or as a dogma, maybe in a non-pejorative sense. It is also a constituent of the kārmic world-view, as is the belief in rebirth. Even the kārmic world-view is to be taken as an article of faith, or dogma, again, maybe in a non-pejorative sense.

Ordinarily one of the main reasons for doing an action is the desire to produce some effect in the case of an instrumental action, and in that of an intrinsically desirable one it is simply the desire to indulge in the activity the action concerned consists in. If all desires are shunned, and along with them the sense of agency, i.e., the sense of being the doer of the action one does, is also shunned, what reason there would be for doing any action? One reason for doing it could be its being a duty. Kṛṣṇa asks Arjuna to do his duties, i.e., obligatory actions. This can be taken to mean that, if an action is his duty, then he is to do it only for the reason that it is a duty, and not at all with a desire to produce a particular kind of effect. He has to have no attachment for the likely result or results of the action. If its being a duty is a reason for doing it, then, on Kṛṣṇa's theory, there would exist a reason for doing duties, or, obligatory actions. But all actions which one may do, or may have to do, are not obligatory. This means there cannot be any reason for doing a non-obligatory action. Cannot we treat all actions as duties? Certainly not, for the simple reason that all actions neither are, nor they can be, duties. Fighting the battle is Arjuna's duty but running away from the battle is not, even though it would be an action none the less. Moreover, to call all actions duties would amount to making the notion of duty uninformative. To call an action a duty would then not be different from calling it an action.

But the *niṣkāma* theory does not require one to give up only all of his desires. It requires him to give up attachment for the objects of senses, or all sense-object contacts, and all emotions. This is quite logical too. Desires are so closely linked with sensations and emotions that with their departure neither sensations, nor emotions, can maintain themselves. Kṛṣṇa admits all this when he says that dwelling on sense-objects (which include mental objects as mind is also a sense in Indian philosophy) leads to attachment for them, attachment leads to desiring, or hankering, for them, hankering produces anger (when not satisfied), anger causes delusion, delusion causes loss of memory, and loss of memory results in loss of understanding, or of cognitive ability, and then the man meets with his ruination.[13] In brief, one has to stop dwelling on empirical objects, having any desire, and any emotion. This ideal is not the pragmatic, or realistic, ideal of exercising control over one's desire, emotions, etc., in his normal life. It is something much bigger than that. One has to withdraw from everything external into this self and limit himself to himself. By the time he reaches this stage, he would have completely lost his sense of agency, the sense that he did, has done, is doing, or will do, this, or that.

When one has achieved this stage of self-absorption, or enlightenment, Kṛṣṇa says, there is no duty which he has to perform. He is no more concerned with doing, or not doing, anything, nor does he have any self-interest in any object of the world.[14] But

13. *The Gītā*, II.61-64.
14. *Ibid.*, III.17, 18.

this does not mean that he should become idle, or, inactive. Just as Janaka and some other *kṣatriyas*, even after achieving enlightenment, remained active, Arjuna should also continue doing his duties, i.e., fight the battle desirelessly. He should keep doing his duties also in order to set a good example for the common people, or, rather to prevent them from becoming inactive in imitation of him if they find him inactive. What a great man does, or considers authoritative, ordinary men also do and consider authoritative. Therefore, to avoid a wrong imitation of his behaviour from happening, Arjuna, even after knowing the secret of *niṣkāma karma* or becoming *niṣkāma*, should not become inactive.[15] The *niṣkama karmī* is, therefore, active even though he does not have to be. He is to act only in the interest of *lokasaṁgraham*, i.e., to prevent others from going astray, from straying away from the path of doing their *varṇāśrama dhārmic* duties.

The reference to *lokasaṁgraham* has been interpreted by some modern interpreters in a purely altruistic way. They hold that, according to the *Gītā*, although the enlightened person does not need to do anything to fulfil any obligation or desire of his, he acts out of his sense of benevolence and does some positive actions to promote, or contribute to, the welfare, or good, of the unenlightened people. This would imply that he ascertains what is their good, and which actions would promote it, and then does those actions in order that their good be promoted. This would obviously mean that he has the desire to do good to others. This is also what being benevolent means. But even such a desire he cannot have. Any desire to achieve anything whatsoever, including even social welfare, is bondage-causing. The *niṣkāma* theory exempts no desire from being bondage-causing. To be enlightened, therefore, one has to give up all desires,[16] and, therefore, the enlightened, in point of logic, cannot have even a benevolent desire. To behave while keeping his eyes on *lokasaṁgraham* does not mean, as has been explained, to behave with a desire to do *lokakalyāṇa*, i.e., good to others. It only means to behave in such a way that the *loka*, i.e., common people, take his example in the right spirit. He cannot have

15. *The Gītā*, III.20, 25.
16. *Ibid.*, II.55.

a desire for *lokakalyāṇa* (social welfare) because, as far as the bondage-causing potentiality of an action is concerned, every desireful action has it, no matter whether it is intended to promote the good of the agent, or of the *loka*. Therefore, the enlightened *niṣkāma karmī* can neither be an egoist, nor an altruist.

It may happen that his performance of a duty of his accidentally leads to someone else's good, but he cannot intend to do any good to him. An action intended to do good to someone else would be as *sakāma* (desireful) as one intended to do good to oneself, or, even as one intended to harm anyone. Therefore, by remaining active, i.e., by doing his duties, and other actions, which are required to sustain his material existence, he does not do anything in order to, with a view to, or with the intention to, help the common people. He only makes to them available in himself an example of an active enlightened person, or rather, unavailable an example of an idle enlightened person, whom they may imitate to become idle, if he himself is idle. He thus intentionally does *nothing to them*, or *for them* which an altruist does. He cannot even intend to set an example before them. He would do his *niṣkāma karma*s independently of any concern for them, and his mere existence, by itself, would be an example to them, if they ever take it as an example. Kṛṣṇa says of himself that he does not need to do anything, he has no duty to perform, but is active only to make available to people a good example.[17]

It can be said that the *niṣkāma* theory, or the general classical Indian theory of action of which it is an offshoot, allows the *niṣkama karmī* to have *mumukṣā*, the desire for *mokṣa*. This is true but to preserve the universality of the doctrine of *niṣkāmatā*, i.e., to keep unaffected the claim that all desires have to be given up, it has also been said that *mumukṣā* is not like anything which we can call a desire; therefore, one remains a *niṣkāma karmī* even when he has *mumukṣā*. But this is a completely untenable position. If the desire for *mokṣa* is *absolutely* different from all desires, i.e., if it does not mean what we mean by a desire, then the concept of desire is not applicable to it. Then, it cannot be called a desire, and we would not know what 'desire for *mokṣa*' means because 'desire', occurring in

17. *The Gītā*, III.22-24.

the phrase, would have no meaning for us. Its practical mal-implication would be that no instruction can be given to anybody to have the desire for *mokṣa*, or that *mokṣa* cannot be an object of anybody's desire. On the other hand, if the desire for *mokṣa* is like any other desire in the sense that the concept of desire applies to it, differing from others only in having *mokṣa* as its object, then, one who has it is not absolutely *niṣkāma*, or desireless. Śaṅkara admits that one who does *niṣkāma karma* with *mumukṣā*, the desire to attain *mokṣa*, is not really *niṣkāma*.[18]

The concept of '*niṣkāma*' is unidirectional, in the sense that it is directed towards the agent rather than towards the action he does. '*Niṣkāma*' is an adjective of the doer. Only the doer can be desireless, and not any action, though in the phrase *niṣkāma karma*, '*niṣkāma*' qualifies '*karma*'. '*Niṣkāma karma*' means an action done by the doer in a desireless manner, i.e., done by a doer who is desireless in doing it. It qualifies the motivation of the doer, the motivation with which he does it, and not the action which he does. Therefore, the thrust of the *niṣkāma* theory is that whatsoever be the nature of an action, if its doer is desireless in doing it, it would not have any bondage-causing effect. The whore Bindumatī, the tradition says, acquired more spiritual powers by doing her ignoble profession in a desirelss, non-attached, manner than the then saints had because they were not in their spiritual practices as desireless as she was. That is why she could turn back the current of a river which they could not.[19]

Desirelessness cannot be a test for the morality of an action, or that of a person. Why doing something with the sole desire of benefiting another person, when there is nothing against him which would have made him unfit to be benefitted, is not morally of a higher order, or is of a lower order, than doing the same thing desirelessly is not at all clear. And, neither the *Gītā*, nor any other work, gives a satisfactory answer to this question. The only reason that is given in the *Gītā*, or elsewhere, for a desirelss action being higher in merit than a desireful one is that the former is not,

18. See my *Karma, Causation and Retributive Morality* (ICPR), pp. 238-42.

19. *The Milinda Praśna*, tr. by Bhiksu Jagadish Kasyap, (Sugat Prakashan, Nagpur), pp. 147-9.

whereas the latter is, bondage-causing. But this is not a moral reason. In fact, it is a non-moral, call it spiritual if you like, answer to a moral question. This answer would carry no weight with him who does not believe in rebirth, or in the *varṇāśrama dharma*. In judging the moral quality of an action we take into account some features of its agent, or of his character, as well as some features of the action, and we assume the agency of the agent, i.e., his role as the doer of the action. Since he has done it, we consider him responsible, blameable, or praiseworthy, etc., for having done it. But in the *Gītā*, or even in other accounts of the *niṣkāma* theory, the ideal *niṣkāma karmī* has no sense of agency, and as I have already said, only one feature of his character, his desirelessness, is taken into consideration.

Moreover, if a man deserves to get a certain result when he does, or has done, something, say, promotion in rank after having worked very sincerely for the required number of years, there is nothing unethical in wishing to get the promotion. Rather, one may say, it is unethical not to wish for it, or not to ask for it, or even not to resent not getting it. No such things, though ethically in order, can be said if one accepts the theory of *niṣkāma karma*. The *niṣkāma* theory is not a moral theory because an action's being desireless is neither a necessary, nor a sufficient, condition of its being morally right. It is not a necessary condition because a benevolent action is not desireless but morally right. It is not a sufficient condition because one may do a wrong action in a desireless manner. Rather, the latter's being desireless would make it not just wrong but wicked. The desirefulness of an action done as a duty may even improve its moral quality. If one does *X* to *A* as a duty accompanied with a desire to help him out of a difficult situation, his desire would not reduce but add to the moral quality of *X*.

Our normal moral intuitions do consider doing a duty because it is a duty commendable. But then what is meant is that the agent does not have any selfish desire to fulfil by doing it. He wants to do it because he considers it his duty, and not because he wants to gain something personally by doing it. He may be aware of its likely consequences, may even wish that they should occur; but, he is not doing it only, or primarily, to cause their occurrence. And, if in doing the duty he also desires to achieve some altruistic ends of his, unless we have accepted Kṛṣṇa's *niṣkāma* theory, we would not consider his dutifulness, for that reason, downgraded.

Suppose it is *A*'s duty to return to *B* his gun, kept by *B* in his custody, on his explicit promise to return it to him whenever he would ask for it. Now *B* asks him to return it for killing his wife, who, *A* knows, is innocent. If *A* returns the gun to *B*, with complete indifference to what it is going to, or very likely to, result in, he would be doing it for the sake of duty. But this would mean that he is morally obtuse, or callous, because he does not care for the murder of an innocent woman. Had he returned it to him only after ensuring that he would not hurt the innocent lady, the *niṣkāma* theory would say, his fulfilment of his duty would be polluted by his desire to protect the lady. But the very same pollution of dutifulness by a desireful component of it would highten, as ordinarily understood, the moral quality of his dutifulness, or of his character. It is likely, therefore, that some uses of the principle of doing a duty for the sake of duty may not be morally commendable, or may even be uncommendable. The Indian tradition does not, but we would, I think, consider uncommendable, or even reprehensible, Paraśurāma's killing his mother on the order of his father, since he considers obeying his father's order a duty. The principle of *niṣkāma karma*, therefore, for this reason as well is not a moral principle. It is not a moral principle for the other reason, as we have seen, namely, the reason that it is primarily a means to ensure the liberation of the person, who follows it, from his bondage, i.e., from his liability to be reborn. It does not necessarily involve a care for the welfare of others which is a constitutive element of the ethical or moral concern. A desire for the welfare of others, being a desire, would be bondage-causing, and therefore it must not be mixed with the practice of *niṣkāma karma*. This means that ethics, or morality, cannot be mixed with the latter. The latter may be higher than everything ethical. But that would be another matter. Moreover, even if it is, proving that it is would not be as simple as breaking a peanut, as some seem to think.

It is not that the *niṣkāma* theory forbids only selfish, and not altruistic, desires. It forbids all desires. If the *niṣkāma* theory is said to forbid only selfish or self-centred desires, and not altruistic ones, then it would not be different from the common-garden variety of altruism. The only difference between it and ordinary altruism would then be that a life lived according to it would be claimed to lead to freedom from rebirth, whereas no such claim would be made of the latter. And, if such a claim can be made of it, we may retort, why cannot then it be made of ordinary altruism as well? But all this manoeuvre is unnecessary because the kārmic world-view, which is foundational to the *niṣkāma* theory, clearly holds that all desireful actions, altruistic or selfish, produce consequences to experience which the agent has to take rebirth.

It is not the what, the content, of an action, but its desirelessness which makes it non-bondage-causing. It is not necessary that it be a duty. Therefore, Arjuna could have told Kr̥ṣṇa that, if desirelessly fighting the battle, which meant killing relatives and elders, would procure his liberation, why desirelessly living on alms, which involved injury to none, should not? Perhaps it is good that he did not, because Kr̥ṣṇa, who is so deeply committed to the theory of *varṇāśrama dharma*, would not have been able to find an appropriate answer without coming out of that theory. Herein lies one of the weakest spots of the *niṣkāma* theory. It has no criterion to compare meritwise one desireless action with another. Rather, it tends to make all of them equal in merit. Release from bondage is the highest end. Therefore, if one desireless action is as good a means to it as any other, all desireless actions are equal in merit. If of two such actions, *X* and *Y*, *X* is better than *Y*, then there must be a criterion higher than *niṣkāmatā* which *X* satisfies and *Y* does not, or *X* satisfies more than *Y* does. Or, there is another end higher than liberation to which *X* is a means and *Y* is not a means, or *X* is a better means than *Y*. But those who accept the *niṣkāma* doctrine neither accept a higher criterion than *niṣkāmatā*, nor a higher end than liberation.

Among human actions, nothing but the fact of its being done desirelessly makes an action a means to liberation. It needs to be noted that an action can neither have, nor not have, any desire; only its agent may, or may not, have. It is really a case of transferred epithet to call an action desireless, or desireful. The *niṣkāma* philosophy of life is agent-centric. This is also clear from the fact that it is the mode in which the agent does an action, desirefully or desirelessly, which matters, and not what the action *as* an action is. What is important to make an action a means to liberation is not that the agent's desire, or will, in doing it, should be a good desire, or a good will, whatever 'good' may mean here, but that he should have no desire at all to produce anything by doing it. Its being even a duty does not matter. Doing an action, which is a duty, would be a means to *mokṣa* only if it is desireless. What makes it a means is not its being a duty but its being done desirelessly. Therefore, this position downgrades even the notion of duty, or gives to it a lower status than to desirelessness.

In the thought-structure, or conceptual context, of the *niṣkāma* theory a *karma* or action means an intentional action, and not an action done inadvertently, accidentally, or impulsively, etc. It is an intentional, thought-out, action which Kṛṣṇa wants Arjuna to do without any desire for its consequences. Fighting a battle is to do a series of well-planned, well-thought-out, intentional, actions, which Arjuna is advised to do in the *niṣkāma* way. There is no sense in advising anyone to do an inadvertent, accidental, or impulsive, action with no desire for its consequences becuase in such actions the doer's eyes are not set on the consequences. He does not think of them or, more truly, the idea of what they are likely to be does not remain at the centre of his attention. Therefore, to be precise, we should say that Kṛṣṇa's gospel of *niṣkāma karma* enjoins that an intentional action be done with no desire for its consequences. Of an intentional action it is obvious to say that its agent intends to do it. Where we can say he intends to do it, we can surely say he wants, or desires, to do it. Therefore, in Kṛṣṇa's conceptual framework, it is possible to intend, or desire, to do an action without having any desire for anyone of its likely consequences.

Kṛṣṇa also speaks of giving up all desires, and not only desires for the consequences of actions. He attains peace, according to him, who, after giving up all desires, moves about freed from the sense of 'me' and 'mine', from egoism and attachment.[20] As per common experience, an intentional action X is possible without any desire for doing X, if there is another desire for doing something else. I drink intentionally, though I do not want, or desire, to drink,

20. *The Gītā*, II.71.

because I want, or desire, to please my boss who has himself offered me the glass of drink. To do an intentional action, therefore, I must have at least some desire for something, or for doing something. But if I have no desire at all, if I am completely desireless, I cannot do any intentional action. Therefore, if Arjuna gives up all desires, he cannot do any intentional action, and then all of Kṛṣṇa's exhortations to him for doing actions without any desire for their consequences would become infructuous, like the exhortation to a blind man to see paintings without looking at their price tags. Kṛṣṇa would have done his job better without insisting on the abnegation of all desires. But by insisting on it he overshoots his target. He would have missed it completely, i.e., would have failed to convince Arjuna to fight, but does not because of Arjuna's overpliability in his relationship with him. Because of his charismatic influence on him, Arjuna does not notice the subtle logical point that, if he gives up all desires, he cannot do anything intentional, and therefore cannot fight. He rather acquiesces in whatever he is advised to do. But the way he fights and the way the battle progresses make it extremely difficult to believe that he fights the battle with no desire at all, or even with no desire for any of its consequences. Kṛṣṇa could have advised him to have no desire for any of its consequences without advising him to give up all desires. Perhaps he is carried away by the general trend in classical Indian philosophy of looking down upon all human desires.

But let us ignore for the time being the advice to give up all desires and consider only that part of Kṛṣṇa's advice which requires Arjuna to have no desire for any of the fruits of his actions. Then, since even this advice would be meaningful only in the context of an intentional action, it presupposes that one can do an intentional action without any desire for any of its likely consequences. That is, one can say that he is *X*-ing because he wants to, or desires to, but he has no desire for any of its likely consequences. This would be something like saying that he wants to chew a sugar-cube but has no desire to taste its sweetness. It would in this version mean that, to follow Kṛṣṇa Arjuna can have the desire to fight the battle, but should not have any desire for any of its consequences. This may look to be the most charitable way to interpret the doctrine of *niṣkāma karma* and thereby to save it from at least some of the conceptual problems it has, in the above discussion, been shown to be afflicted with. But let us see if this optimism is maintainable.

To hold that one can have a desire for *X*-ing but need not have a desire for any of its likely consequences presupposes that he can completely identify, or individuate, the action called *X*-ing, i.e., can have a complete conception of the action, without referring to what he considers to be its likely consequences. But this is not always possible. In the case of many actions to individuate them accurately necessarily requires referring to their likely, or intended, i.e., desired, consequences. A foot-ball game played between two teams would be two different games if the intended consequences are different in its two instances. Suppose the teams play only to avoid forgetting their manoeuvring skill. Then it is a practising game, and it is because the result they intend it to produce is to give them opportunities for rehearsing in action their manoeuvring abilities on the playgrorund. If, on the other hand, the teams play with the intention to exhibit their relative superiority over each other, i.e., when each party intends to defeat the other, it becomes a competitive game, a football match. That is, in individuating the game as a practising game, or as a competitive game, we have to take into account the consequences it is desired by the teams to produce. Even the teams, in intending to play the kind of game they intend to play, they must take into account the effects, or results, they intend it to produce. Therefore, their conception of the game would be complete only if they include in it the results they desire it to produce. None of the teams can say that it wants, or desires, to play a competitive game with the other team but it has no desire to defeat the other team. If it does not have this desire, it cannot say that it desires to play a competitive game.

What I want to say here is that in some cases it is not possible to desire to do an action with no desire for any of its likely consequences, or with no desire to produce some specific consequence or consequences, because a desire for some relevant consequence, or consequences, is conceptually involved in the notion of the action concerned. I think it can also be shown that in no case it is possible to do that, but it is not necessary to show it here since my objective can be achieved by merely showing it to be true of some actions. If this is so, Kṛṣṇa cannot give a general prescription to do all intentional actions without any desire for their consequences.

What about fighting a battle? This is the kind of action which Kṛṣṇa is immediately interested in persuading Arjuna to do without any desire for any of its consequences. It seems to me that fighting a battle is one of the clearest kind of actions, or series of actions, which cannot be completely identified, or concieved of, without referring to its consequences. A battle is one of aggression if one side fights with the other with the desire to capture some territory which rightfully belongs to the latter. It would be a battle in self-defence for the side which fights it with the desire to prevent the other side from taking something that belongs to it. A battle is retributive, or righteous, if it is fought with the desire to take back from the other side what has been wrongfully retained, or taken, by the latter, etc. Unless we include in the conception, individuation, or description, of the battle what it is desired to yield, we cannot call it aggressive, self-defensive, or retributive. Therefore, it is not conceptually possible to have a desire to fight a battle of a certain type with no desire to produce a certain kind of effect by fighting it, because, in the determination of the character, i.e., the identity, of the battle, the desire for the result it is fought to yield has to be taken into account.

Arjuna is asked to fight the battle because it is a *dharmayuddha* (righteous war). It is a *dharmayuddha* because it is to be fought to take back, or recover, from Duryodhana, his rightful share of the kingdom which the latter has wrongfully usurped. Fighting is an intentional activity, and therefore Arjuna has to have a desire to fight. He cannot have the desire to fight a *dharmayuddha* without having a desire to recover his lost kingdom because it is the latter which makes it a retributive battle. If he fights with the desire to kill Duḥśāsana, whether or not he gets back his lost kingdom, or with no care for anything else which may happen, his fight would become purely, or predominantly, retaliative. It may no longer, then, remain a *dharmayuddha*. The kind of actions which fighting a battle and its ilk, like playing a game, teaching a course, digging into the earth, burning dry fuel with *ghī* sprikled on it, etc., are, they get their identity from the agent's desire to produce the results they are done to produce. That is why the agent of any one of them, when asked why does he do it, may mention only his desire to produce the effect he wants to. He may not mention his desire to do the act *per se*. Rather, it can be said that his desire to produce the effect concerned also explains why he wants to do, or why does he do the actiton concerned. When asked why do you sprinkle *ghī* on the burning fuel, the sensible agent may only say that he wants to please his family deity. He does not have to mention two desires, one to put *ghī* on the burning fuel and the other to please the deity. Therefore, in the case of an action like putting *ghī* on the burning fuel, one cannot be advised to have no desire for any its of consequences, while permitting him to have a desire for the basic act of putting *ghī* on the burning fuel. This is so because the desire to produce the result is the desire for the basic act.

I can conclude this part, therefore, by saying that if, to avoid its being forced to deny the possibility of intentional actions if all desires are given up, we want to hold that the *niṣkāma* theory allows having desires for actions but recommends the abnegation of desires for their results, we cannot, in point of logic, do that. The reason is that the complete conception of an intentional action generally involves some conception of at least some of its likely consequences and the desire for the latter is also the desire for the parent action. Philosophers and non-philosophers alike often claim to derive from II.47 of the *Gītā*[21] a pragmatic argument in favour of cherishing no desire for any of the likely consequences of any of our actions. It may be an important exegetical point to ascertain whether or not II.47 really yields an argument of this sort. But I shall not indulge in that kind of exercise. It seems to me that, since this argument has attained some celebrity status in academic as well as lay circles, in its own right it deserves to be given a respectable scrutiny, no matter whether or not it can justifiably be obtained from II.47.

(K) The argument runs as follows:

> A human being has only the right to do an action. He has no right or control over any of its consequences. Therefore, there is no point in having any desire for any of its consequences.

21. *The Gītā*, II.47.

Looking at it with a non-probing eye, anybody would say that it is an innocent argument, if it means that we must not worry too much about the consequences of the actions we do. Sometimes we may, sometimes we may not, get what we want an action to yield. But if the argument is taken to prove, as it really is, that we should have no desire for any of its likely consequences, then it is neither innocent, or logically sound.

It is not innocent because, if we really believe that we have absolutely no control over any of the consequences of an action, we would turn out to be stark pessimists. For example, a farmer, who sows the best kind of seeds available in the best kind of soil he can possibly have, would then have no right to wish that the seeds sprout and therefore no faith in farming. Arjuna would lose faith in his archery because, in spite of his being the most skilled archer, he would have then no right to expect that his arrow would hit its target. Neither the pessimist farmer would have any zeal in farming, nor a diffident Arjuna in shooting his arrow to kill the killer of his son.

The argument is not logically sound because both the premises are overgeneralisations. The first because we have the right to do some of our actions, but not to do all that we may like to do. There are several things we want to do but we cannot do, and we cannot have the right to do what we cannot do. The second because we do not have control over all consequences of our actions, but we do have on some of them. We have because we do sometimes act in such a way that our actions produce the results we want them to produce. It is this empirical truth which makes us optimistic, and inspires us to work for establishing greater coordination between actions done and results expected from them. Moreover, a staunch believer in morality would say that if he deserves to get *X* by doing *Y*, then he has a right to get *X*, and since he has a right to get it, he has a right to desire that he should get it and to make efforts to get it. If he does not get it, it does not mean that he should not have any desire to have got it. For his not getting it, it is not he but the world to be blamed. Therefore, in place of advising him not to have a desire for any of his actions' consequences, what is needed is to change the world, to reorganise worldly matters in such a way that its inhabitants get their legitimate desires, if not all, most of them, fulfilled. But this kind of reasoning would be out of place if we consider (K) unfaultable.

I think the real value of the argument (K), or its source *Gītā*.II.47, lies not in providing a reason for saying that one should have no desire for any of the likely consequences of any action of his, but in providing consolation to him when he has not got what he wanted or deserved on account his having done a certain action, which is all that he should or could have done. He may get consoled if he is told that, since no one has absolute control over the consequences of any action of his, there is no point in his grieving over his not having got what he wanted to. To use his not having got what he wanted or deserved, i.e., his deprivation, as a reason for telling him that he should not have had a desire for the result he has not got, would amount to adding insult to injury because it would amount to telling him that it was wrong for him to have desired, even when it was legitimate for him to have desired, to get the result he did not get.

If we accept the doctrine of *niṣkāma karma* and try to lead a life which is concordant with it, we can do that only if we know how to ascertain that an action has been desirelessly done. But there seems to exist a great difficulty, almost insuperable, in doing that. No inspection of an action, howsoever meticulous, can help because desirelessness is not a feature of the action, but of the motivation of the agent. Therefore, only by knowing the motivation of the doer we may do that. But we cannot peep into his mind to check whether or not he is desireless. We have only to examine his behaviour. But concluding on the basis of his behaviour that he is desireless would be extremely hard, much harder than ascertaining, in the case of a desireful action, which desire has motivated him to behave the way he has behaved. A desireless action is said to produce no bondage-causing effect. But this too we cannot know. We have therefore either to be satisfied with whatever guess we can make from his behaviour, or with his own personal statement which may not always be dependable. But can an agent know with certainty about an action of his own that it has been done, or is being done, in a desireless manner? Even this question cannot be answered in a definitive way because he may deceive himself, or may have a desire he is not distinctly or clearly aware of. I have mentioned all this only to make visible the inherent difficulties in applying the criterion of desirelessness to an external agent, or even to oneself. It is true that some people have been charmed by it. The reason for that seems to be their *ṛṣi* bias, or their not being seriously interested in applying it to a concrete case in their own life history, or in that of someone else.

Kṛṣṇa also tells Arjuna to take shelter in him, who is god, giving up all of his *dharmas*, i.e., rights and duties, and not to grieve. He will free him from all sins.[22] At another place, at an early stage of the dialogue, he tells him to fight in a tensionless manner, without any expectation and egoism, with his mind concentrated on the self, dedicating all of his actions to him (i.e., to Kṛṣṇa).[23] He not only makes references to his being god at so many places, but also shows to him his cosmic form. These devices do work on Arjuna and motivate him to agree with Kṛṣṇa that he should fight and to actually fight. They, thus, have their role, but do not seem to strengthen the *niṣkāma* doctrine. If acting desirelessly can free Arjuna from bondage, causing no sin to him, irespective of the nature of the actions he desirelessly does, then it does not matter whether or not he dedicates his actions to god or even believes in god's existence. But if desirelessly done actions free the doer from bondage only if dedicated to god, then dedicating an action to god becomes a necessary condition for obtaining release. And, if only an action, which is *both* desirelessly done and dedicated to god, can cause release, then what is the comparative share of each one of its two features in causing release? Neither Arjuna raises the question, nor Kṛṣṇa answers it on his own.

The way the *niṣkāma* doctrine has been developed by Kṛṣṇa, it sometimes does give the impression that, if one leads a life in accordance with it, and does nothing else, i.e., does not even think of god, he would get emancipated. But on some other occasions, he says, the desirelessly done actions have to be surrendered to god. If this is the case, then an atheist cannot be emancipated even if his life has been led in accordance with the *niṣkāma* doctrine. But the thrust of the Indian ethical tradition seems to be in the direction of

22. *The Gītā*, XVIII.66.
23. *Ibid.*, III.30.

holding that leading a *niṣkāma* life is an effective means to attain salvation.

Some scholars think that the *niṣkāma* way to attain emancipation becomes smoother, or more convenient, when it is made to involve a reference to god. But this need not happen. The concept of a desireless action has already got, we have seen, some problems of its own. In their solution the concept of god would have been helpful if it were relevant, clearer, and unprone to create any additional problem. But it is neither. It has its own problems which are in no way less intractable than those involved in the concept of *niṣkāmatā*. History of philosophy has very well shown that it is neither easy to believe that god exists, nor to have a conception of what kind of being he is, if he exists. Therefore, I shall not dilate on the theistic reference, if any, involved in the doctrine of *niṣkāmatā*.

It is fair, thus, to conclude that the ultimate justification for the prescription of leading one's life in a *niṣkāma* manner, for doing whatever he does desirelessly, has to be teleological, or consequentialist, i.e., in terms of its purportedly being a means to *mokṣa* which is claimed to be desirable in an ultimate, intrinsic, sense. It is a prescription about *how*, about the *manner* in which, a duty, or any action, should be done. It is meaningful to say of a duty that it should be done in a desireless manner for the consequentialist reason mentioned above. It is not possible for the *niṣkāma* doctrine to get rid of consequentialism, i.e., to give a purely deontological reason for doing a duty desirelessly.

Suppose one avoids the consequentialist route and says that a duty is to be done desirelessly not because of its consequences but because doing a duty desirelessly is itself a duty. Saying this would not only be circular, but would also involve the fallacy of infinite regress. It would involve the latter because, if doing a duty desirelessly is itself a duty, one can very well ask why should he do this duty desirelessly, i.e., the duty of doing a duty desirelessly, and can go on asking it *ad infinitum*. Such a question would not be illegitimate because, if it can be asked of any duty why should it be done desirelessly, it can also be asked of the duty of doing a duty desirelessly when doing a duty desirelessly is also said to be a duty. Therefore, doing a duty desirelessly cannot itself be called a duty.

This does look paradoxical, but the paradox arises only if the *niṣkāma* doctrine is claimed to be deontological, which, as has been shown here, it is not and cannot be. I think to interpret the doctrine in this way is also fair to the Indian tradition, or at least to the tradition which Kṛṣṇa represents.

Final salvation is said to be the release of the self from its embodiment after the *jīva's* (individual's) death (*videhamukti*). But from the point of view of leading a *dhārmic*, a moral, life, i.e., of practising morality, the prospect of one's reaching, in his lifetime, the state of the highest kind of self-fulfilment, possible for a living being, is more important and attractive. The concept of *jīvanmukti* (salvation or self-fulfilment attained by an individual while he is alive) is said to refer to this state. Many classical Indian thinkers hold that it is attainable by leading a *niṣkāma* life, i.e., a life devoted to doing desirelessly whatever one does. If it is, it would justify the latter. But it would do only if it itself is normatively absolutely non-defective and conceptually non-vacuous, i.e., free from any built-in logical deficiency which would make its application or instantiation impossible. To see whether or not it is competent to do the job it is claimed, or expected, to do, let us turn to the next chapter.

3
Jīvanmukti
Probelms of Normativity and Instantiation

JĪVANMUKTI is said to be the highest ideal for a living individual to attain, an ideal much higher than any mundane one, social, political, or moral, etc. It is one of those topics in one's comprehension, or discussion, of which his *ṛṣi* bias is very likely to be operative, if it has taken hold of his mind. *Ṛṣi* bias, as has been shown in chapter 2, is an attitude of mind which forbids its possessor to try objectively to understand and evaluate any view of an alleged *ṛṣi* on the ground that it cannot suffer from any sort of defect. The only thing we can do is, he would say, to try to describe and interpret it, but comment on it we should not, or dare not.

In this chapter, I would approach the topic of *jīvanmukti* in a philosophical or logical manner without the *ṛṣi* bias. I would first show, after some exploration, that, of the various features of *jīvanmukti*, cessation of the *jīvanmukta*'s liability to be reborn[1] is, as per the intention of the Indian philosophical tradition, the most necessary one. Every individual who is in bondage necessarily possesses the liability to be reborn after his physical death. When he becomes a *jīvanmukta* this liability of his, therefore, must cease to exist. But, I will then proceed to show, this feature cannot be predicated by anyone of anyone, including himself. This would mean that the concept of *jīvanmukta*, or of being a *jīvanmukta*, is uninstantiable, or inapplicable to any individual, and even if it is applicable to someone, nobody can say that it is. We cannot say of anybody that he is a *jīvanmukta*, even if he is. I will thereafter argue that an appeal to Śruti, or a revealed text, won't be of any help here.

1. *Vedāntasāra*, 123: 227.

Śruti can give, if it can give anything, only some common features of *jīvanmukti*, or allegedly some general truths about it. It cannot give us any help in determining whether or not a particular individual is a *jīvanmukta*.

Another thing I will do is to examine the claim, so often made of a *jīvanmukta*, that he is a morally perfect individual. In this connection I will also examine whether or not it is possible for anyone to attain moral perfection. My conclusion will be that it would be attainable only if morality is considered to be a closed system. But to do the latter would be counter-intuitive because, as ordinarily or generally understood, morality is an open-ended, or open-textured, phenomenon.

I shall explain below how I shall be using certain terms which play key roles in the essay. I hope this will ensure better understanding, or at least minimise misunderstanding, of the position taken by me. I do not think my use of any one of these terms is incongruent with their, or their equivalents', prevalent usage in the literature. But even if it is, it would not matter if I am using them consistently and the reader knows how I am using them.

I shall use 'individual' as the equivalent of *jīva*, and by the latter I shall mean a living human being. *Jīva* is also used, I admit, to mean any living being, human or non-human, and therefore even animals can be said to be *jīva*s. But since this chapter is about *jīvanmukti* which is a human value or ideal, and only human beings can be said to be concerned with human values, or ideals, I shall restrict the use of *jīva* or 'individual' to mean a living human being. This does not mean that I am ignoring the importance of animals in this world. To the best of my knowledge no school of classical Indian philosophy, has attributed to any (non-human) animal the ability to seek *jīvanmukti*. Any individual is necessarily an embodied being. It can also be called an embodied Self. In trying to be *mukta* it tries to be the Self unencumbered by the body and bodily pains and pleasures. That is why to be *mukta* is also to realise the Self. In *jīvanmukti* it realises the Self but, since it remains embodied, it still has bodily limitations, though it is not controlled or dominated by them. This is so because it knows that they are not necessary for the Self which it ultimately or basically, is, and would remain when liberated. Therefore, it is the individual who is in bondage and who attains *mokṣa* in *jīvanmukti* or *videhamukti*. Only the individual is subject to birth, death, and rebirth, and exists in time. All this is due to the fact that it has to have a body. In *jīvanmukti* it remains an individual, though liberated, because it has its body, but in *videhamukti* it ceases to be an individual because it has no body. Then it returns to the status of a pure Self.

I shall use 'Self' to mean *ātman*. *Ātman*, in classical Indian philosophical usage, to put it roughly and inexhaustively, is taken to be essentially disembodied, in the sense that to be what it really is it does not, unlike the *jīva*, need any sort of body. It is non-active, or a non-agent, because action requires a body and a mind which it does not have. It does not have anything mental because mind is also, in Indian philosophy, considered to be a part or function of the body. It does not, therefore, have any intention, will, passion, or emotion, etc. It is unsullied or pure, perfect in virtue of just being what it is. Therefore, we cannot say that it can be improved in any way, i.e., made better than what it at any time actually is.

What is important to note is that the Self, as it naturally or originally is, is never in bondage. It is neither born, nor it dies, and therefore it cannot be reborn. Therefore, it is not to be liberated. Only the individual is. We can at the most say that the Self in the individual, in the latter's physical death, shakes off its embodiment and comes back to its original, disembodied, state. This is so because the link between it and the body is contingent.

Since 'Self-fulfilment', 'Liberation', 'Salvation', 'Emancipation', 'Release', 'Freedom', etc., have been used in the literature for *mokṣa*, I shall use either one of these terms for the latter, depending on contextual or linguistic suitability.

Mokṣa is said to be the highest human value or ideal (*parama puruṣārtha*), the most important of the things a human being can and ought to aim at. Śaṅkara says that the dull-headed, who does not have a desire for *mokṣa* (*mumukṣā*), or does not try to attain it, is his own destroyer.[2] *Mokṣa* is freedom from bondage. Bondage means the chain, or cycle, of birth-death-rebirth. An unliberated or

2. *Vivekacūḍāmaṇi*, p. 8:4, Gita Press.

bonded (*baddha*) individual is born, lives for a short or long duration of time, dies and then is reborn in a form and environment determined by the actions (*karma*s) done by him in his previous life. With his new birth another cycle of birth-death-rebirth begins. This process continues until the individual attains his *mokṣa*.

It is impossible to say of any individual when was he born for the first time. Therefore, his bondage, or his cycle of birth-death-rebirth, is beginningless. Every individual, unless he emancipates himself from it, is subject to, or bound to be a victim to, this process of triple rhythm, and as long as he is subjected to it, he is in bondage. The redeeming feature is that, though beginningless, the process is not endless or interminable. The state of bondage is a state of unhappiness (*duḥkha*). As long as one remains caught up in the cycle, he has to experience at least some suffering. The bonded individual acquires, because of his intentional actions, the liability to be reborn, and when reborn, he has to experience the pleasures and sufferings he deserves on account of the actions done by him in his previous life. His pleasures are generally of a mixed character and short-lived. He cannot get rid of his sufferings without getting terminated his liability to be reborn, i.e., without emancipating himself from the cycle of birth-death-rebirth. Since the state of emancipation, or emancipatedness, is nothing but the return of the Self-in-the-individual to the Self's original state, every individual has in him the built-in capability of attaining it.

I do not intend to suggest that there is one and only one conception of *jīva*, or *ātman*, or *mokṣa*, in Indian philosophy. Its different schools do, in some respects, differ among themselves in their views on each one of them. But they also agree in some other respects. To the objective of this chapter their agreements are more relevant than their differences. Therefore, in each case, I have presented an account which would be acceptable to all the schools which accept *mokṣa* as the highest value and the possibility of its realisation in life. That is, I have mentioned only those features of *jīva*, *ātman*, and *mokṣa* which are held to be true of them by all the schools I shall be concerned with.

That the termination of suffering is an intrinsic good, and therefore the experience of suffering an intrinsic evil, is taken by

Indian thinkers as an obvious, intuitive, truth. Therefore, they do not see any need of giving any detailed, argumentative, defence of it. Some of them do occasionally refer to the fact that no normal person prefers having a suffering to having a happiness, or even to getting the suffering terminated. By appealing to this fact they do not intend to *prove* that suffering is an evil, something which ought to be gotten rid of, *because* it *is considered* to be an evil, or *is* disliked. There is nothing, in the appeal, like deducing an 'ought' from an 'is'. Rather, it is made only to show the obviousness of the claim that suffering is an evil, or the oddity of disputing or denying it.

It would be a safe generalisation to say that all human beings want to get rid of their sufferings, or to lead a life free from suffering. But this does not mean that all human beings have *mumukṣā*, the desire to attain *mokṣa*. If *mumukṣā* were such a common desire, Śaṅkara would not have exhorted the aspirants after *mokṣa* to have it and called those who did not have it self-slayers.

Mumukṣā is not just the desire to get rid of a suffering, or even of all sufferings one has or can possibly have. It is the desire for *mokṣa* which is release from bondage, from the cycle of birth-death-rebirth, running according to the provisions of the law of *karma*. Therefore, only he can have *mumukṣā* who believes in the law of *karma* and rebirth and in the disembodied reality of the Self because to be *mukta* is to return to the latter. The state of liberation is a state of complete sufferinglessness because the Self in its original, disembodied, state is completely sufferingless. The average human being does want to get rid of his sufferings but he need not be aware of the working of the law of *karma*, of the theory of rebirth, or of what the Self in its original state is. Moreover, his desire to get rid of sufferings is not necessarily one to completely get rid of all them. What happens is that he has, what we may call, the normal standard of a happy, comfortable, life. According to the latter a few sufferings, or certain types of them, do not make a life unhappy, just as some illnesses, or some types of them, do not make a man unhealthy. This norm does not require that there be no suffering in life, but only that the sufferings one has do not exceed a certain limit. The average person possesses a rough, but a fairly clear, idea of the limit. What I mean to say is that the normal, commonsense, standard of a happy life does not mean a life of absolutely no suffering. But the state of *mokṣa* means the latter. Therefore, a man's normal desire to get rid of his sufferings is not the same as *mumukṣā*. *Mumukṣā* can be had only after inculcating the beliefs mentioned above.

We cannot, therefore, build an argument of the following type:

(1) (1a) Everyone has a desire to get rid of his sufferings and therefore he has *mumukṣā*.

(1b) Attainment of *mokṣa* alone can satisfy *mumukṣā*.

(1c) Therefore, everyone ought to attain *mokṣa* (to satisfy *mumukṣā*).

(1) claims to establish the substantive thesis of the universal prescription of attaining *mokṣa*. But it is a deceptive argument. It (mis)takes *mumukṣā* for one's normal desire for getting rid of his sufferings, keeping in view, as explained earlier, his common-sense conception of a happy, or suffering-free, life. *Mumukṣā* is very different from this desire. It is one for *mokṣa*, for getting permanent release from the chain of birth-death-rebirth and thereby for becoming absolutely free from all kinds of sufferings. Therefore (1a) is false. (1) is a prudential argument and had (1a) been true, it would have been valid and would have proven its conclusion. This would have been something very important because it would have proven then that the universal obligatoriness of seeking *mokṣa* is as obvious as the truth of a common-sense belief of our daily consumption.

But we can of course have an argument of the following type, using *mumukṣā* in its correct sense, meaning the desire for *mokṣa*:

(2) (2a) Attaining *mokṣa* alone can satisfy *mumukṣā*.

(2b) Therefore, if one has *mumukṣā*, he ought to attain *mokṣa* (to satisfy *mumukṣā*).

(2) is an innocent argument but it does not take us anywhere. (2a) says truistically that the attainment of *mokṣa*, being the object of *mumukṣā* (the desire for *mokṣa*), alone can satisfy *mumukṣā*. (2b) is also truistic. It is an exemplification of the truism that if one has the desire to get *X*, to satisfy

it he ought to get *X*. (2), thus, does not make any substantive claim, not even the claim that everyone ought to attain *mokṣa*.

It is important to distinguish between arguments (1) and (2), and to note that none of them establishes the claim that everyone ought to attain *mokṣa*. The latter is a fundamental claim entailed by the honourable position of the *parama puruṣārtha* (highest human end) given to *mokṣa* by the Indian theory of value.

Both (1) and (2) are prudential arguments. A prudential argument can be of the form (1) '*A* has a desire for *B*, therefore he ought to have *B* to satisfy his desire', or of the form (2) '*A* has a desire for *B*, therefore, he ought to have *B*.' (1) is truistic because it, in a sense, only explicates the meaning of 'having a desire for *B*'. It does not make any claim about the propriety of having *B*. (2), on the other hand, makes such a claim because it does not have the phrase 'to satisfy his desire' in its conclusion. It gives the impression that having a desire for *B* is a justifying reason for having *B*, and this, one may say, is wrong. To have a desire for *B* is indifferent to the desirability of having *B*. If it is considered to be a justifying reason, then one can claim to have a justifying reason for having anything whatsoever on the ground that he has a desire for it. He may claim to have a justifying reason for killing someone, or having his beautiful wife, or his newly built house, etc., on that ground.

It is true that one's having a desire for *B* has nothing to do with the desirability of his having *B*. But sometimes we do say that he ought to have *B* because he wants to have it. This we normally do when having *B* is in itself a desirable thing. When having something is desirable in its own right then a desire for it also becomes desirable, and therefore it is right to say that one ought to have it when he has a desire for it. But it is clear here that his having a desire for it has not made his having it desirable. Rather, the reverse is the case. Since having it is itself a desirable thing, his desire for it has become a good, desirable, desire. Therefore, satisfying the desire by giving it to him also has become a desirable thing.

It is in the case of such a thing, having which is desirable, that we sometimes say of a person, who does not have a desire for it, that he ought to have a desire for it. This we do only when having it is relevant to him, i.e., to his personhood, profession, social status, physical condition, etc. *Mokṣa* is said to be the highest ideal for every human being in the sense that there is nothing better than it which he may aim at. Therefore, those who accept it say that everyone ought to have a desire for it. When it is said that one who has *mumukṣā* ought to attain *mokṣa*, his having *mumukṣā* is not made a reason for prescribing the attainment of *mokṣa* to him. The latter is prescribable in its own right. *Mumukṣā* is, thus, said to be the highest kind of desire because its object, *mokṣa*, is the highest value.

The way Indian philosophers speak of suffering in human life, it seems that they think of suffering as a necessary constituent of the latter. That is, as long as one is alive, it is impossible for him to be completely free from suffering. He can be free only after becoming freed from the cycle of birth-death-rebirth, i.e., only after becoming liberated. Almost all the modern interpreters of classical Indian philosophy have taken all the schools of it, which accept *mokṣa*, to hold both of the two views: (a) that suffering is necessarily linked with life and (b) that complete freedom from suffering is necessarily a feature of the state of *mokṣa*, i.e., of the liberated state of the individual (*muktāvasthā*). This interpretation has acquired so much of respectability that questioning it is not likely to get an unbiased reception. But to me it seems that both of (a) and (b) need to be questioned and rejected.

(a) The link between suffering and living is non-symmetrical because suffering implies living but living does not imply suffering. One can have an experience of suffering if and only if he is a living being; dead creatures cannot suffer. The link between living and suffering is empirical and not logical. It is empirically true that almost every human being experiences at least some suffering sometime in his life. But the concept of a living being does not imply that of a suffering being. This is a common-sense truth. But that it is also a truth for classical Indian philosophy has not been recognised. To say that the link between the two is empirical, and not logical, is to say that it is logically possible for a human being to have no suffering in his entire lifetime. This we can do without contravening any of the basic principles, or postulates, of classical Indian philosophy, or rather, to put it a little more forcefully, as required by one of them, namely, the law of *karma*, or the kārmic world-view, as I would prefer to call it.

According to the kārmic theory, the next life of an individual is determined by the actions done by him in his previous life. His actions could be of two broad kinds: desireful (*sakāma*) and desireless (*niṣkāma*). Desireless actions yield no consequences which he would have to bear in his present or future existence. But desireful actions do. They are of three kinds: *śukla*, *kṛṣṇa*, and *śukla-kṛṣṇa*. *Śukla* (white) actions yield pleasurable consequences, *kṛṣṇa* (black) actions unpleasurable consequences, and *śukla-kṛṣṇa* mixed consequences which are partly pleasurable and partly unpleasurable.

It is logically possible that a man does in his present existence only one type of actions, say, of the *śukla* type, which would yield only pleasurable consequences. In that case, in his next life he would have only pleasurable or happy experiences and no suffering. Since *śukla* actions yield consequences, their doer would have to experience in his present or future existence, the doer is still caught up in the cycle of birth-death-rebirth. He is still in bondage and would have to be reborn to enjoy in the next life unmixed pleasures. His would be a completely happy life of a man in bondage, of a man living a life of no suffering. And, luckily, if he does only *śukla* actions in this happy life as well, his next life would also be sufferingless. This cycle may go on and on endlessly. It would stop only when he does only desireless (or *aśukla-kṛṣṇa*) actions which do not yield any consequence he would have to experience, and therefore create no liability for him to be reborn. He would obviously then become liberated.

It is clear, thus, that it is logically possible for an individual to be in bondage, to be liable to be reborn again and again, and still have no suffering at all. Whether or not it would be sensible to call him an individual in bondage, a self-slayer because he has no desire for *mokṣa*, and to advise him to seek *mokṣa*, is another matter. I can very well imagine him to retort 'why should I return to the status of a non-active, bodyless Self, even to that of the lonely *saccidānanda*, when I can have a completely happy life in a world replete with opportunities for exploring the secrets of nature, enjoying beauty, and serving the needy?' It seems to me that, had this implication of the kārmic view, drawn and elaborated here, been well utilised, the Indian philosophers, or their modern interpreters, might have given to us a theory of values without *mokṣa* and without many metaphysical beliefs for accepting which there is no ground except the (questionable) authority of the Śruti.

(b) As per the generally accepted interpretation, all the schools of classical Indian philosophy, which accept *mokṣa* as the highest *puruṣārtha*, agree in at least attributing two interrelated features to it. They are (i) complete freedom from suffering and (ii) non-liability to be reborn. The liberated individual, in *videhamukti* (post-mortem liberation), when he returns to the original state of the Self, is free from all suffering and from the liability to be reborn, i.e., freed from the cycle of birth-death-rebirth. Both of these features have absoluteness and eternality in them. The Self in this state is absolutely and eternally free from suffering and absolutely and eternally non-liable to be reborn. (i) and (ii) are interrelated, the received interpretation says, in the sense that absolute freedom from suffering can be had only after getting freed from the bondage of birth-death-rebirth. The heart of *mokṣa* it locates in freedom from suffering and treats freedom from the bondage of birth-death-rebirth as a precondition for attaining the former. But, as I have shown in (a) above, freedom from suffering cannot be said to be impossible when the individual is liable to be reborn. Moreover, the liberated individual, as conceived by the Nyāya school, cannot be said to be free from suffering. This is not to say that it experiences some suffering. Rather, it is a thing to which neither any experience of suffering, nor any experience of the absence of suffering, can be attributed because no experience can be attributed to it. This is so because it is a non-conscious substance.

For the Nyāya, consciousness is an accidental, non-essential, property of the Self. The Self has to be associated with a body to become conscious and to have all those things which a conscious being can have. In the *videhamukta* stage, — and the Nyāya does not accept the possibility of *jīvanmukti* — the Self comes back to its original, non-conscious, state, a state in which it is pure substance having no attribute (*guṇa*). Since it is non-conscious, it makes no sense to say that it experiences some (pleasure or) suffering or that it experiences no suffering. It makes no sense to say of a non-conscious substance that it experiences *X*, whatever *X* may mean. Absence of suffering is an experience which can be attributed only to a conscious substance.

All modern interpreters of the Nyāya describe this state of the Self, or *mokṣa*, as one of complete absence of pain or suffering. According to them it is a negative state of painlessness and not a positive one of pleasure or bliss, as the *advaitins* hold. But this mode of characterisation is not conceptually correct. Absence of any experience can be predicated of a substance only if it has the potentiality to have experiences. It can have the potentiality only if it is conscious. It is meaningless to say of a piece of marble that it feels, or that it does not feel, hurt when a sculptor cuts out of it the statue of an ass. Therefore, if *mokṣa* is what the Nyāya says it to be, then its attainment cannot be prescribed on the ground of its being a state of painlessness or sufferinglessness, because the latter can neither be affirmed nor denied of the non-conscious Self which the liberated individual is. But the latter can still preserve its non-liability to be reborn.

It seems to me it is the non-liability to be reborn which is, for all Indian philosophers, the essential feature of *mokṣa*, and not the much advertised freedom from suffering. The heart of the matter seems to be that, for all of them, to be *mukta* the Self-in-the-individual has to come back to its natural condition in which it is non-liable to be reborn, i.e., to be associated with a body. Therefore, *mokṣa* denotes simply the natural state of the Self. Depending upon how differently the systems conceived of the natural state, they gave different concrete contents to their characterisation of *mokṣa*. Thus, the Advaita Vedānta speaks of it as a state of absolute bliss since it conceives of the Self as *saccidānanda* (existence-consciousness-bliss), and the Sāṁkhya calls it pure consciousnenss abstracted from all objectivity, because of the self-being consciousness as such, and not the consciousness of anything in particular. Since it is pure consciousness, the Sāṁkhya can say that it is absolutely painless or sufferingless in the sense that it is not the consciousness of any pain or suffering. An experience of a pain is the consciousness of a pain though we do not ordinarily speak of it this way. We cannot therefore object to the Sāṁkhya's calling *mokṣa* a painless state. We may object to the viability of its conception of pure, objectless, consciousness on the ground that consciousness is always consciousness of something, but that would be an objection of a different kind. But the Nyāya cannot call *mokṣa*, as conceived by it, a state of painlessness because the Self, according to it, is non-conscious.

That complete freedom from suffering is not an essential feature of *mokṣa* is also testified by the acceptance of the possibility of *jīvanmukti* by some systems. All these systems admit that the *jīvanmukta* is to live until he exhausts experiencing the consequences of his *prārabdha karma*s. These are the actions which were done by him in his past life and which, because of having matured, have started yielding their consequences bearing which he cannot avoid. Some of these consequences may themselves require him to experience some suffering. Besides, since he has a physical body which is under the governance of the laws of physical nature, he may have to experience pain on account of the effects of some physical phenomena on his body. For example, he may feel pain because of the effects of extreme heat or cold on his body, pangs of hunger when his stomach is empty for a long time, etc., etc. But his non-liability to be reborn remains unaffected by his having his body, i.e., by being a living being. It is because of this non-liability that he is a *mukta* while alive, and not because of his having been completely freed from all kinds of suffering. If having been the latter were a necessary condition of being liberated, then no one can be liberated while alive. This would make *jīvanmukti* impossible.

Let us then accept that a *jīvanmukta* is a person who, after the death of his body, would not be reborn again. This is not to imply that he attains this non-liability by fluke or by doing nothing. Rather, he has to attain knowledge of ultimate Reality and follow a very rigorous discipline an important part of which is leading a flawless mortal life. It is maintained that he attains moral perfection, and also acquires several other excellences. He attains complete detachment in the sense that all of his actions are desireless (*niṣkāma*). He bears no ill-will against anybody, does not mind whether he is respected, insulted, or ignored, has his heart full of benevolence, exercises complete self-control over his passions, emotions, wants, etc. In spite of some differences, the various systems of Indian philosophy agree a lot about the excellences possessed by the *jīvanmukta*, as well as about the methods of attaining *jīvanmukti* (or *videhamukti*).

Since my inquiry is mainly conceptual, I shall not discuss the nature of the methods of attaining *jīvanmukti*, nor the nature of all the individual excellences attributed to the *jīvanmukta*. I shall take up only some of them, the presence of which in an individual is necessary if the concept of being a *jīvanmukta* is correctly applicable to him. I have already mentioned that (a) his non-liability to be reborn is one. Another feature which has been given prominence is (b) his moral perfection. Modern interpreters attach great significance to it.[3] But it seems to me that the non-liability to be reborn is the decisive feature. The reason is that if one does not have it, i.e., if one has done anything which makes him liable to be reborn, then he would be a bonded, an unliberated, individual. And, to accept that he has acquired the non-liability to be reborn is *eo ipso* to accept that he has become *jīvanmukta*.

While admitting that the *jīvanmukta* is a morally perfect individual, it is also held that he is a much more elevated being than a merely morally perfect one. In the classical Indian ethos there is nothing higher than *mokṣa* of which the ultimate form is *videhamukti*. The *jīvanmukta* automatically attains it after the death of his body. This means that he surely occupies the highest

3. Bāl Gaṅgādhar Tilak, *Gītārahasya*, chapter 12.

status which a living being can, and therefore higher than one who is only morally perfect (and not *jīvanmukta*).

Even in our ordinary understanding, moral perfection is not the highest kind of perfection because it does not make its possessor the most perfect individual. For example, one, who possesses any other kind of perfection, say, perfection in creating a work of art, in addition to moral perfection, is certainly a higher kind of being, or more perfect, than him who possesses only moral perfection. This is the reason why those who call god the most perfect being attribute to him not only moral but other kinds of perfection as well. Rather, they realise that if their list of his perfections is perchance incomplete but is taken by others to be complete, and if there is a being with a longer list of perfections than that of god's given by them, then their god would not be considered the most perfect being. The other one with the longer list of perfections would be considered more perfect than the latter. To rule out this eventuality, or this type of misunderstanding, some of them claim that god has infinite number of perfections. Then obviously no entity can be more perfect than him because none can have more than infinite perfections.

However, even if it is granted that the *jīvanmukta* is necessarily a morally perfect individual, that being a *jīvanmukta* implies being a morally perfect individual, the converse is not true. It is not true that if one is morally perfect, then necessarily he is also *jīvanmukta*. Morality is a social, earthly, this-worldly, phenomenon. In characterising the concept of moral perfection, it is not necessary to make any reference to that of rebirth, or of the survival of the Self after the death of the body. One can even reject the possibility of rebirth and post-mortem survival, and still elucidate or elaborate the concept of moral perfection. Whether or not it is empirically possible to be morally perfect depends on the nature of the world, including human nature, and on how much high one keeps his standard of moral perfection. It has nothing to do with the belief in rebirth, survival after death, etc.

The concept of *jīvanmukti* (or of *videhamukti*) necessarily involves reference to the concepts of rebirth and post-mortem survival. If, for example, the possibility of rebirth is rejected, there is no sense in calling anyone bonded because of being caught up in the cycle of birth-death-rebirth, nor in exhorting him to become *jīvanmukta*, or *mukta*, i.e., to become non-liable to be reborn. But there would still be sense in believing in the possibility of moral perfection and in exhorting someone to be, or to try to be, morally perfect, if there is no insuperable hurdle, logical or empirical, to anyone's becoming morally perfect, i.e., if otherwise the possibility of moral perfection is not questionable.

Thus, since the concept of moral perfection does not, while that of *jīvanmukti* (or *mukti*) does, involve reference to the concept of rebirth, or of post-mortem survival, the concept of moral perfection is independent of the concept of *jīvanmukti* (or *mukti*). Obviously, then, the former cannot imply the latter. This is also clear from the position of the schools which do not admit the possibility of *jīvanmukti*. They admit that, in order to become *videhamukta*, one has to attain, in his lifetime, moral perfection. Even the smallest immorality committed by him would make him liable to be reborn and therefore stop him from becoming *videhamukta*.

On the other hand, if he has attained moral perfection while alive and does not lack any other condition for attaining *videhamukti*, he would attain the latter after his bodily death. But, though morally perfect in life, he would not be *jīvanmukta* for the simple reason that, they would say, *jīvanmukti* is not possible. It is clear from this discussion that, according to the classical Indian philosophies, *jīvanmukti* implies but is not implied by moral perfection.

Now let us assume that a *jīvanmukta* is both, or at least both, (a) non-liable to be reborn and (b) morally perfect, in the sense that we can apply the concept of being a *jīvanmukta* to a putative individual, say *A*, if and only if we are sure that *A* is (at least) both. I shall take up (a) and (b) separately and try to explore the problems which their attribution to *A* is likely to give rise to.

The concept of *jīvanmukti* is a technical one evolved out of the needs of a set of theories about man's nature, his destiny, and the world. It is not an ordinary concept evolved from ordinary usage. It stands for, we have seen, what the theorists think to be the highest ideal an individual can attain in his life-time, or the highest kind of being he can become while alive. For him, to become *jīvanmukta* is to become non-liable to be reborn after his physical death, to become freed from the cycle of birth-death-rebirth. Since his first birth cannot be located because the cycle is beginningless, every birth can be called a rebirth. That is why non-liability to be reborn means non-liability to be involved or entangled in the process of birth-death-rebirth.

Technical, or theory-generated, concepts, because of their genesis, are always precise. The concept of *jīvanmukti* seems to be one of the luckiest among them. The condition an individual has to fulfil to be called a *jīvanmukta* is very neat and unambiguous: he has to be non-liable to be reborn. Nothing else would entitle him to deserve the crown.

Non-liability to be reborn is a very precise notion. It suffers from no vagueness. There cannot be the borderline case of an individual about whom we cannot definitively say whether he is, or is not, liable to be reborn. Nor can there be one who is neither, nor both. Everyone must be either liable, or not liable, to be reborn. Secondly, non-liability to be reborn is an absolutist notion, and so is its opposite, the liability to be reborn. Either one is, or is not, non-liable to be reborn. He cannot be partly non-liable, or more or less non-liable, to be reborn, because he cannot be partly, or more or less, reborn; he is either reborn or not, i.e., born, or not born. In ordinary, normal, conceptual affairs, it is generally quite easy to decide whether or not a precise and absolutist concept applies to a putative case. But the situation is entirely different with the concept of *jīvanmukti* because of an epistemic impossibility involved in the non-liability-to-be-reborn requirement.

Who can say, or how can anyone say, whether *A* is, or is not, non-liable to be reborn? Nobody, not even *A* himself, can do that. There is no way to know whether or not he would be reborn. Therefore, nobody can say of anybody that he is *jīvanmukta*. This means that the concept of *jīvanmukti* is uninstantiable or unexemplifiable.

To say of *A* that he is *jīvanmukta* is to say that, after his physical death, he would not be reborn. The latter is a future-tense statement which we can call true only if we find, after his death, that he is not reborn. But there is no way to do that when he is alive, a *jīvanmukta*, nor will it be any easier after his physical death. We cannot even say it of the basis of induction. If we knew that so far no *jīvanmukta* had been reborn after death, we could have inferred from it that *A* would also not be reborn. When it is impossible to test, or confirm, one individual's non-liability to be reborn, it is obvious that we cannot have an inductive generalisation of the type mentioned above. Moreover, if we take *A*'s non-liability to be reborn as an inductive inference from a generalisation, we can at the most say that it is highly probable that *A* would not be reborn. We cannot say that *A* would surely not be reborn, which is what, according to the tradition, *A*'s becoming *jīvanmukta* means.

To speak in terms of induction, or empirical inference, does not seem to be very relevant here. To say that a *jīvanmukta* would not be reborn is not to make an empirical, or synthetic, statement. Rather, it is analytic because to be *jīvanmukta* means to be non-liable to be reborn. It is not that we somehow come to know that *A* is *jīvanmukta* and then try to find out whether or not he would be reborn. Rather, the issue is to decide whether or not we can call *A* *jīvanmukta*, to ascertain whether or not *A*, who has been claimed by some to be *jīvanmukta*, is really *jīvanmukta*. To decide this way or that way, we have to find out whether or not he is liable to be reborn. This is an impossible task. Therefore, it becomes impossible for us to decide whether or not he is *jīvanmukta*. That is, because *jīvanmukti* means non-liability to be reborn and because it is impossible for us to confirm or disconfirm anyone's non-liability or liability to be reborn, we cannot, in point of logic, call anybody *jīvanmukta*. We cannot even call anybody *baddha* (bonded), the opposite of being a *jīvanmukta*, for the same reason: to be *baddha* means to be liable to be reborn, and it is impossible for us to confirm or disconfirm the liability. Being *jīvanmukta* and being *baddha*, therefore, are equally uninstantiable.

Not even the *Śruti*, or any revealed text, can be of any help here. A *śruti* can only say, if it can say anything at all, that it is possible to be a *jīvanmukta*. A possibility statement is always a hypothetical one. In this case it would be something like this: If an individual leads a life of type *T*, he would be non-liable to be reborn, a *jīvanmukta*. This would be a causal or a means-end hypothetical. Such a hypothetical would be true if the effect, or the end, is actually achieved when the causal, or the means — end, condition is fulfilled. But even if *A* leads a life of type *T*, there is no way for any one to know that he has, or has not, become non-liable to be reborn. This means that the possibility statement given by the *śruti* cannot be known to be true or false in the case of any individual. No *śruti* can tell us which particular individual was, is, or will be, a *jīvanmukta*. *Śruti* is not history which can tell us that *A* became, or has become, or will become, *jīvanmukta*. It would be pointless to look into any book, admitted to be a revealed one, a *śruti*, to find out whether Gandhi was a *jīvanmukta* or became *videhamukta* after his murder.

But does not a *śruti* statement enjoy the special status of being exempt from satisfying a truth condition which a non-*śruti*, an empirical, statement, is required, or expected, to satisfy? Some would answer this question in the affirmative. They would say that the *śruti* causal, 'If one leads a life of type *T*, he would become non-liable to be reborn' (*S*), has to be taken as true without being required to satisfy the condition required of empirical, causal, hypothetical, statements. But even if we accept this position, and accept *S* to be true, our inability to use it to decide whether *A* is, or is not, *jīvanmukta* would remain as irremovable as it otherwise is. This is so because there is no way to ascertain *A*'s non-liability to be reborn because of the nature of this non-liability. And, if we cannot ever be sure if *A* has become, or would become, non-liable to be reborn, *S* would have no practical value: it would remain an inapplicable or unusable 'truth'.

S, whether taken as a *śruti*, or a non-*śruti*, truth is intended to be a practical truth, a truth providing us guidance in choosing the kind of life by leading which we can allegedly attain what is claimed to be the highest ideal attainable by a living human being. It is meant to be used as a premise in a practical argument of the following type:

(3) If you lead a life of type *T*, you would become *jīvanmukta* (i.e., non-liable to be reborn). You ought to (try to) become *jīvanmukta* (because *jīvanmukti* is the highest *puruṣārtha* for a living being). Therefore, you ought to lead a life of type *T*.

This argument would have no practical value because we do not, or rather would never be in a position to, know how to ascertain whether or not anyone has become *jīvanmukta*, i.e., we cannot exemplify the concept of *jīvanmukti*. A stickler for the classical Indian style of argumentation may even say that the above does not have a valid argument form, because not only it does not have an *udāharaṇa*, but it cannot have one.

One may say here that examples of *jīvanmukta*s are given in the Indian mythology. Janaka is said to have attained *jīvanmukti*. But mythology is not history, and a mythological example cannot be taken as an actual example. Moreover, when we cannot think of a way of ascertaining whether or not one has become *jīvanmukta*, we cannot accept that someone did become on the authority of mythology. Mythology has no authority to overrule logic. What we cannot think of we cannot accept even if mythology accepts it.

Since one cannot say of anybody that he is *jīvanmukta*, he cannot say it even of himself. This means he cannot say that he has, would, or can, become *jīvanmukta*. Attaining *jīvanmukti* cannot, then, be anybody's *puruṣārtha* because one cannot aim at attaining a goal of which he can never say that he has attained it. Nor can someone else help him in this regard because everybody is equally handicapped. Therefore, there is no point in advising or exhorting anyone to try to become *jīvanmukta*. Neither the teacher nor the disciple would see in the precept 'Be a *jīvanmukta*' anything of practical value. The practical argument (3), mentioned above, thus, not only cannot have an *udāharaṇa*, but it cannot have its second premise as well: 'You ought to (try to) become *jīvanmukta*.'

The problem posed here has become insoluble, one may point out, because the non-liability to be reborn refers to a post-mortem condition which we certainly cannot know or ascertain in any empirical or logical way. This is the case with all such concepts, as those of *videhamukti*, rebirth, heaven, hell, etc. We have to accept them, if we want to, on some non-rational, non-empirical, grounds. The appeal to *śruti* is one such ground. We accept them also because we find them to have great practical or inspirational, utility.

But I have already shown, in the case of the concept of *jīvanmukti*, that, because of its being unsayable that one is *jīvanmukta*, the belief in the attainability of *jīvanmukti*, or the advice to anyone that he ought to try to become *jīvanmukta*, cannot have much of practical utility. The handicap the concept suffers from, i.e., the handicap of being unpredicatable, is not trivial. It cannot be removed by doing some tinkering in the theory of *mokṣa*, or of rebirth, or even in some other component of the philosophies which accept *mokṣa*, in the form of *jīvanmukti* or *videhamukti*. It is difficult to imagine how a theory, with so handicapped a concept as that of *jīvanmukti* (or *mukti*) as its core concept, can provide to a thinking individual any inspiration to live this or that sort of life.

What is true of the concept of *jīvanmukti* is true of all concepts which involve reference to post-mortem existence in any form, for example, the concept of being a citizen of heaven or hell, an enjoyer of god's company, etc.

Even the concept of rebirth involves some reference to something post-mortem, because, according to the theory of rebirth, the individual does not cease to exist after his death. He is reborn in some form, which would not have been possible had he ceased to exist. None of such concepts can be definitively, or authentically, predicated of anyone. We can have applications of them in myths, but not in statements which can be known to be true or false. We can still have beliefs which involve their use but they will be beliefs which cannot be converted into knowledge.

I do not intend to deny that many people hold some beliefs to be true even though they know that they can never be confirmed to be true. Beliefs in *jīvanmukti* or *videhamuti*, heaven, hell, etc., are such beliefs. They are what I once called privileged hypotheses[4] in the sense that their holders consider them exempt from the requirement of being confirmable. They are sometimes considered to have been confirmed in some extraordinary manner by some extraordinary people. Ordinary people have to accept them on their authority. If they require that they should be confirmable in the manner of ordinary mundane beliefs, they would be dishonouring them and the *ṛṣi*s who have handed them over to the world. These beliefs thus provide a rich field for the operation of the *ṛṣi* bias.

4. See "Religious Belief", in my *Regularity, Normativity and Rules of Language*, (Poona University, 1989).

Almost all religions have a set of such beliefs. Their adherents may be deriving some inspiration or solace from them, and even some motivation to lead a morally commendable life. But they can also be used to defend even morally undesirable practices. As the *Mahābhārata* recounts,[5] Dharmavyādha uses his belief in rebirth and kārmic theory to defend his running a butcher's shop. He tells the saint Kauśika that because of his past actions he has been born in a butcher's family. The *varṇadharma*, or *kuladharma* (caste or family ethics), of a butcher is to run, in an honest manner, a butcher's business which he is doing. By doing the butcher's business honestly he hopes to be born in a better family after his death. By doing one's business, one's *kuladharma*, whatever it is, even if it is a butcher's business, honestly and leading a good moral life in other respects, one can, he believes, improve his status in the next birth, or even get *mokṣa*. These beliefs, for him, do not need confirmation; they are as true as, or even truer than, ordinary true beliefs.

Beliefs of the type mentioned above, of which the belief in *jīvanmukti* is one, can work as long as the believer has not probed into them with a critical, mature, and objective reason, bereft of the *ṛṣi* bias. They can buckle down any time under the logical pressure of a probing reason. When they do, no calamity need occur because a healthy reason can provide stable beliefs for leading a balanced, morally commendable, life. Even when these beliefs work, they work more as make beliefs than as tested beliefs. Even to let them work, one has to keep his reason subdued, and subduing reason would surely benumb his overall critical alertness. Theirs is very much like a placebo effect which reduces tension by dulling normal sensitivity. Dharmavyādha's reason has become subdued. A man with a subdued reason can even say that selling honestly the meat of animals killed for that purpose has the same moral worth as selling honestly medicines for curing sick animals' ailments has. A normal reason would, on the other hand, say that a person, who does honestly medical business and leads a morally good life in other respects as well, is morally better, or more commendable, than a Dharmavyādha.

5. *The Mahābhārata*, Vol. 2, (Gita Press) pp. 1548-57.

To make any belief previleged is like putting a particular candidate for a prestigious job in the reserved quota and thereby exempting him from meeting the requirements of merit which one in the non-reserved quota has to do. In the case of a belief it would really mean locating it in a zone with the 'No Admission for Philosophy' sign at its entrance. Even some philosophers plead for respecting the sign, and sometimes more loudly than others. This is very much true of the belief in *mokṣa*, *jīvanmukti* or *videhamukti*. Whether or not it is fair to put it, and some others, in a no-entry zone for philosophy, cannot be discussed in detail here. It is obvious that this essay is written on the assumption that nobody has the authority to do that.

Leading a well-disciplined moral life and acquiring knowledge of reality are said to be the two necessary prerequisites for becoming a *jīvanmukta*. Therefore, after becoming *jīvanmukta*, the tradition says, the individual becomes a living exemplar of morality. It becomes his second nature to do what is morally right and to avoid doing what is morally wrong or forbidden. It is his second nature in the sense that his moral behaviour is always spontaneous and tensionless. His wisdom never fails him in telling him what is the right thing to do; his self-control over his passions and desires never lets any emotion or desire rise against his natural inclination to do the morally right, and his completely unakratic moral will never fails in taking and implementing the right moral decision. He never has a moral conflict or struggle. What is a moral law for others, which they have to obey and which they sometimes fail to obey because of akrasia, is a law of *jīvanmukta*'s nature. It has become natural for him to do what the law requires him to do. He does not deliberate on what he ought to do; he just does what, as someone else would say, he ought to. Deliberation is required when one does not know what is the right thing to do, or has a conflict between a duty and an opposing desire, or between two competing duties. But such eventualities are not to arise in his life.

Whatever the *jīvanmukta* does, he does in a desireless manner, only out of his sense of duty, and not with the intention to produce any specific result. Desireful actions, as we have seen in chapter 2, cause bondage because their consequences have to be borne by their doer for which he may have to take another birth. The *jīvanmukta* has no desire to fulfil, and has acquired the exemption from being born again after his bodily death. All of his actions, being motivated only by his sense of duty and not by any desire, or any other non-moral inclination, are like roasted seeds. They would produce no effect to be borne by him and are therefore bereft of a desireful action's rebirth-causing potentiality.

He may do a lot to ameliorate the conditions of the suffering humanity. But even such actions of his would be desireless, done not with the intention to achieve something, even the well-being of the beneficiaries, but only as duties. A desireful action, whatever may its motivating desire be, a desire to save a drowning man by lifting him up, or to make him die soon by pushing him down into the water, is always bondage-causing.

A duty arises only in a social set-up in which the members of the set are related in a certain manner. It is this network of social relations which generates duties or obligations the fulfilment of which, by the members of the set, is considered necessary for their well-being as well as for that of the set they compose. The duties or obligations of a person exercise a binding, necessitating, influence on him. In some sense he is bound to fulfil them, even if he does not want to. The *jīvanmukta* has also a society, small or large, but the duties applicable to him do not bind him. This is so because fulfilling them has become natural to him. Just as an unliberated man proceeds naturally towards the object he wants to have, lying in front of him, the *jīvanmukta* proceeds to fulfil his duties spontaneously, without feeling constrained in any way.

Normally we classify actions into four categories and call them obligatory, permissible, forbidden, and supererogatory. The obligatory has to be done, the permissible may be done, the forbidden must not be done, and the supererogatory is such that its omission carries no moral demerit but doing it carries more moral merit than even doing an obligatory one. Since the *jīvanmukta* has only one motive for doing any action, namely, his sense of duty, he does only that which he considers to be a duty. Therefore, his actions can all be called his duties, i.e., actions done as duties. If anyone of us shows kindness to an unknown stranger, we would call it supererogatory and not obligatory. But if the *jīvanmukta* does it, he would do it as his duty, and therefore it would not be supererogatory for him. We can say that the *jīvanmukta* does all his duties and only his duties and nothing which is forbidden. He takes his duties in a broad sense so as to include in them even supererogatory actions.

I admit that several things could be added to the account of the nature of the *jīvanmukta* given here. But I think the essentials have been included in it. For the limited purposes of this essay, let us take it, even if it is not, as a fair enough characterisation of the *jīvanmukta* as the tradition depicts him. The tradition takes him to have achieved moral perfection. The features on the basis of which it calls him morally perfect have all, I think, been included in the present account.

Suppose we come across a person who satisfies the above description. Would we call him, would we have the authority to call him, *jīvanmukta*? Certainly not, unless we have a good reason to believe that after his death he would not be reborn. From his moral status, however elevated it may be, we cannot validly infer his non-liability to be reborn and without being sure of that we cannot say that he is *jīvanmukta*.

But can we call him morally perfect? For anyone to be morally perfect (rather perfect in any way) means that he cannot be better than what he is, nor can anybody else be better than him. Therefore, unless we watch a person carefully until the moment he dies, we cannot say that he is morally perfect. A simple moral lapse done anytime by him, even a minute before he dies, would make him morally imperfect. But in the tradition it is said, almost as a necessary truth, that a *jīvanmukta* is morally perfect; as if it was impossible[6] for him to do a moral lapse, impossible to do anything morally wrong, or to miss doing anything morally obligatory. That he is morally perfect seems to have been made definitional. But if that is the case, then it would be uninformative to say that the *jīvanmukta* is morally perfect. One of the purposes of calling him morally perfect is to make the ideal of *jīvanmukti* more lustrous, more attractive and prizable. This cannot be done if calling him morally perfect is analytic. And, it would be analytic if being morally perfect is made a part of the definition of being a *jīvanmukta*.

6. *Gītārahasya*, p. 479.

Secondly, it is not absolutely safe even to call moral perfection an empirical property of the *jīvanmukta*. I have already mentioned one difficulty in doing that: unless we watch the full career of a *jīvanmukta*, from the time he becomes a *jīvanmukta* til the moment he dies, we cannot validly make an empirical claim that he is morally perfect. But a more serious difficulty meets us when we realise that the statement 'The *jīvanmukta* is morally perfect' occupies, in the tradition, the status of a general truth, a generalisation, about all *jīvanmukta*s. Now, if we take it as an empirical generalisation, we can call it reliable only if we have generalised from some unquestionable instances of *jīvanmukta*s who are also morally perfect. These instances must have been identified as *jīvanmukta*s on empirical grounds and in some other way than by means of their moral perfection. If they are identified as *jīvanmukta*s on the basis of their moral perfection, then generalising that all *jīvanmukta*s are morally perfect, or asserting it as a general truth that *jīvanmukta*s are morally perfect, would be viciously circular. But it is impossible to make this sort of generalisation because it is impossible to have unquestionable instances of *jīvanmukta*s. The other necessary feature of the *jīvanmukta*, on the basis of which we could have identified one as a *jīvanmukta*, is his non-reliability to be reborn. We have seen that this is a feature we have no means to attribute to anyone. Therefore, we cannot identify anyone as a *jīvanmukta* on the basis of finding him non-liable to be reborn. This means we cannot have any instance of a *jīvanmukta* and therefore any empirical generalisation about *jīvanmukta*s.

Moreover, there would be another great risk in making moral perfection an empirical feature. If we do, then, as we have seen, the statement that the *jīvanmukta* is morally perfect would become an empirical generalisation. The possibility of an empirical generalisation turning out to be sometime false cannot be ruled out *ab initio*. But if this is so, if it is possible for the *jīvanmukta* to commit sometime an immorality, in thought, word, or deed, what would then happen to his *jīvanmukti*? Would he get de-liberated? *Jīvanmukti*, or liberatedness, is an absolutist concept. Either one is, or is not, liberated; he is never more or less liberated. If he is once liberated, he is liberated for ever. The *mokṣa* state, in *jīvanmukti* or *videhamukti*, is 'attained once for all and is permanent'.[7] Therefore, he would remain liberated or become de-liberated; we cannot say that because of his immorality he has become a lesser *jīvanmukta*. This possibility of getting de-liberated does not seem to be available in the tradition.

The possibility of a *jīvanmukta*'s committing an immorality, it may be said, is unreal, Therefore, the problem I have raised is also unreal. But it is a possibility and it would be an important one if the claim of the *jīvanmukta*'s moral perfection is empirical. The hypothetical or theoretical possibility of an empirical statement being sometime false cannot be rejected. This is all that I need for my argument. To be tenable, the theory of *jīvanmukti* must be able to take care not only of a real possibility but also of a hypothetical or theoretical one, going against it.

However, it does not seem to be an unreal possibility. The tradition gives several examples of great *ṛṣis* committing some sexual lapses which are immoralities. *Ṛṣi* Parāśara's[8] episode with the virgin Satyavatī, fathering her son, the great *ṛṣi* Vyāsa, *maharṣi* Viśvāmitra's[9] with Menakā fathering her daughter Śakuntalā, and *ṛṣi* Nārada's unsuccessful infatuation with Viśvamohinī[10] and Viṣṇu's befooling him, are well-known to students of Indology.

Perhaps neither Parāśara, nor Viśvāmitra, nor Nārada were *jīvanmukta*s. The tradition's position about them does not seem to be very clear. But considering the way they have been extolled, it is also not safe to say that they were not. And, about Nārada the traditional view seems to lean towards depicting him as a *jīvanmukta saṁnyāsī*. But whether they are, or they are not, *jīvanmukta*, all of them are morally very highly elevated individuals. If such men can commit sexual lapses, it seems anyone can, and therefore the theoretical possibility of a *jīvanmukta*'s committing a moral lapse does not seem to be unreal.

One commits a moral lapse, or is guilty of an omission, not

7. M. Hiriyanna, *Art Experience*, p. 27.
8. *The Mahābhārata*, (Gita Press) Vol. I, pp. 172-80.
9. *Ibid.*, pp. 207-13.
10. Tulsīdās, *The Rāmacaritamānasa*, Bālakāṇḍa, (Gita Press) pp. 140-54.

always on account of some weakness in his character. Sometimes he may do that because the available ethical theory is not clear about what is the right thing to do in the situation he is in, or does not have the solution to the problem he is facing. The great scholar and moralist Bhīṣma could not answer Draupadī's question whether Yudhiṣṭhira had the moral right, after having lost his freedom, to put her on the stakes. Bhīṣma's reason for not answering the question, and thereby letting Duḥśāsana continue trying to derobe her, is that he finds the meaning of *dharma* so deep and subtle that he does not know how to answer her question.[11] A *jīvanmukta* may also face such a situation.

The Indian tradition does not pardon even immoralities done inadvertently or unknowingly. Śravaṇa Kumāra was killed by Daśaratha[12] unknowingly but still the victim's father cursed him to die on account of the agonies caused by the separation of his son from him. Even the gods did not tone down the punishment, nor did the cursing *ṛṣi* was influenced by Daśaratha's entreaties. The result was that the curse did come out to be true. Similarly, Karṇa killed a *brāhmaṇa*'s calf unknowingly, thinking it was a killer animal. In spite of Karṇa's pleadings and promises to compensate for the loss of his calf, the *brāhmaṇa* gave him the curse that cost him his life in the Mahābhārata war. The curse was that the wheels of his chariot would sink into the earth when he would be fighting and trying to defeat the man he was most envious of.[13] Unless the *jīvanmukta* is omniscient, such eventualities may take place in his life. To take care of such possibilities, it seems to me that the theory of *jīvanmukti* has to have a mechanism of de-liberation, or of the suspension of liberatedness, to be inflicted on the defaulter for a short or long while, depending upon the nature of his lapse. This would mean reconstructing the theory to a certain extent. I think the theory needs to be reconstructed in more than one way. The general direction the reconstruction should take, as it seems to me, is that of converting it into a neat moral theory by retaining only the unavoidable metaphysical-theological paddings, and purging away

11. *The Mahābhārata*, Vol. I, p. 907.
12. Vālmīki, *The Rāmāyaṇa*, Vol. I, (Gita Press) pp. 360-5.
13. *The Mahābhārata*, Vol. V, pp. 4428-30.

those which create some theoretical or practical confusions or unnecessary complications. All this would mean making the theory more rational and less esoteric. But this proposal cannot be developed here. It would require an essay at least as long as the present one. That the scholars with the *ṛṣi* bias may look down upon such a venture as a gross distortion, or plain destruction, of a glorious tradition cannot be denied. But we have learnt to live with it, and I do not think it would deter a critical mind from going ahead.

The concept of moral perfection has also some built-in, indigenous, problems. For a person to act morally is to act according to the principles of morality he acknowledges as valid on some objective grounds, i.e., on grounds which any neutral or rational person is likely to accept. But sometimes a principle or standard accepted in one age is considered to be inadequate or not well-grounded in another. Therefore, evalutions made according to it in the age of its acceptance are rejected or modified in the age which has become sceptical of it. Droṇa's decision that Ekalavya was not fit to be admitted in his school because of his low parentage was not considered unfair in his age. But nowadays such a decision would be considered grossly unjust. Suppose Droṇa to be a *jīvanmukta*. Then, according to the standards of his age, in spite of his rejecting Ekalavya, he would remain morally perfect (if a *jīvanmukta* is morally perfect). But according to the present-day Indian standards, he would not be considered morally perfect. This would also mean that his age, using its own standards, was right when it considered him a *jīvanmukta*, and the present age, using its own, is also right in saying that he was not.

What I mean to say is that if the *jīvanmukta* is said to be morally perfect, then it may happen that the *jīvanmukta* of one age, or of one moral community, may not be accepted to be a *jīvanmukta* by another age, or by another moral community. This would take away much of the grandeur which goes with the concept of a *jīvanmukta*. This objection, it may be said, smacks of a relativistic interpretation of moral standards. Perhaps it does. But the point it makes is very obvious. Our standards of evaluation do sometimes get modified because of our changing needs or perceptions of the social reality. If this fact is kept in view then the possibility of a person evaluated as a *jīvanmukta* in his age and of being not so evaluated in another cannot be ruled out. Which evaluation of his is correct cannot be decided. To decide this issue means to confirm whether or not he was really a *jīvanmukta*, i.e., whether or not he was reborn after his death. But this is a matter, as I have already said, no one can confirm or disconfirm.

Morality, as is commonly understood, is an open-ended, social or societal, phenomenon. It is open-ended in the sense that new moral problems keep coming up on account of changing needs of the society, introduction of new institutions, changes in human aspirations, changing human relationships, etc. For example, in the post-Independence period in India such things as the acceptance of parliamentary democracy, revaluation of the caste-structure, encouragement given to inter-caste marriages, legalisation of abortion, reservation for some sections of the society in some spheres of public services, etc., have brought in a number of ethical problems which were non-existent, or not so prominent, in the pre-Independence period. To solve these problems one may have to modify some of the moral principles or standards considered respectable since classical times. In any case, he may have to do a lot of thinking or deliberation to find out a solution. This means that we cannot give to anybody, howsoever morally perfect and elevated he may be, the credit of knowing the solution of all moral problems which may arise anytime in the immediate and distant future. But this is what we do when we call someone morally perfect. A morally perfect person must be knowing the solution of all moral problems howsoever new or strange they may be and he must be able to give a solution in an effortless, struggle-free, manner.

To grant this sort of moral omniscience to the morally perfect, the *jīvanmukta*, has the pernicious implication that morality is a closed and pre-determined phenomenon. Since he *knows* all the problems which may arise anytime, it means it is pre-determined how many and what type of problems would ever arise. Since he *knows* their solutions, it means that the solutions are also predetermined. All this would make the world of morality dull, drab, and definitively determinate. This is diametrically opposed to our experience with morals. Our experience shows that even in some ordinary cases we have to think, deliberate, argue for and against a position, and then to choose or decide which way to go.

Even then quite often a rejected alternative keeps nagging us and not infrequently the feeling persists that perhaps it would have been morally better had we chosen it in place of the one we actually did. It seems to me, thus, that if we are sensitively aware of the phenomenology of our actual moral life, we must say that moral perfection is impossible. It is impossible because it involves attributing some sort of an omniscience to the morally perfect which would imply that the world of morality is a thoroughly predetermined one in which there is no place for any kind of choice or decision-making. If moral perfection is impossible, there is no point in calling the *jīvanmukta* morally perfect. We can definitely call him morally very elevated, even a pradigm or examplar of morality, because he can be all that without being morally perfect. We can put him on the highest moral pedestal without calling him morally perfect. But we have to keep in mind that the position of the pedestal is not unalterably fixed. It may slide to a higher, or even to a lower, level, depending upon the condition of the social reality and man's understanding of it. The world of morals is extremely complex. It is a world in which moral considerations act on, and are acted on by, many others, such as social or societal, political, economic, environmental, hygienical, scientific, etc. In an intellectually mature surrounding even conceptual or logical considerations also join the fray. A new moral principle or problem may cause some change in a social reality, and a new social or societal situation may bring some change in an existing moral principle or practice, leading to a changed assessment of some existing moral issue or issues. And, to add to the complexity, a change in man's understanding of any one of the components of this world may also bring some change in that component and even in some other one or ones related or contiguous to it. In fact, each one of the components is a potential agent for ushering some change in some other or others.

There is a trend of thinking in the tradition which puts the *jīvanmukta* in a zone beyond morality. He is said to be beyond good and evil. Perhaps this trend got initiated because of the problems, some of which have been discussed above, which may arise on account of calling him morally perfect. To call him morally perfect is to keep him well within the bounds of morality.

The ideal of *jīvanmukti* is rated to be higher than any moral ideal. This is clear from the claim that the cultivation of morality is a means to it. To become *jīvanmukta* one has to lead a morally good life. This point is made sometimes by saying that *mukti*, whether *jīvanmukti* or *videhamukti*, is a spiritual, and not just a moral, ideal. One cultivates the highest kind of morals, uses his moral achievement to get *jīvanmukti*, and then transcends, or goes beyond, the world of morality. The *jīvanmukta* is not just morally elevated, he has also become something more, i.e., non-liable to be reborn after death. To call him just a moral exemplar, even morally perfect, is to underrate his status.

It is true that *jīvanmukti* (or *videhamukti*) is not a moral ideal for the simple reason that one can lead a good moral life, a life as rigorously moral as the human world permits, without even believing in the possibility of *jīvanmukti* (or *videhamukti*). Moreover, the essence of leading a moral life consists in having a care or concern for the welfare of others. But *jīvanmukti* is a personal ideal; to attain it is to attain one's own salvation, his own freedom from the chain of birth-death-rebirth. "It must be admitted", says Hiriyanna, "that individual release is the prevalent ideal in Indian philosophy on the whole."[14]

Some Indian philosophers do speak of *sarvamukti* (liberation of all) and we can locate some theories of *sarvamukti*, though they are not available in a developed or well-constructed form. The admission of the possibility of *sarvamukti* may suggest that *mukti*, or *jīvanmukti*, does not mean an individual's liberation. But when the theory is properly understood, it becomes obvious that to hold it as suggesting any such thing would be unjustified. Without going into historical details I will briefly state here some of the important positions in this regard.

(i) Some hold that there is only one Soul, which dreams that there are many other souls. This, i.e., dreaming that there are many other souls, is its bondage. Therefore, when it stops dreaming, recognises the dream to be a dream, it gets liberated.[15] Since it is the only soul, its liberation means the

14. M. Hiriyanna, *Indian Conception of Values*, (Kavyalaya Publishers, Mysore, 1975), p. 293.

15. *Ibid.*, pp. 295-6.

liberation of all. This is not really *sarvamukti* because here 'all' means nothing more than one.

(ii) Some hold that there are infinite number of *jīva*s and one *jīva* cannot be liberated unless all the others are liberated.[16] If this view is tenable, then an individual's liberation would not be a mere personal liberation. But it really makes anyone's liberation, and therefore all's liberation, impossible. Let us call the number of individual *N*. *N* would mean infinity as the number of individuals is *exhypothesi* infinite. Then, any individual *A* can be liberated only if *N-A* individuals are liberated. Since *N* is infinite, *N-A* would also be infinite. Therefore, the liberation of *N-A* individuals would never be completed. This means *A* would never be liberated. This theory of *sarvamukti* would thus be a theory of the liberation of no individual instead of being one of all individuals.

(iii) Some[17] hold that an individual can attain his liberation alone, — and it would be his, a personal liberation — but he should refuse to have it for serving the world, for helping the other unliberated individuals to become liberated. No one, therefore, is to remain in the state of liberation unless all others are liberated. But for this theory also the number of individuals is infinite. Therefore, as is the case with (ii), the number of unliberated individuals would never be zero. This means that, although one can attain his liberation, he should not have it. He may decide to have it, but then he would be shirking from his responsibility of helping others to become liberated. Since shirking from the responsibility would mean earning a great demerit, he may not then be able to retain his liberation. According to this theory also, all individuals cannot be liberated, and any individual who is liberated is not allowed to retain his liberation unless all are liberated. This means that none would have liberation. Each one can try for his and for others' liberation, for *sarvamukti*, which would never be achieved.

16. *Indian Conception of Values*, p. 297.

17. *Ibid.*, p. 303.

(iv) There is another view[18] according to which there is only one soul, which may be called the cosmic soul, manifesting itself partially in many individual souls. This cosmic soul would be liberated only when all the individual souls are liberated. Each individual soul by liberating itself contributes to the liberation of the one, cosmic, soul. All individual souls should strive for the common end, which is the liberation of the cosmic soul.

Sarvamukti, on this view, is the *mukti* of the cosmic soul and each individual soul contributes to it by liberating itself. An individual soul, thus, does not contribute to the liberation of other individual souls, but only to that of the cosmic soul. Therefore, an individual soul's liberation remains his individual, personal, liberation. It is a component of the cosmic soul's liberation which occurs only when all the souls get liberated. Moreover, if the number of individual souls is infinite, then, as has been already pointed out, the liberation of all individual souls and consequently that of the cosmic soul, would be impossible. If the number is finite, the latter would be possible. But then one can ask how many are they. To mention, or guess, any specific number would be only an exercise in myth-making.[19] Moreover, the general spirit of Indian Philosophy would revolt against making the number of individuals, or souls, finite.

To conclude, the *jīvanmukta* may, or, rather, would, have a care for others' welfare, but what he finally aims at is his own salvation. Morality is for him a pre-condition of *jīvanmukti*. But it is obvious that the latter is not a pre-condition of the former. One can lead a good moral life without even believing in the possibility of any kind of *mukti*. Morality is thus independent of *jīvanmukti*. An ideal moral person would care for the welfare of others without ignoring his, and if he has to choose between his and another man's welfare, he would choose the latter. In no case he would use morality as a means to his own welfare. It would put a lot of strain on our common

18. *Indian Conception of Values*, pp. 305-7.

19. Hiriyanna attributes (i) and (ii) to Śāṅkara Advaita Vedānta, (iii) to Mahāyāna Buddhism, and (iv) to Bhartṛprapañca. *Ibid.*, chapter XIII.

sense, or moral sense, if we call such a person inferior to one who leads a good moral life to attain his own salvation, to free himself from the cycle of birth-death-rebirth. But there is a halo around the ideal of *jīvanmukti*. Classical as well as contemporary writers on Indian philosophy would shrug their shoulders at the very idea of putting morality and *jīvanmukti* on the same level, what to speak of putting the former a little higher than the latter.

Some philosophers have attempted to show that the state of *jīvanmukti* is exemplifiable in some of our normal experiences. For example, *advaitins* claim that the experience of deep, or dreamless, sleep (*suṣupti*) exemplifies it in a limited way. Among modern Indian philosophers, M. Hiriyanna has tried to show that the consummation of genuine, or enlightened morality and aesthetic experience in the life of an individual, if achieved, would be a limited analogue of *jīvanmukti* because, according to him, the state of *jīvanmukti* contains both moral perfection and pure joy which is comparable to aesthetic delight. If these attempts are successful, they would show that *jīvanmukti* can be at least partially exemplified. The calim made in this chapter, that the concept of *jīvanmukti* cannot be instantiated because a necessary feature of it — the non-liability of the *jīvanmukta* to be reborn — cannot be predicated of anyone, would still remain valid, as neither any *advaitin*, nor Hiriyanna, denies that the latter is a necessary feature of being *jīvanmukta*. Even then the two attempts to exemplify *jīvanmukti* deserve some detailed discussion and examination. I shall take up the *advaitic* position in the next chapter. I shall not discuss Hiriyanna's in this work because I have discussed it in detail elsewhere.[20]

20. See my *Aesthetics, Morality and Jīvanmukti: Revaluation of an Indian Perspective a la Hiriyanna*, Prasaranga, Karnatak University, Dharwad, 1992.

4

Dreamless Sleep as Empirical Analogue of Jīvanmukti: How much Appropriate?

THE highest truth or value, for an *advaitin*, which a man can and ought to achieve in his life time is the identity of the Self (in him) and the *Brahman*. To achieve it is to realise it, i.e., to have a direct experience of it. The Self is identical with the *Brahman* in the sense that both the terms denote the same entity which is *saccidānanda*, i.e., existence-consciousness-bliss (ECB). It is because of ignorance that the individual (*jīva*), who is an embodied being, thinks of himself as one among many kinds of beings and believes in a plurality of realities. The truth is that only the Self or *Brahman* is ultimately real. When the individual attains the direct cognition of this truth, he attains his salvation. He becomes *jīvanmukta*, liberated while alive. To become *jīvanmukta* is to become, in the sense of returning to one's original state, ECB. Therefore, it is not really a case of his becoming something he earlier was not, but realising that he is ECB, which he really is, or the Self-in-him is. He had only forgotten that he is ECB because of his ignorance. This realisation is achievable by leading a life of impeccable morality and acquiring right knowledge of reality, which is nothing but the Self. To say that the Self is existence-consciousness-bliss is not to say that it is a collection of three things. It is pure unity, literally one entity. 'Existence-consciousness-bliss' does not, in Advaitic usage, denote trinity, i.e., any kind of plurality. This means that even if we simply say that it is existence, or consciousness, or bliss, it would mean that it is existence-consciousness-bliss. It is because of linguistic inadequacy that we have to use a term, which appears to mean a group of three things, to mean pure unity.

To call something ultimate Reality is not *ipso facto* to make it the ultimate value. When a materialist says that the ultimate reality is pure, unqualified matter, he does not mean, or imply, nor does he have to mean, or imply, that human beings, who have a sense of values and can realise them, ought to aim at becoming, or returning, to their primal state of pure matter. Therefore, it is not an illegitimate question to ask an *advaitin* why the individual ought to realise that he is the Self or *Brahman*. To put it in a more general form, why ought he to know what is the ultimate Reality? The classical Indian tradition, including the Advaitic, admits the legitimacy of the question, and *formally the same answer* is given by all the schools of philosophy. Their answer is that he ought to in order to attain freedom from bondage. As long as he does not know the reality, he is in bondage. To be in bondage is to be liable to be reborn after his physical death. To remain caught up in the cycle of birth and death is to have a painful existence. Their *answers differ in content* inasmuch as they differ in their conceptions of reality. For the Advaita Vedānta, the only way for the individual to get salvation from bondage is to know that he is really the Self which is ECB, because the ultimate Reality is the Self or *Brahman* and the latter is ECB. Therefore, realising the identity of the Self and *Brahman*, or the truth that the Self is ECB, is the ultimate value because then and then alone the individual can be freed from bondage and the suffering the latter is associated with. Quite naturally, then, freedom from bondage would mean not merely freedom from suffering, but absolute bliss, because the Self is bliss.

To think rightly of the Advaitic Self as ECB is not to think of it as an existent object which is eternally conscious and blissful, i.e., as one which always enjoys undisturbed, unmixed, bliss. It does not enjoy, but is, bliss. It cannot, because it is nonsensical to say that bliss enjoys bliss. To be bliss itself is to be categorially different from being an enjoyer or experiencer of bliss, and so is to be existence itself from being an existent object, and to be consciousness itself from being a conscious being. To think of the Self as ECB is, thus, not an easy feat. When a philosophically unsophisticated person is won over by the Advaitic doctrine of the Self as *saccidānanda* at the very first blush, it is very likely that he takes it to mean an eternally conscious being eternally enjoying pure bliss, without realising that *saccidānanda* is not a being of this type, nor realising how difficult it is to think of it as what it is claimed to be. His would be a case very similar to another person's having been attracted by the Platonic Idea of Beauty, taking it to mean the most beautiful being anyone can think of. All this is so because an ordinary person has experiences of enjoying happiness, of being a happy individual, but not of cognising, happiness as such, i.e., happiness which is not the happiness enjoyed by an individual. We meet with happy, or beautiful, individuals, not with the entity called 'happiness' or 'beauty'. The same is the case with the notions of existence and consciousness. It is no problem to think of an existent object, or to be conscious (or aware) of an object. But it is not at all easy to think of existence as such, i.e., of existence which is not the existence of something, or of consciousness as such, i.e., of consciousness which is not the consciousness of anything whatsoever, which is absolutely objectless, or rather, the consciousness of nothing.

The above difficulty with the Advaitic notions of existence, consciousness and bliss, as figuring in the notion of the Self as ECB, is not merely theoretical. It is bound to affect the intelligibility of the Advaitic notion of *mukti*, *jīvanmukti* and *videhamukti*. If one cannot think of what is it to become pure existence, or pure consciousness, or pure bliss, he cannot think of what it is to become *jīvanmukta*. It is the notion of bliss in that of existence-consciousness-bliss which makes the notion of Self-realisation or *jīvanmukti* obviously attractive to an ordinary individual. But when he would notice the insuperable difficulty in comprehending the notion of bliss, or of his becoming bliss, which is very different from his becoming blissful, he would find it difficult to retain the initial attraction the ideal of *jīvanmukti* had for him. This is natural because he wants to enjoy bliss, to become blissful, and not to become bliss, simply because he finds it almost impossible to understand what becoming bliss would be like. All this is due, the *advaitin* would say, to his ignorance. This may be true; but it is also true that the ignorant individual needs to be given some idea of what it is like to be ECB, if he is to be motivated to realise the Self, i.e., to have *mumukṣā*, the desire to attain *mokṣa*.

A *sādhaka*, as the result of his successful *sādhanā*, may get in his spiritual experience called *turīya* a confirmation of the Advaitic claim that the Self is ECB. But everyone is not a *sādhaka*. Rather, to be one, or to proceed on the path of attaining Self-realisation, one needs to be convinced of the attainability of the ideal. Appeal to *Śruti* may be made to convince him. But by itself it may not be able to produce a conviction strong enough to make him a *mumukṣu* (desirer of *mokṣa*). Reasoning could be another way. But in the case of such matters it is not likely to be conclusive, or persuasive enough, to move him to proceed in the direction of attaining Self-realisation. The *advaitin* does appeal to *Śruti* and also tries to give a rational vindication of his doctrine; but he is also aware of their limitations.

I think the *advaitin* realises that the most natural way to give an ordinary individual an idea of what Self-realisation is would be to show to him that there is an analogue, even a limited one, of the state he is advised by him to reach to, in his normal life. This sort of analogue, he thinks, is available in *suṣupti*, the experience of deep, dreamless, sleep. His belief is that even an ordinary individual, one who is ignorant of what, according to the Advaita, are the basic truths, has, or can have, this experience. Therefore, his answer to the question 'What is the experience of Self-realisation like?' is that it is like that of dreamless sleep, though the latter examplifies it only in a very limited, or minimal, way. Therefore, the concept of dreamless sleep is one of the basic concepts of Advaitism. If it is shown to be untenable, or incapable of doing what the *advaitin* thinks it does, it will mean a lot for him because there is nothing else in an individual's experience besides it which, according to him, can exemplify Self-realisation. In what follows, I shall try to examine whether or not the concept can do all that the *advaitin* claims it to do. This will be a purely logical or coceptual exercise. I will not try to give any developmental or historical account of the Advaitic treatment of it. My conclusion would be that the *advaitin*'s claim about it is not as invulnerable as he thinks it is.

The concept of *suṣupti* has not been discussed, by modern writers on Indian philosophy, as well as some other Advaitic concepts like those of *māyā*, *Brahman*, *adhyāsa*, *ātman*, etc., have been, and, to the best of my knowledge, no critical assessment of its role has been done. Andrew O. Fort has given a good, scholarly, historical, account of it in his *The Self and Its States* (Motilal Banarsidass, 1990), but it is almost exclusively exegetical and not at all assessive.

The Advaita Vedānta holds that there are four states of which the first three are the states of the *jīva* under the domination or direction of ignorance. They are the states of waking, dreaming or dreamfully sleeping, and deepsleep, or dreamlessly sleeping (*suṣupti*). For brevity's sake I shall call the latter two simply dreaming and sleeping. It is obvious that dreaming here does not include day-dreaming. The fourth state is called *turīya*, a state in which the *jīva*, after having become enlightened has the non-dual experience of the Self as ECB. This sort of *jīva*, since it has become enlightened, has come back to its original selfhood, is now the Self, though still embodied. Therefore, *turīya* is not really a state of the *jīva*, but of the Self. It can be said to be an epistemic state or experience which realises the non-dual nature of the Self, and also an ontological state, the state of the Self as it is, or even the Self itself. This is so because, for the *jīva*, to know the Self is to be the Self which it really is.

Attaining *turīya*, or *jīvanmukti*, is the highest ideal for a living human being. It is higher than moral perfection because the latter could be called a means to it, a ladder the *sādhaka* may use for climbing to the state of *turīya*. After attaining the latter he is not subject to moral injunctions. Good and evil do not touch him. Morality does not elevate his status since he has already attained the highest, and immorality does not defile him either. *Pañcadaśī* quotes the *Kauṣitakī Upaniṣad*, saying that "Killing of parents, stealing, causing abortion and such other sins do not affect his illumination, nor is the colour (serenity) of his countenance marred."[1]

That the *jīvanmukta* is beyond good and evil, or that he has no further duty to perform, since he has attained the highest that can be aspired after, etc., have been said to extol, in a hyperbolic

1. मातापित्रेर्वधः स्तेयं भ्रूणहत्यान्यदीदृशम् ।
न मुक्तिं नाशयेत्पापं मुखकान्तिर्न नश्यति ।। १७ ।।

Svāmi Svāhānanda's translation,(Sri Ramakrishma Math, Madras), p. 541.

manner, the highest spiritual attainment he has been blessed with. It is better not to take them as literal statements expressing his indifferent, or it-does-not-matter-to-me, attitude towards morality. It cannot be denied, however, that too much insistence on his status being higher than, or on its transcending, morality, on morality's being a mere means to attaining *mukti*, on *jīvanmukta*'s having been freed from all moral obligations, etc., is available in some classical texts and has been very much highlighted by some modern writers on Indian philosophy as well. This sort of insistence has built into it the potentiality to make one think that morality is a disposable vessel which, after use, can be thrown away, without any loss. The only way to make it benign, or ineffective, is to take the insistence as a hyperbolic characterisation of the status of a *jīvanmukta*.[2] The attainment of no ideal can make morality superfluous. It is dangerous to consider the latter to be a dispensable commodity. Whenever two proposed ideals, referring to any sphere of life, conflict, or are at variance with each other, the only way to determine which one is to be preferred is to find out which one has more moral merit, or moral considerations in its favour.

The Advaitic Self is "the witness of the presence and absence of the states of waking, dreaming and deep sleep."[3] It itself is never in any one of the three states. All the three are the states of the *jīva*. How to convince the common man that there is in him a witnessing consciousness observing always the functioning of his empirical consciousness? In his waking experiences his sense-organs and mind are active, supplying him information about the external world and his inner, mental, states or moods. In observing what happens in the external or the internal world of his, he not only is the agent, but also knows that he is. When he recollects sometime

2. धन्योऽहं धन्योऽहं दुखं सांसारिकं न वीक्षेऽद्य ।
धन्योऽहं धन्योऽहं स्वस्याज्ञानं पलायतिं क्वापि ।। २९३ ।।
धन्योऽहं धन्योऽहं कर्तव्यं मे न विद्यते किञ्चित् ।
धन्योऽहं धन्योऽहं प्राप्तव्यं सर्वमद्य संपन्नम् ।। २९४ ।।
Pañcadaśī p. 342

3. जागरस्वप्नसुप्तीनामा गामापायभासनम् ।
यतो भवत्यसावात्मा स्वप्नकाशचिदात्मक: ।। ५८ ।।
Ibid., p. 493

later any of his waking experiences, he recollects it as an experience of his. Therefore, his waking experiences do not seem to need, or imply, any agency which witnesses or observes their life-history, though, according to the *advaitin*, the witnessing consciousness is not absent from them.

Dreaming also seems to be similar to waking in not obviously requiring reference to a witnessing consciousness. When an individual dreams, he is aware of his dreaming, and when he recollects a dream, he recollects it as *his* dream, as something he himself dreamed. He does not seem to need an observer of his dreams to enable him to recollect them. But the phenomenon of dreamless sleep does obviously need, the *advaitin* thinks, reference to the witnessing consciousness. Therefore, he uses it as a corner of the common man's normal life demonstrating or implying the reality, or the necessity of admitting the reality, of the witnessing consciousness as ECB.

In dreamless sleep the sleeper has no dreams, and as dreams are the only kind of things which could be the content of sleep, dreamless sleep has no content. There is nothing in it of which the sleeper could obviously be said to be aware of. But when he wakes up he says he had a very sound sleep. As Vidyāraṇya puts it, "A man from deep sleep remembers his happiness and ignorance and says: I was sleeping happily: I knew nothing then."[4] Since he recollects that he slept happily, the *advaitin* argues, he had the experience of sleeping happily because recollection presupposes a prior experience. But the sleeper also confesses his unawareness or ignorance, as he says he knew nothing; i.e., he was not aware, or conscious, of anything. And, even common experience shows that in deep, dreamless, sleep the sleeper is conscious of nothing. But if he is not conscious of anything, how could he be said to have had an experience of sleeping happily, which he later recollects? This puzzle, the *advaitin* holds, can be solved only by understanding properly the nature of the consciousness present in it *and* admitting

4. सुखमस्वाप्सामाभाहं न वै किञ्चदवेदिषम् ।
इति सुप्ते सुखाज्ञाने परामृशति चात्थितः ।। ५९ ।।
Pañcadaśī, p. 452

the reality of the Self as the witnessing consciousness.

For the *advaitin*, dreamless sleep is an experience. Therefore, there is consciousness in it. The latter is very different from the consciousness present in waking and dreaming experiences. It is different because it is undifferentiated (*ekībhūta*) mass of consciousness (*prajñānaghana*), containing no differences or distinctions, no multiplicity, of any type. It is effortless and therefore blissful because the miseries, which making an effort involves, are absent from it. The *supta* (sleeper) does not have any desire for getting anything. Hence the question of making any effort to fulfil it, or of feeling unhappy because of failing to fulfil it, does not arise. Waking and dreaming experiences misapprehend reality, but *suṣupti* does not apprehend or misapprehend any reality. What is there in it is mere consciousness, making no discrimination of any kind.[5]

Since there is consciousness in *suṣupti*, there cannot be any objection to calling it an experience. This consciousness is blissfull. Therefore, there cannot be any objection to calling it a happy or blissful experience. But there is still the question of explaining the recollection of happiness with the confession of ignorance, of not knowing anything. The Advaitic answer seems to run as follows:

The consciousness present in *suṣupti* being an undifferentiated mass, though blissful, cannot be said to recollect the happiness and to report it when the sleeper wakes up. Rather, the question of its recollecting does not arise because it vanishes when the sleeper wakes up. Recollection is done only when he wakes up and then he has the waking consciousness which is different from it. But the happiness is recollected and reported. This implies that, when *suṣupti* was being experienced, some agency was observing, as an outsider, that it was an experience of happiness under the cover of ignorance, of knowing nothing. This agency is nothing but the witnessing consciousness, the noumenal Self, which observes, without participating in, what is experienced, or done, by the phenomenal or

5. यत्र सुप्तो न कञ्चन कामं कामयते न कञ्चन स्वप्नं पश्यति तत्सुषुप्तम् ।
सुषत्पस्यानः एकीभूतः प्रज्ञानघन एवानन्दमयो ह्यानन्दभुक्येतोमुखः प्राज्ञसतृतीयः पादः ।। ५ ।।
Māṇḍūkya Upaniṣad with Gauḍapāda Kārikās and Śaṅkra's Commentary, (Gita Press), p. 15. For Śaṅkara's commentary, see pp. 15-17.

empirical self. Waking, dreaming, dreamless sleep, all are the experiences of the phenomenal self observed, in a detached or uninvolved manner, by the noumenal Self. We do not have perforce to refer to it to account for recollecting or reporting any item belonging to waking or dreaming experiences. But we have to in the case of dreamless sleep. The *advaitin* has his agruments for admitting the presence of the witnessing consciousness in waking and dreaming experiences as well. But we need not go into them here. To do that would amount to going much deeper in the Advaitic metaphysics than we presently need to.

Suṣupti is, thus, for the *advaitin*, an experience which is non-dual and blissful. Because of the consciousness present in it being an undifferentiated mass and its being recollected, after its termination, as a blissful experience under the cover of ignorance, it is an indicator of the Self as a witnessing consciousness. Therefore he takes it to be an analogue, of course a limited one, of the experience of Self-realisation, or *jīvanmukti*, because the latter too is a non-dual, blissful, experience, revealing the witnessing, non-participant, character of the Self. It is a limited analogue because it is short-lived, whereas the latter is ever-lasting. And, it is a sleeping experience when the latter is a waking one. To conclude, the *advaitin* makes three claims about it: That it is (a) non-dual, (b) blissful, and (c) indicative of the Self as witnessing consciousness. I shall examine them in what follows, taking up (c) first.

Every living human being (rather any living being) is a conscious being. Therefore it is not at all difficult for him to have an idea of what consciousness is. But the consciousness he is acquainted with is a participant consciousness, one which is always a consciousness of something or other, which moves him to action, functions as the hinterland for his desires, feelings and emotions, aims and aspirations, doubts and beliefs, etc. None of these things can be said to be true of the witnessing, objectless, consciousness which the Advaitic Self is said to be. Therefore, it is not at all easy for him to form an idea of the Advaitic Self. Therefore, if *suṣupti* indicates a witnessing consciousness, it would be doing a great service to Advaitism and be of great help to the ordinary individual by giving him a good reason to believe in the reality of witnessing consciousness.

The Advaitic argument for the reality of a witnessing consciousness, or of Self-realisation or *jīvanmukti* derived from the experience of *suṣupti*, can, using some of the things the *advaitin* says in talking about the latter, as already mentioned, be formally reconstructed as follows:

(1) *Suṣupti* is a phenomenal (or empirical) reality.

(2) That it is blissful and under the cover of ignorance is recollected by the *supta* when he says, after waking up, that he slept happily and knew nothing.

(3) Recollecting anything implies a prior experience of that thing.

(4) *Suṣupti* is an experience.

(5) An experience implies consciousness.

(6) There is consciousness in *suṣupti* which is just a non-discriminating or undifferentiated mass.

(7) Such a mass of consciousness, a bare consciousness, cannot account for the post-*suṣupti* recollection of what *suṣupti* is.

(8) Therefore, there must be another agency observing what goes on in *suṣupti* without interfering with, or participating in, it. This agency is what is called a witnessing consciousness, a noumenal reality, unaffected or unpolluted by the phenomenal reality of *suṣupti*, to know which is to be *jīvanmukta*.

Let us see what this argument really amounts to.

One way to respond to it, though a little crude but not logically impermissible, would be to deny the truth of the first premise. One may say that *suṣupti* is not empirically real. We never have sleep without dreams. When we seem to have one, the truth is that we have forgotten the dreams we had, because dreams are, as psychologists say, very soon forgotten.[6] If this is so, the argument

6. A very knowledgeable neurosurgeon once said, in course of a lecture on the neurology of sleep, that we never have sleep without dreams. By instrumentally observing the mevements in the eyes of a sleeping subject, it has been confirmed that he has dreams all the time he sleeps. (R.P.)

will collapse because it is built on the assumption that dreamless sleep is as natural a human phenomenon as waking or dreaming is. But the *advaitin* can counter it by saying that, even if an ordinary person does not have it, a *yogī* or *yati* (recluse) does have it, and therefore the first premise cannot be called false.

Let us then assume that (1) is true; (3) is obviously true; (4) follows from (1), (2) and (3); (1) and (3) we have accepted as true. Therefore, if (2) is also true, then (4) will obviously be true. But (2) does not seem to be as innocent as it seems to be. Let it also be granted that the sleeper, on waking up, says 'I slept very happily, I knew nothing'. The *advaitin* takes the quoted sentence to be a memorial report, given by the sleeper, of what happened in the *suṣupti*. But it may be an expression of the after-effect of the deep-sleep he had. It is a well-known empirical truth that the after-effect of a sound sleep, when it ends in a natural way, is to make the sleeper feel cheerful and refreshed, and equally well-known is the other truth that one knows nothing when he is having sound sleep. Only when his sleep had been disturbed off and on, he could have heard, or half-heard or mis-heard, something being talked about by the inmates present in the room. It is also possible that the sub-sentence 'I knew nothing' has been used by the sleeper as an expressive, and not as an assertive sentence, that is, only to express emphatically how well he slept and not to assert that he did not know anything. In fact, if he had said that, though he had sound sleep, he still heard what was being talked about in the room, our natural reaction would be that he was not really sleeping.

But if 'I slept happily, I knew nothing' is taken as an expression of the after-effect of the sleep on the sleeper, or of the impression the sleep has left on him, and not as a recollective report of what happened during his *suṣupti*, then it would not imply that *suṣupti* is an experience. And, if it is not an experience and the sentence 'I slept . . . nothing', not a recollective report, then we would not need an agency to observe what happened in the *suṣupti* to enable the sleeper to make about it any recollective report. Obviously, then, *suṣupti* would not indicate and thereby give a reason for admitting the reality of an witnessing consciousness.

But let us grant this also that the sentence 'I slept . . . nothing' is a recollective report and that *suṣupti* is an experience and then examine whether or not *suṣupti* gives a good reason for admitting the reality of any witnessing consciousness.

For the Advaita, *suṣupti*, like waking and dreaming, is a state of the *jīva*, the empirical or phenonmenal Self, and not of the Self, or the noumenal Self. The latter neither sleeps nor wakes up, neither remembers nor forgets anything, neither initiates nor participates in any programme, neither obstructs nor cooperates with any other agency, because nothing other than it is real. It is completely non-dual. There is not even the duality of it and its object because it is pure, objectless, consciousness. This seems to be the reason for the *advaitin*'s giving more weightage to the consciousness allegedly involved in dreamless sleep than to that involved in waking and dreaming. In both of the latter consciousness has some object. It has external or internal objects in waking, and dreams in dreaming, experiences. But it has no object at all in dreamless sleep. *Prājña*, the third quarter of the Self, which has dreamless sleep as its sphere, is said to be the Lord of all (*sarveśvaraḥ*), omniscient, the inner director and source of all, the place of origin and dissolution of all beings.[7]

It is the phenomenal Self which has *suṣupti* and which, on waking up, recollects and says 'I slept . . . nothing'. This means that the experience of bliss and the ignorance of everything in *suṣupti* are also had by it, since one can recollect only one's own past experience, or such a total ignorance, and not that of anyone else. Therefore, there seems to be no need to refer to the noumenal Self, or to its observation of what goes on in the phenomenal Self's experience of *suṣupti*. It may be said that, the consciousness involved in *suṣupti* being just an undifferentiated mass, the phenomenal Self's experience is too indistinct or inarticulate to be recollected. Therefore, it is the witnessing consciousness which is to be referred to in order to explain the phenomenal Self's recollection and utterance of the sentence 'I slept . . . nothing'. This would mean that the witnessing consciousness tells the phenomenal

7. एष सर्वेश्वरः एष सर्वज्ञः एषोऽन्तर्याम्येष योनिः सर्वस्य प्रभवाप्ययौ हि भूतानाम ।। ६ ।।
Māṇḍūkya Upaniṣad, p. 18

consciousness that the latter had in its *suṣupti* the experience of bliss, etc. But this is not possible. The witnessing consciousness, being the noumenal Self, cannot tell anything to the phenomenal Self. To assume that it can is to assume that both can co-exist at the time of the former's telling the latter. But they cannot co-exist, in the case of the same individual, at the same point of time because that would entail the duality of the two Selfs. They are not two reals. The phenomenal Self is only the noumenal Self under the influence or domination of ignorance. The moment it hears and recognises the voice of the noumenal Self, it knows the noumenal Self. For the phenomenal Self to know the noumenal Self is to *be* the noumenal Self, or to return to its original state in which it is the noumenal Self. The two cannot have a dialogue with each other, or face each other, because if they do, there would be two reals which, for Advaitism, is not possible. If follows from all this that the experience of *suṣupti* cannot be used to indicate or imply that there is a witnessing consciousness, or that the noumenal Self is a witness and not a participant.

Even if the argument (A) is taken to have proved (8), its conclusion, when we look at the latter, we find that what is proved is that there is a witnessing consciousness behind every experience of *suṣupti*. This means that there are as many witnessing consciousnesses as there are experiencers of *suṣupti*. But the *advaitin* holds that there is one and only one witnessing consciousness and that alone is real. His is a theory of absolute monism. This does not, I admit, mean that his monism is disproved by the present analysis because he has some other reasons also for upholding it. But, I think, it is also to be admitted, as shown above, that the experience of *suṣupti* cannot be used to prove the kind of monism he holds.

I will now turn to the other two features of *suṣupti* which also are said to contribute to its being analogous to the experience of Self-realisation. They are its (a) non-duality and (b) blissfulness. As far as non-duality is concerned, it is by definition non-dual because it is said to be dreamless and only dreams can be the objects of a sleeping experience. Therefore, it is non-dual in the sense that the awareness which exists in it is just awareness, and not the awareness of something. It is an experience only, and not an experience of doing, receiving, giving, or cognising something. It is non-dual in the sense of being objectless, or non-objective, i.e., non-intentional (in Brentano's sense). But there is another kind of duality which it has. That is the duality of the *supta* and *suṣupti*, the sleeper and the sleep, as it is a state or experience of an individual, and not a self-maintaining state or experience. The Advaitic concept of Self-realisation is doubly non-dual. It is non-dual in the sense that to realise the Self is to *be* the Self, which means to be existence-consciousness-bliss. It is just existence, *not the existence of* something; just consciousness, neither *the consciousness of some object*, nor the state or *property of a conscious* individual; just bliss, neither the bliss *experienced by an individual,* nor the bliss *occasioned by any object* or individual.

Since *suṣupti* is claimed to be only a limited analogue of Self-realisation, its being non-intentional only, i.e., only partially non-dual, may be conceded to be enough to make it deserve the honour given to it by the *advaitin*. But its not being under the control of an ordinary individual's will makes it, to all intents and purposes, primarily a theoretical or hypothetical analogue. It is not that he can experience *suṣupti* when he wills, or tries, to have it in order to get an idea of what the Advaitic Self-realisation is like. Just as we cannot choose to have dreams, or dreams of a certain type, we cannot even choose to have no dreams. This means that the practical utility of the analogue cannot be very great. We have some control only on our waking experiences. Therefore, if something belonging to our waking life is found to be analoguous to Self-realisation, it would be more easily usable and therefore of more practical value than *suṣupti*.

The other feature of *suṣupti* which is referred to in this connection is (allegedly) its blissful nature. I raised, a little earlier, the question whether *suṣupti* itself is blissful, or its after-effect is blissful. Let us probe this question a little further. One quite often says that he had last night a pleasant dream. Suppose he dreamed that he and *A*, a very dear friend of his, were sitting on a branch of a mango tree in his orchard, plucking and eating some real sweet mangoes and gossiping about their childhood days in a care-free, uninhibited, manner. Now, did he and *A* eat mangoes in his dream, or did he dream that he and *A* ate mangoes? We might sometimes say they ate . . .. But actually what we mean is that he dreamed that he and *A* ate . . .. It is quite obvious that one *cannot eat anything in a dream*; he can definitely *dream of eating* something, alone, or in the company of *A*. This is so because the level of consciousness one needs to have to sit on a branch of a mango tree, to pluck mangoes, and eat while gossiping with a friend *A*, etc., is not present in him when he is sleeping. Moreover, it is absurd to say that *A* ate mangoes, etc., in his (i.e., someone else's) dream. If we grant the locution that they ate mangoes, etc., in his dream, we would have also to grant this absurdity.

Similarly, it seems to me that the level of consciousness one has in *suṣupti* is not of the type one needs to have the experience of bliss. Experiencing any kind of pleasure is possible only when the person concerned has an undiffused, clear and distinct, responsive, consciousness. It requires him to be in a certain kind of mood which is a mood of alertness, and not one of indifference, unconcernedness, or sleepiness. On the *advaitin*'s own admission what is present in *suṣupti* is a mere, or bare, consciousness, an undifferentiated mass (*ekībhbūta, prajñānaghana*), non-discriminative, or indistinct. This level of consciousness does not seem to be of the kind which can enable one to experience bliss, or to *be* blissful.

For the *advaitin* both waking and dreaming experiences deal with unreality or appearances. The objects known in waking experiences, whether they are external or internal objects, are all unreal, and so are the dream-objects of dreaming experiences. *Suṣupti* has no object, as if the Self takes rest in the state of *suṣupti*. But if this is so, the *advaitin* may say, *suṣupti* is like the state of *mukti* because the latter too is a state of rest for the Self, a much more durable state than *suṣupti*. Therefore, the *advaitin* may assert, *suṣupti* is a limited analogue of *jīvanumukti*. But there could be a hitch in allowing him even to do that. The state of waking is very different from that of deep-sleep which *suṣupti* is. The state of *turīya* is waking state, and so is that of *jīvanmukti*, though the *jīvanmukta* can be sometimes asleep as well. Then, can a state of deep-sleep, which *suṣupti* is, give a correct idea of a waking state in which a *turīya*-experiencing individual, a *jīvanmukta*, may be? Can the bliss of *suṣupti*, a sleeping state, assuming that *suṣupti* is blissful, give an idea of the bliss of *turīya*, or *jīvanmukti*, a state of waking? It seems to me that it may not, for the simple reason that a sleeping state is very different from a waking state.

Kāvyānanda, the pleasure obtained from reading a poetic work understandingly, has been claimed by aesthetic writers to be a limited analogue of the pleasure obtained in the state of *jīvanmukti*, a *Brahmānanda-sahodara*. But *advaitin*s, to the best of my knowledge, do not use the example of *Kāvyānanda*, or that of human love. Even Śaṅkara does not do that though he was a very good poet, as is obvious from his devotional hymns.[8] It is not simply because most of them, being recluses, did not like to refer to either one of the two on account of the element of attachment or emotionality involved in both of them. I think the reason was the element of duality essentially involved in them. The duality of the enjoyer and the object enjoyed, the reader of a poem and the poem in Kāvyānanda, and that of the lover and his beloved in human love, have to be there. The Advaitic bliss is non-objective, and therefore Kāvyānanda, or human love, cannot be its analogue.

There is a theoretical compulsion for the *advaitin*'s offering only *suṣupti* as an analogue of liberation, as an example from the life of the individual to give to him an idea of what *jīvanmukti*, *Brahmānanda* or *Ātmānanda*, is like. As has already been said, in Advaitic ontology, the Self in itself and as itself is alone real. It is also the highest value for the unliberated individual. It is true that the latter is an embodied being. But this embodiment has the peculiarity that it is not really real. It looks as if the individual is the Self in a fallen form. But there is no real fall of the Self. The causation of the appearance of the Self as the unliberated individual, the empirical Self, is attributable to *māyā*. But the causation itself can be called a *māyā*, or an appearance, because the Self does not really become an embodied being. In the categoriology of the Advaita, *māyā*, which is said to be the cause of appearances or illusions, is itself a *māyā* and not a reality because nothing other than the Self is real. Everything else, including *māyā*, is only a *māyā*.

8. See the hymns appended to his *Ātma-Bodha*, (Sri Ramakrishna Math, Madras).

The highest ideal for the *mumukṣu*, therefore, is to reverse back his movement from worldly affairs towards the Self and finally to *be* the Self. This he can do by absolutely withdrawing himself from the (apparent) non-Self and centre himself into himself, into the Self in him. It is extremely difficult to effect the withdrawal in waking experiences. That he can do only after becoming enlightened. His success in it would be the end-product of his *sādhanā*, his liberation or Self-realisation while alive. This happens in *turīya*. Therefore, *turīya* is not an analogue of Self-realisation experienced by an unliberated, ordinary, individual. Rather, it is the state of Self-realisation. In every waking experience the individual interacts with the external world, or experiences some impressions caused by such an interaction on his cognitive apparatus. Even in dreaming, he is not completely withdrawn into himself. He experiences dreams and dreams are caused by his *vāsanās* (desires or passions) generated in waking experiences. It is only in *suṣupti*, the *advaitin* holds, that he is completely withdrawn from the not-Self, or completely drawn into himself, because he does not even experience any dream which alone could be experienced in this state. Thus *suṣupti* is, for the *advaitin*, the only state of an individual which can be said to resemble the state of Self-realisation, if anything from the latter's life can be said to do that even in the minimal way. This is the reason why he speaks of it in a highly appreciative, or laudatory, manner.

In his commentary on the *Bṛhadāraṇyaka Upaniṣad*, IV.iii. 32, Śaṅkara, *via* Yājñavalkya's instruction to Janaka, says:

> In profound sleep the self, bereft of its limiting adjuncts, the body and organs, remains in its own supreme light of the *ātman*, free from all relations. . . .[9]

He says something similar in his commentary on the *Chāndogya Upaniṣad*, VI.8.1:

> For the knowers of *Brahman* do not admit attainment of its own nature by the individual soul, in any state other than deep sleep.[10]

9. Svāmi Mādhavananda's translation, pp. 475-6, (Advaita Ashrama, Calcutta).
10. Swami Gambhirananda's translation, p. 455, (Advaita Ashrama, Calcutta).

That is, as far as the individual or *jīva*, who is not yet liberated, is concerned, *suṣupti* is the only state of his which, as per the Advaitic understanding of it, comes nearest to Self-realisation. In the context of the Advaitic ontology, among the experiences possible for the individual, no other experience can do this job. In *suṣupti* alone he cognises neither anything external nor anything internal. Therefore, quite naturally, being dictated by the demands of his theoretical structure, the *advaitin* has to give to *suṣupti* the place of high honour he in fact gives to it. The pessimistic implication of this fact is that, if the concept of *suṣupti* is shown to be, as has been done in this chapter, incapable of playing the role the *advaitin* holds it actually plays, he would have nothing in his conceptual stock to illustrate to the unliberated what Self-realisation, as conceived by him, is like. He would have nothing to illustrate it even to a philosopher who is not liberated, or not already converted to Advaitism.

In the very beginning of this chapter it was mentioned that for Advaitism the highest reality is also the highest value. In fact, every school which holds *mokṣa* to be the highest value — and all schools except the Cārvāka do that — holds that reality as the self is the highest value for the individual (*jīva*). *Mokṣa*, as *jīvanmukti* or *videhamukti*, is for everyone of them the return of the *jīva* to its original selfhood, no matter whether its ontology is pluralistic or monistic. To be *mukta*, liberated, while alive or after death, the *jīva* has to realise, or regain, its sense of non-identity with its body, i.e., to realise the Self it really is. Therefore, the Self as a reality for pluralistic systems, and as the reality for monistic systems, is the highest value. In all this thinking the common presupposition, thus, is that reality is also value. The classical schools do not discuss it as an issue in its own right but take it to be obviously true. But, as has been shown in this chapter, it is not obviously true and needs to be established. In modern times, Śrī Aurobindo has tried to do that. Since he works in the broad framework of classical Indian metaphysics and axiology, his treatment of the identity of reality and value can be taken as a renovated characterisation of the classical Indian position. Therefore, discussing it would amount to, or be very close to, discussing the classical presupposition. This will be done in the chapter that follows.

5

Commonly Presupposed Identity of Reality and Value

Aurobindo's Renovated Characterisation Stated and Examined

In classical Indian philosophy, as has been mentioned in the previous chapter, the identity of reality and value is assumed to be an obvious truth. It is true that 'reality' in the identity statement means an ultimate Reality and not any sort of reality whatsoever. Further, the statement does not mean that an ultimate reality is a value because it satisfies some criterion or criteria, but that it is because it is an ultimate reality. The self is the ultimate value for the Advaita because it is *the* ultimate reality and for the Nyāya and Sāṁkhya because it is *an* ultimate reality, as both of the latter hold the theory of ontological pluralism. Why an atom is not an ultimate value is not taken to be an important question by the Nyāya, and why *prakṛti* is not by the Sāṁkhya. But these questions can be asked and asking them is a pointer to the logical fact that some reason has to be given for the claim that an, or the, ultimate reality is also an, or *the*, ultimate value.

One may say that the Advaita gives such a reason when it says that the self is bliss. But, as has been shown in chapter 4, that is not the case. To say that the self is bliss is not different from saying that the Self is existence, or that it is consciousness. That is why the self is said to be existence-consciousness-bliss. And, it is a good question to ask why existence, or consciousness, or even bliss, is an, or the ultimate value.

Any value is a value for a human being or a *jīva*. Therefore, any value is a human value and so is an ultimate value. Since only a *jīva*, or an individual, can be said, or advised, to seek a value, the classical thinkers assumed that nothing could be a higher value for it than returning to its original status, i.e., to its selfhood. The question of giving a reason for this view remained almost undiscussed. But as modern ethical studies show, to be real is not to be *ipso facto* a value. Aurobindo tries to ronovate the classical characterisation by giving to it a religious colour. His stand is not very much different from the classical position, but since he discussed the issue in some detail it is worth examining. It is also worth examining because it shows how a modern thinker, sympathetic to the classical position, handles the issue or issues involved in it and also because it shows that he fails to satisfactorily answer the question 'why is to be real to be a value?' because he is not prepared to question the classical way of looking at it.

Philosophy, according to Aurobindo, is 'the intellectual search for the fundamental truth of things', and religion 'the attempt to make truth dynamic in the soul of man'. They 'are essential to each other, a religion that is not the expression of philosophic truth, degenerates into superstition and obscurantism, and a philosophy which does not dynamise itself with the religious spirit is barren light, for it cannot get itself practised'.[1]

The above characterisation of philosophy may give the impression that it does not cause any diminution of the large area philosophy has, in its long history, been allowed to occupy as its legitimate owner. But it does because everything which has been called a philosophic truth cannot be called a fundamental truth about something and therefore any search which can be called a philosophic search cannot be called an intellectual search for some fundamental truth about something. For example, the philosophic truth (if it is one) that all *a priori* propositions are analytic is not a fundamental truth about *a priori* propositions and a search for it, therefore, not an intellectual search of the above type. Aurobindo adds that philosophy has to dynamise itself with the religious

1. Śrī Aurobindo, *The Supramental Manifestation and Other Writings*, (Sri Aurobindo Ashram, Pondicherry, 1971), p. 314.

spirit. But everything which has been called philosophic cannot, in point of logic, be required to be dynamised with the religious spirit. It makes no sense, for instance, to require the philosophic thesis of, or the search about, the analyticity of *a priori* propositions, to be so dynamised. This means that a large part of philosophy has to be called non-philosophic if Aurobindo's characterisation of philosophy is accepted.

An objection might be raised that I am unfair to Aurobindo because I have tried to apply his characterisation to a philosophic doctrine (or search) belonging to Western philosophy, when it was intended to represent only the spirit of classical Indian philosophising. This would be a very lame objection for more than one reason. There are several theses, admitted to be philosophic truths by classical Indian philosophy which, on Aurobindo's characterisation, would require us to call them non-philosophic. For example, all the classical schools[2] admit that *anumāna* (valid inference) is a *pramāṇa* (a source of knowledge) only if it contains a *vyāpti* of a certain type (an incontrovertibly true and contextually relevant universal proposition). This doctrine, thesis, or truth, as one may choose to call it, is not categorially very different from the Wittgensteinian doctrine of the analyticity of *a priori* propositions. It makes no sense, again in point of logic, to require it to be dynamised with the religious spirit. Aurobindo, therefore, seems to draw the boundaries of philosophy in such a manner that a large part of philosophy, Indian as well as Western, is left out.

He wants philosophy to be dynamised with religion because, if it is not, it 'cannot get itself practised'. The obvious implication is

2. Many interpreters of classical Indian philosophy would object to this statement by saying that the Cārvākas reject *anumāna* or inference as a source of knowledge. This is a standard charge against the Cārvākas. But to me it seems to be based on the non-recognition of a very important distinction, namely that between inference and a theory of inference. The Cārvākas reject the then prevalent theory of inference and not inference, just as Hume rejects a certain theory of causality and not causality. The theory of inference they reject is that according to which every inference which is valid, or which can deservedly be called *anumāna*, must have, as a constituent of it, a *vyāpti* in the sense of an incontrovertibly true universal proposition. They need not reject *anumāna* if *vyāpti* is allowed to mean a universal proposition with only a high, or very high, degree of probability.

that he wants it to be 'practisable' in a very specific way, which may be called the religious way; otherwise there is no reason for requiring it to be dynamised with religion and not by anything non-religious. It is not that philosophy, for him, has to be practisable in a broad, general way; rather, it has to be in one specific way which is the religious way. A non-religious, secular, advocate of practisable philosophy could have required it to be dynamised with, for example, the spirit of social justice, or of moral upliftment, or of material well-being. When a Marxist wants to make philosophy a powerful instrument of economic or social change, he wants it to be practisable, and therefore dynamised. But his dynamising agent is not the spirit of religion; rather, it is some economic/social theory or a set of some eeconomic/social theories.

According to Aurobindo, dynamising philosophy with religion 'is at least a fundamental principle of the ancient wisdom', — the wisdom of the East and by the East he definitely means ancient or classical India — that 'philosophy ought not be merely a lofty intellectual pastime or a play of dialectical subtlety or even a pursuit of metaphysical truth for its own sake, but a discovery, by all right means, of the basic truths of all existence which ought, then, to become the guiding principles of our own existence'.[3] It is this sort of wisdom on which he claims to have founded his own thinking or philosophising.

Philosophy, for Aurobindo, as the lines quoted above show, is a discovery of the basic truths of all existence and these truths are not merely intellectual truths. Rather, they are truths which ought to become, i.e., which we ought to make, the guiding principles of our own existence. It is here, in helping them become, or in enabling us to make them, our guiding principles that philosophy's dynamisation by religion would be, according to Aurobindo, effective, and dynamisation by no other, secular, agent, would be. Aurobindo does not discuss, why only religion and no other agent would accomplish this feat.

Let us grant that philosophy discovers by the use of all right means the basic truths of all existence, and that *P* is such a truth.

3. Śrī Aurobindo, *The Synthesis of Yoga*, (Sri Aurobindo Ashram, Pondicherry, 1970), p. 367; cited hereafter as *SY*.

Since *P* is a basic truth of all existence, by definition, it is a basic truth of our existence because our existence is not outside all existence. Because *P* is a basic truth of all existence, and therefore of our existence, no existence, including our own, can violate it, flout it, or go against it, in very much the same way as no segment of nature can flout a law of nature basic to all nature. But when *P* is inviolable by any, and therefore by our, existence, there is no point in saying that it ought to be, or we ought to make it, a guiding principle of our own existence. It makes no sense to admonish anyone for making any principle a guiding principle when he cannot violate or break it.

Aurobindo seems to think that if something is a basic truth of all existence, then it is obvious that it ought to be made a guiding principle of our existence. But the logical consequence of calling any *P* a basic truth of all existence is that we cannot speak of making it a guiding principle of our existence. It is in the very logic of 'ought', of normativity or prescriptivity, that we can meaningfully say that one ought to make a principle a guiding principle only if it is possible that one may not be guided by it, or may violate it. Therefore, if philosophic truths are basic truths of all existence and consequently inviolable, philosophy cannot be said to be practisable in the sense that it gives principles or truths we ought to make our guiding principles.

Behind Aurobindo's insistence that philosophy should be dynamised by religion is the classical view or assumption that the religious or spiritual life is the highest kind of life, i.e., some religious or spiritual goal is the highest goal one ought to aim at. This he takes to be the same as realising what is also the highest, most basic, or ultimate, reality. He considers the ultimate religious goal as also ontologically ultimate. It is here, in his identification of ultimate reality with ultimate value (or *vice versa*), i.e., in conceiving ultimate reality as ultimate value (or *vice versa*), that we can reasonably hope to locate the roots of the idea of dynamising philosophy with religion. He thinks that this step makes ultimate reality more attractive or appealing, and provides an unshakable base for the highest value anyone ought to seek.

The highest reality, which is the object of *yogic* knowledge, the highest kind of knowledge, is called by Aurobindo 'the Self, the Divine, the Supreme Reality, the All, the Transcendent', or 'the one in all these aspects.'[4] He also calls it the Infinite, the Absolute, God, etc. It is the 'summit of existence', i.e., it occupies the highest place among things which are real. 'To reach the spiritual consciousness and the Divine' is 'the ultimate goal and aim of our being and therefore of the whole development of the individual and collectivity in all its parts and activities. . . .'[5] This is a scalar conception of reality according to which one real thing can be more or less real than another, and the Divine is the highest reality.

When a concept, *C*, is considered to be scalar, one can legitimately ask of any *X* and *Y*, when *X* is claimed to be more *C* than *Y* is, what is it that makes *X* more *C* than *Y*, or why is *X* given a higher place on the *C* ladder than *Y*. For example, if both *X* and *Y* are pen-knives, we can ask what is it that makes *X* a better pen-knife that *Y*, if someone says that *X* is better than *Y*. The concept of a good pen-knife is scalar and therefore our question is in order. If 'real' is also used as a scalar concept, then, if both *X* and *Y* are real, and not toy, pen-knives, we should be able to say meaningfully that *X* is a more real pen-knife than *Y* and also be able to ask meaningfully why this is so. But we are not and the reason is that 'real', as ordinarily understood, is not a scalar concept. It is therefore that 'real pen-knife' is also not a scalar concept. 'Good', on the other hand, like any other value-term, is scalar and it is therefore that 'good pen-knife' is. Value-predicates are scalar. Therefore, one way to eliminate the ring of oddity surrounding the use of 'real' or 'reality' in the scalar sense is to treat them as value-terms. Whether or not doing so is logically or conceptually fair is another matter, and many modern philosophers would say it is not. Aurobindo does treat 'real' or 'reality' as a value-predicate, otherwise he would not have asserted that the Divine, the ultimate reality or 'summit of existence', is 'the ultimate goal and aim of our being'. His theory of ultimate reality is thus, as already pointed out, a theory of the identity of reality and value.

4. *SY*, p. 286.

5. Śrī Aurobindo, *The Human Cycle*, (Sri Aurobindo Ashram, Pondicherry, 1970), p. 162; cited hereafter as *HC*.

If 'real' is an ontological as well as an axiological predicate, then to call the Divine the summit of existence would also amount to calling it the summit of value, or the highest value. To call its realisation the ultimate aim or goal of life would then need no further justification. But by making 'real' axiological, though we can rule out the question why the Divine, which is the ultimate reality, is also the ultimate value, we cannot rule out the question why is the Divine to be called the ultimate reality. This question is not very much different from asking why is the Divine to be called the ultimate value, because calling it by one name is also to call it by the other name in Aurobindo's scheme of things.

Identifying ultimate reality with ultimate value cannot make it illegitimate to ask for the justification of calling the Divine either ultimate reality, or ultimate value. The question why is the Divine considered to be the ultimate value may be (mis)taken to be identical with the question how is it known that the Divine is the ultimate value, but they are two different questions. The first can be answered by mentioning the reason or reasons, if there be any, for calling it ultimate value, and the second by mentioning the method or methods of knowing the reason or reasons. It is possible that there exists some reason but we do not know it or only inadequately know it, though if we know what it is, then it certainly exists. But though conceptually the two questions are different, one may try to answer both of them by answering the latter, by explaining how he knows that the Divine is the ultimate value, provided his claim to its knowledge is valid.

It seems to me that Aurobindo cannot say that the Divine is the ultimate value *because* it is the ultimate reality, since anything's being real is neither a sufficient nor a necessary reason for its being or having a value. Perhaps he would say that in being the ultimate reality it is also the ultimate value, which would be tantamount to saying that 'being the ultimate reality' and 'being the ultimate value' mean the same thing. But the two do not normally mean the same thing. Using them to mean the same thing, therefore, would neither prove that the Divine is the ultimate reality, nor that it is the ultimate value.

Aurobindo quite often says that the Divine, God, or the Self, is pure bliss or *ānanda* '. . . the idea of a joyless God is an absurdity, which only the ignorance of the mind could engender'. 'When the *ānanda* comes into you, it is the Divine who comes into you, just as when the Peace flows into you, it is the Divine who is invading you, or when you are flooded with light, it is the flood of the Divine himself that is around you.'[6] 'The Divine whether it manifests itself in All-Quality or in No-Quality, in Personality or Impersonality, in the One absorbing the Many or in the One manifesting its essential multiplicity, is always in possession of self-bliss and all-bliss because it is always *saccidānanda*. For us also to know and possess our true Self in the essential and the universal is to discover the essential and the universal delight of existence, self-bliss and all-bliss.'[7]

But though the Divine is bliss or *ānanda*, Aurobindo does not seem to consider its *ānanda* a reason for its being the ultimate value. Rather, 'being the *ānanda*' and being the ultimate value', as is the case with 'being the ultimate Reality' and 'being the ultimate value', seem to be used by him synonymously. Therefore, the Divine's being the *ānanda* cannot be used as a reason for its being the ultimate value, and if it is, then Aurobindo would have to prove that *ānanda* or bliss is at least a necessary determinant of all (positive) values, which also he does not.

But it would be unfair to conclude that Aurobindo has no reason to call the Divine the ultimate reality or value. His reason is his *yogic*, spiritual, experience. 'Spiritual experience tells us that there is a Reality which supports and pervades all things as the Cosmic Self and Spirit, can be discovered by the individual even here in the terrestrial embodiment as his own self and spirit, and is, at its summit and in its essence, an infinite and eternal Being, Consciousness and Bliss of Existence'.[8] That there is the Divine and that it is the ultimate reality as well as ultimate value, both are, for Aurobindo, revelations made by spiritual experience. Similar position, or positions, differing from it in some not very significant details, have been taken by classical Indian philosophers.

6. Śrī Aurobindo, *Letters on Yoga*, (Sri Aurobindo Ashram, Pondicherry, 1970), p. 173; cited hereafter as *LY*.

7. *SY*, p. 363.

8. *HC*, p. 158.

The *advaitin* Śaṅkara too appeals to spiritual experience. He also makes use of highly sophisticated logical analyses but only to clarify his revealed truths, and not to prove them. Aurobindo, on the other hand, not only does not indulge in logical sophistication, but seems to hold that logic is of no use in this regard. This is clear from his critique of reason. Reason, according to him, is destined to end in agnosticism. It is because of its dependence on reason or intellect that he accuses European thought of inevitably ending in agnosticism. 'European metaphysical thought', he says, 'does not in its method and result go beyond the intellect. But the intellect is incapable of knowing the supreme truth. . . . At the end of European thought, therefore, there must always be Agnosticism, declared or implicit. Intellect, if it goes sincerely to its own end, has to return and give this report:

> I cannot know, there is, or at least it seems to me that there may be or even must be something beyond, some ultimate Reality, but about its truth I can only speculate; it is either unknowable or cannot be known by me.[9]

Aurobindo's wholesale condemnation of European thought as merely intellectualist and therefore agnostic may be an expression of his attachment to some philosophical or religious traditions of ancient India, but certainly it cannot be justified on factual grounds.

When Aurobindo claims that something is the case on the ground of its being revealed in his mystic or spiritual experience, his pattern of thinking can be presented as follows: Since in my experience *D* seems to be the ultimate value (Reality, Bliss, etc.), *D* is the ultimate value (Reality Bliss, etc.). He does not seem to notice the logical possibility of a gap between *D*'s *seeming to be* and *being* the ultimate value. He seems to compensate for this apparent, logical, oversight by attributing to mystic or spiritual experience some sort of infallibility, by claiming that it can never go wrong. It thus becomes definitional to hold that what seems to be real in mystic experience is real. But there is another logical insensitivity in not noticing that by defining mystic experience in a certain way, nobody, even if he is a mystic, can make the gap between 'seems to be' and 'is' non-existent.

9. *LY*, p. 157.

Let us assume, however, for the sake of argument, that the Divine is the highest value and that Aurobindo knows that it is, and let us then try to understand the nature of this knowledge. To emphasise the uniqueness of this knowledge he calls it *yoga*. It is 'not merely an intellectual conception or clear discrimination of the truth, nor is it an enlightened psychological experience of modes of our being. It is a 'realisation', in the full sense of the word, it is the making real to ourselves and in ourselves of the Self, the transcendent and universal Divine, and it is the subsequent impossibility of viewing the modes of being except in the light of that Self and in their true aspect as its flux or becoming under the psychological and physical conditions of our world-existence![10] For anyone to have this knowledge, then, is to realise the Self or Divine in himself. Consequently, it becomes impossible for him to consider any other thing except in the light of this reality. It culminates in a kind of identity or becoming. 'We must not only see God and embrace Him, but become that Reality.'[11] It is 'the knowledge by which we *become* what we know'.[12]

To know the Divine is to know what it is and to know what it is, is to become the Divine. But what sort of claim is it? Is it a logical or an empirical claim? It cannot be an empirical claim because then the possibility of its being sometimes false cannot be ruled out of court. But Aurobindo will not allow that it can ever be false. For him it is impossible that one knows the Divine but does not find that it is the ultimate reality or value, or does not become it. Can we then call it a logical or definitional claim? Does Aurobindo make it definitional that only he can be said to know the Divine who agrees to call it ultimate reality and value and who becomes the Divine? This would amount only to redefining the word 'know'. It cannot be said to be used in its standard, normal, sense because what is meant by knowledge here is not what it ordinarily means. It amounts, in effect, to saying that there is a special kind of knowledge by having which one becomes the Divine and thereby is convinced of the identity of the highest reality and highest value.

10. *SY*, p. 290.
11. *SY*, p. 292.
12. *LY*, p. 160.

There are several possible ways in which one can react to Aurobindo's account of the identity of ultimate reality and value. His reactions would very much depend on the kind of person he is. If he is a tender-minded, devotional, person, he may take it as a sacred truth, as a not-to-be-questioned revelation, and try to mould his life-style according to it. If he is himself a mystic, a *yogī*, he may try to relive the relevant experience to test it. But what if he finds his experience not supporting Aurobindo's claim? This is not an impossibility since mystics do sometimes disagree among themselves about the verdicts of their mystic experiences. There is no way to decide which mystic is right, or more right than some other one. But if he is a mere philosopher, he can only try to understand what Aurobindo reports on the basis of his mystic experience.

Since any experience is private, to the philosopher would be available only the set of statements or utterances made by Aurobindo, and not his experience. Therefore, he can make only the former the raw materials of his philosophising. But he cannot test their truth-claim because he is not a mystic and therefore lacks the ability to have the needed mystic experience. He can only try to ascertain how cogent, how sensible, how logically or pragmatically defensible, they are. In doing all this, he has to use his normal, professional, logical tools. If it is held that they can be properly understood only by another mystic, or by one who is devotionally oriented towards mysticism, or that the philosopher's logical, conceptional tools are inapplicable to them, there is no alternative for the philosopher but to keep off the scene. On the other hand, if it is said that a genuine philosopher need not care for logic, or be guided by any logical consideration, in his study of the mystic discourse, or that the mystic alone is a genuine philosopher and not he who subjects the mystic's utterances to logical scrutiny, then the issue becomes a verbal one as to how should the word 'philosopher', or 'philosophy', be used.

Aurobindo offers his statements about the Divine as reports of his spiritual experience, and since they are claimed to be reports, he does not have to, one may like to say, give any argument or reason for them. Even a sense-empirical report, an observation-report, does not need to be supported by any reason. Therefore, when a mystic-empirical report of Aurobindo is not accompanied with a reason or ground for accepting it, it need not be taken as an indication of any intrinsic deficiency in it. When I taste sugar and find it sweet, it would be absurd to say 'Sugar tastes sweet because . . .' Similarly, when he finds in his spiritual experience that the Divine is the highest value, it would be absurd to expect him to say 'The Divine is the highest value because. . . .' All this is sayable, but there is a basic difference between an ordinary observation-report and a mystic report.

The logical possibility of sugar sometimes not tasting sweet is not rejected *ab initio* by the sense-empiricist, but Aurobindo seems to rule out the logical possibility of any of his mystic-empirical reports ever being untrue. If his mystical utterances are like ordinary empirical reports, the logical possibility of their being untrue must be granted, and if they are unlike the latter, they cannot be exempted from the requirement that they must be accompanied with supporting reasons on the ground that they are like empirical reports or observation-statements.

To know the Divine is, for Aurobindo, as has been mentioned earlier, to become the Divine. This kind of knowledge is, in the mystical, religious, tradition, rated as higher than the ordinary, common, variety of knowledge, the acquisition of which does not consist in the knower's becoming the known. One consequence of the former conception of knowledge is to efface the conceptual distinction between knowing what is the ultimate value and attaining or acquiring it. Since the Divine is the ultimate value and knowing it is to become it, only he really knows what the ultimate value is who has become the Divine, i.e., who has attained the ultimate value. Ordinarily we think that knowing what one ought to be is a necessary condition of being, or trying to be, what he ought to be. But Aurobindo's conception of knowledge makes it impossible for anyone to fulfil it before actually being what he ought to be. In fact, for him knowing what one ought to be is isomorphic with being what he ought to be, and therefore it cannot be called a condition, necessary or sufficient, for the latter.

Perhaps one would like to say, in support of Aurobindo, that he who has not yet known the Divine by *becoming* it can have a second-hand knowledge of it from the utterances of Aurobindo (or of any other mystic), which he has to take on trust, and proceed, as required or directed, to attain the first-hand knowledge which would be a kind of becoming. But then one comes back to the starting point of the orthodox. Vedic, systems of classical Indian philosophy: one has to start by accepting on trust the statements or utterances of some authority, some Vedic sage, or an Aurobindo. It is a relevant question to ask which mystical authority one should accept since all authorities do not say the same or similar things. This question cannot be answered because their differences are based on their differing experiences and there is no way to decide whose experience is more authentic.

Aurobindo has said more than once that the higher activities of man express his seeking for God.

> In all the higher powers of his life man may be said to be seeking, blindly enough, for God. To get the Divine and eternal in himself and the world and to harmonise them, to put his being and his life in tune with the Infinite reveals itself in these parts of his nature as his concealed aim and his destiny. He sets out to arrive at his highest and largest and most perfect self, and the moment he at all touches upon it, this self in him appears to be one with some great Soul and Self of Truth and Good and Beauty in the world to which we give the name of God.[13]

One may read in the above words an argument for the claim that the Divine or God is the ultimate value: Since we always seek to realise God, God is our ultimate value or destiny. It is true that if Aurobindo shows that man always, as a matter of fact, seeks God, God can be said to be, in a factual sense, his ultimate value. He does not give any empirical support for the claim that man always seeks God, but accepts it on the authority of ancient sages. 'The truth that all active being is a seeking for God' is 'a truth on which the sages have always agreed, though by the intellectual thinker it may be constantly disputed.'[14] If we accept all this, it would only mean that man really seeks God, the ultimate Reality, and not that God or the

13. *HC*, p. 145.
14. *HC*, p. 136.

ultimate Reality is also the value he ought to seek. Therefore, the classical, or Aurobindo's, claim, that the ultimate Reality is ultimate value in the sense of being a normative ideal or value one ought to seek remains unproved. It has to be taken on trust, on the faith that what Aurobindo says, or what classical thinkers say, is true. But if there is a logical gap between being real and being a value, faith, or even mystic experience, cannot bridge it. Only logic can, and if logic cannot, it cannot be bridged.

Part II

Ethics in Practice

6

Inculcating Secularism
The Buddhist Way

A VIABLE society, using 'society' in a liberal, or broad, sense in which even a government, or an academic institution, is a society, has to provide two sorts of opportunities to everyone of its members. They are: (a) opportunities for his earthly well-being (*abhyudaya*) and (b) opportunities for his spiritual upliftment or fulfilment (*niḥśreyasa*). Providing these opportunities does not merely mean abstaining from creating any obstruction in the way of his pursuit of the two goals. Rather, it means helping him to understand what these goals are and to understand why they should be pursued, and providing him those facilities to pursue them which he cannot manage to acquire by the use of his own personal resources.

What is normally believed is that sciences provide the means to acquire earthly well-being. To some extent it is true but not completely true. Religion too provides means for earthly well-being, though its primary objective is to motivate and help an individual to secure his spiritual goal. It contributes to his spiritual flourishing by strengthening his motivation to know that there is something in him over and above his bodily and social capabilities which is subtle and more important than the latter, and thereby refining his attitudes towards his surroundings and towards himself. To refine his attitudes is to lead him to have healthy, constructive attitudes towards everything he is concerned with. This is largely the task of the spiritual content of it.

Every religion has as a basic, or core, constituent of it a set of moral beliefs and principles. The moral content of a religion aims at developing or strengthening the individual's moral sense, i.e., his sense of care or concern for the welfare of others. And, leading a morally commendable life is considered by every religion to be a necessary condition for making progress in the direction of spiritual development. This means that one who is genuinely interested in his spiritual upliftment cannot ignore morality. Some religions do sometimes say that to attain his spiritual goal the aspirant should severe his connection with his society which would entail that he would have to suspend even his moral commitments, his duties towards others. But quite often such religions also say that, before giving up his social connections, he must have fulfilled his social and moral commitments. Some others, on the other hand, say that after his enlightenment, he would naturally serve the society in a much better way. Buddhism goes to the extent of holding that the enlightened must, or ought to, serve the society by helping the unenlightened to become enlightened, as per Buddha's own example, and if necessary, he should even postpone his *nirvāṇa* for serving the suffering, ignorant, people around him. There is a trend of thinking, though, in some religions, or religious thinkers, that the enlightened may, or would generally, serve the society, but he has no obligation to do that. He has no duties left to fulfil.

Frequent conflicts are not likely to occur between morality and religion, but the occurrence of one is not impossible. Moral ideas change, and therefore a religion may have in its moral core an idea which is considered to be untenable, or not acceptable, at sometime, or by some people belonging to another religion, or even by some belonging to the same religion. For example, non-vegetarianism, considered permissible by a religion may be considered morally impermissible by an adherent of it, or by an adherent of another religion. The institution of *satī* was considered by some Hindus morally commendable, while by some other Hindus, as well as by the adherents of (almost) all other religions, it was considered barbarous. Therefore, sometimes a conflict between the moral and the non-moral, (i.e., religions, in a narrow sense of the term) constituents of a religion do arise. The religion concerned has to solve it this way or that way. A conflict sometimes becomes really serious and assumes a cross-religious, or inter-religious form. Every religion is an individual, historical, phenomenon, in the sense that to be religious is to belong to a particular religion, and what that religion requires in its spiritual sphere is a concern only of its adherents. For example, if a religion sanctions idol-worship, it is a matter with which only the adherents of that religion are concerned. It has nothing to do with any other religious group, and an adherent of another religion, which does not allow idol-worship, in principle, is not concerned with it. But morality is universal, and a moral person does not belong to a particular moral group, since it is the entire humanity which constitutes the moral community. Therefore, a Hindu who believes in the *satī* custom cannot tell a non-Hindu that it is not the latter's concern to condemn it, even if it is morally condemnable. If any Hindu, or non-Hindu, custom is morally wrong, then anyone can oppose it, and can try to get it stopped. He has only to see that his attempt does not cause a confrontation between one religious group and another. To avoid that, or to restrain recalcitrant adherents of one religion from sticking to an immoral custom, recourse to get it legally banned generally is resorted to.

But suppose one says of a practice, which is morally wrong but is sanctioned by a religion, that, since it is a permitted religious practice, it has to be done by an adherent of the religion even if it is morally impermissible. Suppose, further, that it enjoins the adherent to pour as much milk as he can procure on the head of a deity on a certain day in the year, with the consequence that, if he collects all the milk available in the locality, then either no milk remains available for children and sick people, or that the scantily available milk becomes so expensive that the children of poor people, and the poor sick, have to go without it. We have now a case in which a religious consideration or reason is in favour of pouring all the available milk on the head of the deity and a moral consideration against it. The general question which arises here is this: Which one of the two reasons, religious and moral, when they prescribe two incompatible courses of action, should override, or be given preference over, the other? An answer to this question would determine whether the answerer is a (religious) fundamentalist or a secularist. One, who answers it by saying that a religious consideration is more authoritative than, and therefore overrides, a moral consideration, is a fundamentalist, and he, who answers it by calling the moral consideration more authoritative, is a secularist. The two terms 'fundamentalism' and 'secularism' can be and have been defined in so many ways. But this mode of defining, and distinguishing between them seems to me preferable to others because it helps us to solve some of the problems, associated with the current Indian controversy between secularism and fundamentalism, in a better way than the others.

Secularism can be conceived as a theory, and reasons, good or bad, can be advanced in its favour. But to adopt a secularist attitude in life is to do something more than accepting it as a tenable theory, and one can adopt this attitude even when he is not in a position to give fully conclusive reasons to prove its tenability. In fact, one who has this attitude may not bother about the inconclusiveness of the reasons he has for believing in secularism. The fact of the matter with him may be that he finds the secularist attitude facilitating the task of living well, or of living well a socially cohesive life. There is no conclusive reason for anybody to believe that he won't die the next moment. But everybody believes that he won't, and he, who does not, is considered to be abnormal, or a sceptic, in a pejorative sense of the term. The same thing may happen with one's adoption of the secularist attitude.

Secularism and fundamentalism have become topics of active discussion in the last few years in the country. The reason for it is neither ethical nor religious, but political. The allegedly secularist politician claims to be unbiased towards every religion by which he simply implies that he is not against the religion of any minority community, or speaking affirmatively, that he is favourable to the religions of the minority communities, even though he himself does not belong to anyone of them. His obvious aim is to thereby tempt the members of minority communities to cast their votes in his, or in his party's, favour in any election, regional or national. Secularism has thus acquired a market value, and it has become fashionable for a person to claim that he is a secularist and that his opponent is not, or only pretends to be one. In such a situation it is possible that the number of people genuinely having the secular attitude is very small, and, that most of those who claim to have it do so only to procure some electoral, or some other sort of benefit, personal or political, which they do not even deserve. It is natural for such claimants to take advantage of unclearities, or ambiguities, existing in the concept of secularism, or, in that of the secular attitude. Almost every politician claims that he is a real secularist and he who disagrees with him is a non-secularist. Rather, 'non-secularist' has become a term of political rebuke. If you want to condemn some opponent, call him a non-secularist, or a promoter of non-secular forces.

'Secular' and 'non-secular' have thus ceased to be terms of netural, non-emotive, or merely academic, characterisation of people, so much so that one may feel insulted if he is called non-secular. What has promoted this situation is the pluralistic nature of the Indian society, particularly its religious pluralism. Indian democracy is claimed to be secular, and therefore to call someone non-secular is, in effect, as derogatory as to call him non-democratic. A non-secular person, like a non-democrat, is, the argument goes, against the national policy of political administration. Therefore, he must not be elected by an electorate to any regional or national body, to a *pancāyat* or a parliament. When such things are argued about in political, or social, controversies, a lot of unclarity remains unnoticed, or unanalysed, with the result that it is left undecided who is a genuine secularist, and even those who vote for anyone do that without being sure of the secular attitude of the person they vote for. Quite often they vote for some other reason than for the secular or non-secular affiliation of the candidate. Confusions prevail even in the minds of a large number of highly educated people about the distinction between secular and non-secular attitudes. It is also true, and sad too, that logically sophisticated philosophers, or social scientists, have not taken as much pains to clarify the issues involved as they should have.

In the last fifty years of its post-Independence, the too slow progress which India has made to contributing to the *abhyudaya* and *niḥśreyasa* of its people is not due to a single cause. But one of the most important of the causal factors is the overall downgrading, or devaluation, of the ethical concern. It has so happened that a good moral character has ceased to be a necessary consideration for getting, or becoming, anything, and the morally fallen has ceased to experience any kind of shame, or guilt-feeling. A morally denuded person can neither be genuinely secular, nor genuinely religious. It would be sheer foolhardiness to claim that intellectuals can get morality salvaged, or genuine secularism inculcated. But they can, by non-partisan analysis, make clear the concept of secularism, and that of fundamentalism which is the opposite of the former. If the analysis reaches a sizeable section of the Indian people, hopefully, it would help them to distinguish the genuine from the sham among those who claim to be secularist. I shall make a modest attempt in this direction by giving a precise sense to secularism and thereby to fundamentalism. To illustrate my conceptual points I would choose my illustration from some non-technical works of Buddhism. Buddhism is, *par excellence*, an ethical religion, i.e., a religion built on the conviction that religion cannot supersede ethics but the *vice-versa* is possible. Therefore, it very well demonstrates that one can be genuinely secular and genuinely religious by accepting the primacy of the ethical over all other considerations, including religious considerations. A religious consideration, in being overriden by a moral consideration, does not cause any humiliation to the religion it belongs to but makes it purer and therefore brighter and stronger.

A religious fundamentalist, who holds that a religious consideration, or reason, for doing, or believing, something is not to be overriden by *any other* consideration, or reason, against doing, or believing, it, would be one of the extreme type. If, on the other hand, one holds that it can override considerations of only some sorts, and not those of some other sorts, he would be a moderate fundamentalist. Not very often we come across an extreme fundamentalist. Most of the fundamentalists would admit that religious considerations should not override legal, or economic, considerations. But that it can override at least some ethical considerations is also admitted by all, or almost all, fundamentalists. If some of them do not consider it permissible to sacrifice a human being to please a deity, when their religion requires that an animal sacrifice should be done on a certain day to please, or quench the wrath of, the deity, they would agree to sacrificing a non-human animal, say, a goat, or a buffalo. This religious requirement conflicts with the ethical principle of doing no injury to an innocent animal, human or non-human, the classical principle of *ahiṁsā*. The fundamentalist, when reminded of it, may respond by saying that the religious consideration has the right to override the ehical one, or that killing an animal as an offering to the deity is not real killing (*vaidikī hiṁsā hiṁśā na bhavati*). But it is clear that even in saying the latter he is letting the ethical principle overriden in not calling the killing real killing when it is real killing. His reason for not calling it real killing is religious, for example, the belief that an animal killed as an offering to the deity is given a place in the heaven, or that getting killed to please the deity is better for the animal than being allowed to remain alive, or that he who kills, or gets killed, the animal to please the deity, incurs no sin, etc. These beliefs work like an excuse, or a rationalisation, and not a real justification, of the supremacy of the religious over the moral.

In practical affairs the moral consideration, in principle, is the most primary in the sense that if there is a moral consideration for doing something, to justify its doing we do not need to give any other kind of consideration or reason. For example, if it is morally right to extricate a man from the clutches of some terrorists, a political consideration in favour of getting him eliminated cannot justify letting him to be killed by his captors. Similarly, if it is morally wrong to kill an innocent animal, a religious injunction to kill it to please a deity cannot make it right or justified. But, for the religious fundamentalist, a religious consideration can supersede a moral consideration, because, for him, religion is of higher authority than morality.

Even a religion can be secular if it acknowledges the primacy of the ethical over the religious in case there is a conflict between the two. Such a religion would be an ethical religion, a religion which does not simply have a moral core but one which does not allow anything to have a religious value if it goes against a moral principle. It may have a religious doctrine, belief, or practice, which is morally neutral, i.e., neither required, nor forbidden, by a moral principle. But it cannot have any which goes against, or is forbidden by, a moral principle. This to me seems to be the general approach of Buddhism. Even Buddha's indifference to discussing abstruse metaphysical questions seems to be inspired by his belief in the primacy of the ethical. Suffering, for him, is not only something bad, but a moral evil, and it is more important, or obligatory, to devote one's time to find out ways and means to remove it than to discussing metaphysical questions.

What moved Gautama to leave his kingdom was not his thirst for knowledge of the nature of ultimate reality, but the desire to find out a way to the removal of suffering. To conceive of it as a moral evil is fraught with the implication that it is the moral duty of everyone to try to remove it. The solution, 'Get rid of your craving to get rid of your suffering', which he offers, is also a moral one because craving is a trait of one's character and a trait which is morally demeritorious. And, there is nothing else, in Buddhism, like the performance of a Vedic *yajña*, or that of one's *varṇadharma*, or god's grace, which can help one to get his salvation, or freedom from suffering, while letting morality to be overriden by a religious, or non-moral, consideration. Therefore, one can be secularist while remaining Buddhist, i.e., religious in the Buddhist way, which is non-different from being secularist in the ethical way. Rather, he cannot be genuinely religious unless he accepts the primacy of the ethical, i.e., unless he is a genuine secularist. This means that his secularism would not stand in his way of attaining his spiritual flourishing, if he is otherwise equipped to do that. I am not suggesting that the Buddhist way is the only way to combine secularism with religiosity. I only want to emphasise that the way Buddhism shapes itself, it makes the secularisation of religion a natural process. I have referred to Buddhism only to make the general point that, instead of there being any incompatibility between being religious and being secular, the fact is that a religion itself could be secular. All references to Buddhism in this chapter are, therefore, only illustrative, and not expressive of the superiority of any Buddhist view over any non-Buddhist one.

Buddhism's rejection of the Vedas, the caste-system, and the belief in god contributed to making the process natural. Each one of the three has the potentiality of throwing up non-moral, including religious, considerations or reasons for the supersession of morality. To illustrate only very breifly, if there is a Vedic injunction to debar a *śūdra* from reading the Vedas, the latter ought to be debarred even though it is immoral; if it is Arjuna's caste or *varṇadharma* to fight the Kurukṣetra war, he ought to even if he would then have to do the immorality of killing his elders; if Ajāmila's uttering 'Nārāyaṇa', the name of god, even though by it he meant the name of his son, can save him from being subjected to the tortures of the hell which he deserved on account of a large number of immoralities done by him, then one can flout morality not only with impunity but with great rewards. And he would remain, even then, fully religious. The follower of the Vedic instructions, the performer of caste-*dharmas*, and the utterer of god's names, all would, in spite of their immoralities, be called religious persons. It was a bad luck for Arjuna, as well as for the world, that instead of having a Buddha to answer his querries, he had Kṛṣṇa. Had the former been his preceptor, Arjuna would have become a moral hero, instead of a war-hero, and justice would have been restored to him without any bloodshed.

Anyone who is not a fundamentalist is, thus, a secularist. He may, or may not be religious. If he is not, the question of conceding overriding authority to a religious consideration would not arise for him. But if he is, then it becomes important. And, then the question of being, or not being, a secularist would also become important. It would assume extra importance if he lives in a society in which religious pluralism exists. As I have said, to be a secularist, one does not have to be non-religious, or a-religious. He may very well belong to a particular religion with the belief that, in respect of matters to which morality is relevant, a moral consideration would have the primacy over a contesting religious consideration. As long as a man of another religion does not, to satisfy a requirement of his religion, himself do, or promote doing by someone else, anything morally wrong, he would not mind. He would not mind even the former's doing, or asking someone else to do, something which his own religion does not recommend, or even prohibit, if it is morally neutral. For example, his religion may believe in an impersonal, non-creator god, and therefore may not recommend, or may even prohibit, the performance of an ornate ritual of worship. But his neighbour's may believe in a personal, creator god and prescribe the performance of a very ornate programme of worship. Both of these, opposed beliefs in, and consequential attitudes towards, rituals of worship are compatible with leading a morally good life.

Problems arise when one religion requires something to be done while another considers it morally forbidden. The *satī* custom is a good example. Suppose a follower of the religion *R* follows this custom. What then a follower of *S*, which considers this practice grossly immoral and cruel, should do? If he believes in the primacy of the ethical, he would naturally resent against the practice. But he would not need to use violence to stop a follower of *R* from observing the practice. One who believes in the primacy of the ethical would not like to use an unethical means to get it stopped, and violence is an unethical means. His method could, therefore, be that of rational, moral, argumentation and persuasion. He may try to convince the former of the immorality of the custom by an appeal to his moral reason. If persuation fails, he may take, as already suggested, recourse to getting a legislation passed which would make it illegal and punishable. This is the way the *satī* custom got banned.

To follow a religion sincerely is to be commited to follow its basic tenets. A basic tenet of one religion may be incompatible with that of another. If this incompatibility is also likely to motivate the adherents of the two religions to adopt incompatible, i.e., opposed, courses of actions, it may lead to violence between them. To eliminate the possibility of such occurrences is needed an inter-religious dialogue between the two groups, held sometimes formally but more often informally, with an attitude secular and non-fundamentalist, but respectful of both the religions. If the two sides believe in the primacy of the ethical, such dialogues, when conducted in an unprejudiced manner, are bound to be successful, because the two sides would then only need to decide which of the two tenets is ethically superior to the other. But suppose they do not accept the primacy of the ethical and stick to their positions fanatically. It may then become a law-and-order problem and the state may, on that account, adopt legal, preventive, methods, or permit one side to perform its relevant religious ceremony in such a manner that it does not provoke resentment from the other side. Such solutions are, however, not likely to be durable, and when governmental efforts slacken, the opposing sides may come to blows.

There is another, a more durable, way to mollify such extreme types of fundamentalism or fanaticism, and this is the scholars' way. Scholars neutral to the contesting sides can provide a way out by rationally examining the fundamentals of the two religions and discovering some meeting points if they are there, or something else in their fundamentals which shows the ethical, or even logical, superiority of one side over the other. I have already talked about ethical superiority. The logical superiority of a tenet or idea over another means that there are stronger reasons, or arguments, in favour of the former than in that of the latter. A problem very similar to the one involved in such cases is raised in the *Milinda Praśna* (113.43). The king wants to know what is the most subtle thing and whether there is anything which can cut it, i.e., override it. The reply given by the saint is that religion is the most subtle but it can also be cut, or crossed over, i.e., superseded by, *prajñā*. *Prajñā* is stated, in 44, the same page, to be the ability to properly comprehend. It is what we call deliberative, discriminating reason, which forms a judgement about what ought to be accepted, or done, after properly comprehending and assessing the relevant pros and cons of the issue, or issues, in question. This is to say nothing very obscure or mystical. Rather, it is simply to say that the way to solve such tricky issues is to subject the two conflicting sides to the scrutiny of deliberative, adjudicative reason, and accept its judgement. The most rational, or the rationally preferable, would be that in favour of which reason finds more considerations than against it, or in favour of its contrary. Even in common sense we call a man rational who is disposed to believe, accept, or do, that in support of which he finds more considerations or reasons than he finds against it.

Such an approach to solve religious disputes is not irreligious, or extra-religious, though it can be called secular. Rationality is an important constituent of secularism, as important as the belief in the primacy of the ethical. They are not in fact two constituents but one. A rational person cannot reject the primacy of the ethical. Ethics provides the cement of social cohesion, and therefore a rational person, who considers a cohesive society desirable, would naturally consider being ethical to be of primary importance. And, one who does not consider a cohesive society desirable would not only be unethical but also irrational. It would be unrealistic not to admit that the above suggestion is not easy to implement. It is not easy to find a knowledgeable scholar who can non-committally but respectfully examine the fundamentals of a religion which may be his own, or an alien one. The number of scholars who have an authentic knowledge of even a few of modern Indian religions, an attitude neither biased in favour of, nor against, anyone of them, and the ratiocinative ability to assess which doctrine of which is, or is not, formulated on the basis of sound ethical and logical grounds, is really few. Moreover, even if we locate one, he may not be permitted by the followers of a religion, or by their leaders, to rationally examine the fundamentals, or even non-fundamentals, of their religion. They may consider such an exercise blashphemous, or sacrilegious. In the case of a militant religious group, it may not be even safe to undertake such a work.

The above possibility, if it becomes real, would be a great hurdle to breaking the rigour of, or even to watering down, fundamentalism and fanaticism by adopting what I have called the scholars' way. Governmental, or legal, efforts, too, in such a situation, are not very likely to yield good results of a lasting nature. The most effective, and harmless, method seems to be that which functions through the medium of education imparted from the school to the college stage. If Indian religions are taught in schools and colleges, not necessarily to make students religious, but to make them understand what they say, or prescribe in course of time a dispassionate, rational, attitude towards them is very likely to be developed in the minds of educatees. And, if the scheme is conducted well, it may take time, but it is very likely to usher in, in course of time, a religious climate in the country which would loosen the rigour of fundamentalism and promote liberalism. This liberalism would not be very different from what has been called secularism in this chapter.

It is a redeeming feature that all religious disagreements do not cause conflict, or affect social cohesion. Which day of the year the followers of a religion consider sacred does not matter to those of another. Rather, the latter may even join the former's celebrations. Or, they may feel unconcerned about it. On some other counts, there may be a little serious disagreement, but even that may not cause any kind of confrontation. For example, on a certain day the followers of *R* may consider it obligatory, or auspicious, to eat meat of a certain animal, while those of *S* may consider eating any animal food expect milk prohibited. Even such things generally do not affect social cohesion. The reason is that animals whose meat is considered edible do not always matter to human beings, so much as to cause conflict between vegetarians and non-vegetarians. The former may propagate the advantages of vegetarianism and disadvantages of non-vegetarianism. But they would not normally like to be violent or agressive in stopping someone from killing an animal for food, though they may hold it to be morally wrong to kill any animal for food. This is a kind of moral compromise, and there arise several occasions when, in a society having religious plurality, one religious community has to make compromises with another so that both of them may live in peace with each other. The reason for making a moral compromise is that moral hyper-activism, like any other, is very likely to be (morally) counter-productive.

Suppose an office boss considers immoral a colleague's using an office pin to pin-up some private letters, and therefore puts an adverse entry in his personal file, accusing him of the immorality of misusing official stationery. In a sense it is a lapse, but such lapses have to be taken non-seriously to avoid avoidable friction. It does not mean that all lapses have to be taken non-seriously. Moral maturity consists in the ability to decide which lapses are negligible and which are not. The same is the case with moral disagreements caused by religious reasons. If *A* considers an action of *B* morally wrong, though required by his religion, he has to use his mature judgement to decide how serious a moral lapse it is. The path of morality, as well as that of religious *sādhanā*, has to be, as Buddha says, a *madhya mārga* (middle path), on which every normal person may walk. If it can be used only by a man of extraordinary moral/ religious ability, it won't do what it should be doing. Extraordinary people need no guidance. They can carve cut their own paths. Only ordinary people need to be shown the right path walking on which may enable them achieve their *abhyudaya* and/or *niḥśreyasa*. Only a middle path would do that, and this is what morality, as well as religion, is meant to provide to them.

We normally speak of the equality of all religions, or of the desirability of having equal respect for all religions. As a matter of fact two religions may not be equal because one may contain a belief, or permit a practice, which is undesirable, while the other may not have any such thing. For example, a religion which accepts a caste-system among its followers, or considers one group of them untouchable for others, is inferior to the other which does not admit such things. But every adherent of a religion is committed and devoted to it. To disrespect his religion, or to give some advantage to another religion and deny that to his, is to hurt his feelings. Therefore, to have equal respect for all religions is in effect to have equal respect for the followers of all religions. Another side of saying it is that in matters of public policy, which may be political, economic, etc., the policy-maker must not let a consideration arising from his own religion, or from that of another whose followers have been politically, or in some other way, useful to him, influence his policy-making. If he is so influenced, that would amount to ignoring other religions and therefore to hurting the self-respect of their adherents.

Not letting a religious consideration influence a non-religious decision, say political, social, economic, academic, ethical, etc., is the basic, or at least one of the basic constituents of secularism, or of the secularist attitude. This attitude would be possible only if one does not assume that a religious consideration can override any other consideration. The fundamentalist, or communalist, makes this assumption, and therefore, he would take a decision concerning any matter only if it is supported by, or does not go against, any religious consideration. For him a religious consideration would be unquestionable, but for a secularist it would not be. Rather, there may be a situation in which it may be overriden by a non-religious consideration. I have been speaking all along of the primacy of the ethical consideration, meaning that an ethical consideration can override any other consideration, but cannot be overriden by the latter. This is obvious from the fact that we can say of any morally wrong decision which may be, for example, a political decision, that it is politically wrong *because* it is morally wrong, but we cannot say the converse of it. We cannot say that it is morally wrong because it is politically wrong. To conclude, to be a secularist one has to be a broad-based rationalist. It is reason alone which helps one to weigh the pros and cons of a decision, and therefore only it can help him to decide when a religious consideration should be implemented and when it should be overriden by some other consideration. To be rational does not mean to be devoid of feelings and emotions. It only means to open-mindedly examine the pros and cons of an issue and to take the decision in favour of which are available the best possible reasons in the prevailing circumstances.

7

Inculcating a General Dharma Forgiveness as Moral Cement

Wronging, Rupturing and Rejoining Social Relationships

IN almost all cultures of the world forgiveness is considered to be one of the basic virtues. Its possession is held to be highly desirable for leading a morally commendable life. In the classical Indian conception of the goal of life it is given a place of great honour. Manu mentions it as one of the ten constituents of morality (*dharma*), or of a morally good (*dhārmic*) life.[1] This means that a morally good life would not be complete unless it is imbued with it. The Buddhist classic *Dhammapada* calls the cultivation of a forgiving nature by an aspirant (*sādhaka*) the highest penance (*tapa*).[2] The *Mahābhārata* emphasises its high moral status at so many places. But in spite of the fact that classical Indian works vie with one another in praising it (and some other virtues as well), none of them, as far as I have been able to ascertain, have given an analytical, or conceptual, account of what forgiveness (or any other virtue) is, or of the various things its inculcation (or any other virtue's) or practice involves. Quite naturally, then, such questions as whether it is an unconditional virtue, or a virtue which is to be practised only when certain conditions are fulfilled, whether to practice or exemplify it is obligatory, or only supererogatory, or sometimes obligatory and sometimes supererogatory, whether its exemplification does, or does not, go against the retributive moral intuition that the

1. *The Manusmṛti*, chapter VI.2.
2. Chapter XIV.6.

wrongdoer ought to be given the punishment he deserves, whether or not one can forgive himself for a wrong done by him to himself, or to someone else, etc., have not been critically discussed in anyone of them. Whenever anyone of the virtues has been referred to, the reference is generally casual, or takes for granted several things which should have been probed into.

This need not surprise us because, by and large, the works which talk about virtues are not systematic philosophical treatises. But even the latter have not fared better. Some of them do not talk about virtues, and those which do remain satisfied with emphasising, without adequately discussing, how important they are for enabling a seeker of salvation (*mumukṣu*) to attain his salvation (*mokṣa*). Twentieth-century Indian philosophers too have not turned their attention to them. A good number of them do pontificate that philosophers should do normative ethics instead of doing metaethics and thereby wasting their time in logic-chopping, which, according to them, the latter is. But even they have not tried to give a philosophical account, of any sort, of anyone of the virtues. Coming to forgiveness, the topic of this chapter, I have not been able to locate any philosophically probing discussion, or description, of it, by any classical or contemporary Indian philosopher (or non-philosopher). But even if there exists such a work, or a large set of such works, there is nothing wrong in one's trying his hands on it. As John Stuart Mill has remaked, on all great subjects something always remains to be said.

In this chapter I shall analyse the content of the concept of forgiveness in order to find out what is involved in one's forgiving someone and in one's being forgiven by someone, phenomena with which we are very well acquainted. This would require me to examine the conceptual context in which forgiveness can properly be asked for, granted, or denied, the social role which can be attributed to it, and the kind of virtue it can justifiably claimed to be. In doing all this, I would be discussing at least some of the questions referred to above. My discussion of them, even if sketchy and unsatisfactory, would, hopefully, bring out their real importance and show the direction in which we have to go in order to find out their solution, if not fully satisfactory, at least as much satisfactory as the subject-matter permits.

I shall begin with a simplified version of the inter-personal context or situation in which an act of forgiveness is ordinarily, or standardly, performed. I shall first explain its relevant features and then attend to those aspects of, or complexities involved in, the phenomenon of forgiving which the simplified version does not seem to take note of. My objective would be to give an account of forgiveness which is commensurate with, or does not conflict with, our normal, or ordinary, moral intuitions about what forgiveness is and what is the role it performs in our public and private life. This account, I would try to show, with some minor modification, or tinkering, here and there, is capable of making intelligible even the kinds of forgiveness which seem to be different from the ordinary variety of forgivenes, which I have called the standard variety of it. I call it the standard variety because it is common-sensical, a kind of case with which we are familiar without being aided by any theory.

An inter-personal situation in which forgiveness ordinarily makes its appearance can be schematised as follows: *A*, a normal, adult mature and person does *W*, a morally wrong thing, to *B* who is another normal, adult and mature person. Both *A* and *B* are moral agents in the sense that they have at least a working understanding of what is right and what is wrong. They belong to the same moral community insofar as they, by and large, share a fairly large number of their ideas about right and wrong, desirable and undesirable things, have several common or similar goals and aspirations, and their pictures of a morally good life, or understandings of the value and role of morality in human life, are not drastically, or conspicuously, different from each other. *W* is an intentional action done by *A*. He does it because he wants, or intends, to do it, and has as clear an idea of its likely consequences as the circumstances permit, or as a man of his type or status is expected to have as per the existing norms of his society. It is not something he does unknowingly, i.e., without knowing what kind of action it is, inadvertently or accidentally, being coerced by someone else, under the influence of drugs, in a situation which makes doing it unavoidable, etc. Therefore, quite reasonably, he can be held responsible for it and its consequences. As regards its moral status, he may, or may not, know, or believe, that it is morally wrong. Knowing, or believing, that an action is morally wrong does incline a person to abstain from doing it, though it does not entail that he would not do it. Therefore, he may do it while knowing, or believing, that it is wrong if his inclination to abstain from doing it is very weak and consequently overpowered by a more powerful counter-inclination, say, a non-moral (or even immoral) inclination to attain *X* which can be attained only by doing *W*.[3] He may also not know, or believe, at the time of doing it, that it is wrong even though it is, and may later on realise that it is as a result of his own retrospective reflection, or of someone else's discussion with him.

B, on the other hand, knows, or believes, that *W* is morally wrong and reacts to it by feeling resentment against *A* for having done it to him. His feeling can be characterised as one of having been ignored, disgraced, hurt, ill-treated, injusticed, etc. He thinks that, by doing him *W*, *A* has done him some injustice, or moral injury, or offence, and reacts by feeling angry with him for having done *W*. In brief, his reactive feeling is one of moral anger. He now has an antagonistic, a hostile, contrary, or, con-attitude, towards *A* whom he considers to be a wrongdoer. His reactive feeling is one of moral anger because it has been aroused by *W* which he considers to be morally wrong. He may express it by inflicting some punishment or injury on *A*, by being hateful of him, by avoiding his company, etc. In doing either one of such things he feels morally justified because he thinks that *A* is guilty of a moral wrongdoing by doing *W* to him, and therefore deserves a retaliatory response from him.

The social relation which existed between *A* and *B* before *A*'s doing the offence has now become ruptured. They may not openly fight with each other. But they would no longer remain as friendly, or non-hostile, to each other as they were in the pre-offence days. Some souring of their pre-offence social relationship is bound to have occurred. If there was no pre-existing social relationship between them, if they had met for the first time, *A*'s doing *W* to *B* would surely not sour their pre-existing relationship because there did not exist any. It would, then, foreclose the possibility of their entering into a harmonious social relationship. They can make a beginning to enter into such a relationship only after *A*'s having

3. Obviously a specific theory of moral weakness is presupposed here which cannot be discussed in detail in this essay. For it and other related issues see my *Karma, Causation and Retributive Morality*, chapter 6, pp. 81-108.

apologised to *B* and *B*'s having forgiven him.

A realises, on second thoughts, that he ought not to have done *W* to *B*, experiences a sense of guilt and feels repentant or remorseful for having done *W*. He then acknowledges to *B* that he has done *W* and *W* is morally wrong, expresses his regret for having done it, promises to compensate, as far as he can, for the damage, mental, or material, if any, caused to *B* by *W*, and not to do anything like *W* to *B* in future, and requests *B* to forgive him. *B* is convinced of the sincerity of his repentance, etc., and forgives him. After forgiving *A*, his moral anger, or con-attitude, vanishes, or is reduced to such an extent that it loses its motivating force to make him do anything against *A*. He would not now retaliate, or do anything punitive to *A*, for his having done *W* to him. Forgiving *A* for his wrongdoing and punishing him for the same wrongdoing cannot go together.

B now recovers his peace of mind which had been disturbed by his moral anger, his feeling of having been wronged, etc. *A* also recovers his peace of mind which had been disturbed by his sense of guilt, his consequential fear of a retaliative action by *B*, etc. As a result of all this, the pre-offence social relation between *A* and *B*, which had been disturbed by *A*'s wrongdoing to *B*, is completely, or very greatly, restored. Its complete restoration may take place immediately, or it may take some-time, depending on *A*'s and *B*'s psychology, gravity of the offence, nature of the circumstances in which it was done, etc. But normally it is not expected to take much time. And, even if the full restoration is delayed, a large part of it would be soon achieved in the sense that *A* and *B* would cease to be, after the forgiveness, as hostile to each other as they had become after *A*'s wrongdoing and before his having been forgiven by *B*. In not too distant a future *B*'s con-attitude towards *A*, and *A*'s feeling guilty, or ashamed, for his wrongdoing to *B* as well as his feeling of having become estranged from *B* are very likely to die out, assuming that none of the two does anything else which ruins the prospect of there being re-established a harmonious social relationship between them. After *A*'s doing *W* to *B*, it is not only *A* who feels estranged from *B*, *B* also feels estranged from him. None of them would have any, or any strong, motivation to associate with the other, as they used to have earlier. Social estrangement is unpalatable, or irksome, to both the estranged parties. Since forgiveness removes the feeling of estrangement, not only the receiver of forgiveness, but also the forgiver, is a gainer when the latter forgives the former. In a good number of cases, the victim of a wrongdoing has a desire to get restored or repaired the estranged relation between him and his wrongdoer. In such cases, he welcomes an opportunity of forgiving him when he finds him sincerely repentant for the wrong he has done.

To motivate *B* to forgive him, *A* primarily needs to be sincerely repentant for having done *W* to him. His preparedness to compensate, as far as it is possible for him to do, for the damage *W* has caused to *B*, and promise not to do anything like *W* again to him, almost logically, or conceptually, go with the sincerity of his repentance. It would be extremely odd for him to say to *B* that he is sincerely repentant for his wrongdoing but he would not try to repair the damage he has thereby caused to him, or would offer no assurance to abstain from doing a similar wrong in the coming future. Therefore, *B*'s conviction that *A* is sincerely repentant would offer him the hope that *A* would try his best to compensate for the damage and abstain from doing a similar wrong. *A*'s assurance that he would do both would strengthen *B*'s belief in the sincerity of his repentance, and if *A* fails in either of the two respects, he would conclude that his repentance was not sincere. There is nothing unusual in this. As it happens in many other spheres of human transaction, *B* may discover a little later that he should not have forgiven *A*, he took him to be genuinely repentant when he only pretended to be. But it is also possible that he mistakes *A*'s genuine repentance to be a mere sham, and therefore retaliates, but discovers a little later that *A* was genuinely repentant. He then himself repents for having retaliated, because, in the fitness of things, he should have forgiven him and not retaliated.

Repentance is a good reason for granting forgiveness because, as has been said, it offers the hope that the wrongdoer would not, or is not likely to, do such a wrong again. It, in a sense, makes him a better person, a purer one, than he was when he did the wrong. Even a retributivist, who holds that the wrongdoer ought to be punished, cannot refuse to call it a reason for forgiving him because, in experiencing repentance, the wrongdoer makes himself suffer the pangs of his own guilt-feeling. Therefore, it can be said that he has undergone, or is undergoing, some sort of a self-inflicted punishment.

Sincerity everywhere is a notion not too easy to be sure of. But it is not an unusable notion. We know, — though we make mistakes many times and some of us are more prone to make mistakes than some others, — how to distinguish between a sincere and an insincere love, friendship, promise, attitude of helpfulness, or of revengefulness, etc. Similar is the case with the sincerity of anyone's repentance. As in other cases, the victim of the wrongdoing ascertains the sincerity of the wrongdoer's repentance, not by entering into his mind, or inner self, but by carefully examining, or reflecting on, the ways of his speaking, of his dealing with some of the persons, including the victim, concerned with the affair, state of his mind expressed in his behaviour and way of living, the kind of things he takes interest in, or of people he associates himself with, etc., etc. One can pretend to be repentant, just as one can pretend to be any other thing. But that there are pretenders of repentance does not mean that there are no sincere repentants, or that the sincerity of repentance is an inapplicable notion. Rather, it shows that there are sincere repentants, since unless we know when is someone sincerely repentant, we cannot call anyone pretendingly repentant.

Even forgiveness can be sincere or sham. *B* may say to *A* that he forgives him though he may not really do that. He may pretend to forgive *A* with the hope that *A* would then, fearing no retaliation from him, not remain as alert or prepared, as he is otherwise likely to do, to protect himself from his (*B*'s) retaliatory moves. Therefore, it would be easier for *B* to fulfil his retaliatory desire. Both repenting and forgiving denote the occurrence, in one, of a change, not only in feeling but also in attitude, towards the other. An attitudinal change is expressed in behaviour in appropriate circumstances. Therefore, whether *A* is sincerely repentant, or *B* has really forgiven him, can be ascertained by observing how they behave, or tend to behave, with each other, how either one of the two behaves with other persons associated with the other one, or, in transactions or situations involving the other one, etc. We have to compare how they perceived, or described, each other before the offence with how they do now. Neither 'I repent' nor 'I forgive' is a performatory expression because one may say 'I repent' without really repenting, and 'I forgive' without really forgiving. Repenting and forgiving, both, are assessive. *A* assesses his own action, finds it a case of wrongdoing, assesses his relationship with *B* and finds that he does not deserve to be 'wronged', and then feels repentant. Similarly, *B* assesses *A*'s present mood and behaviour, his own relationship with *A*, finds him, as the saying goes, scorching himself with the flames of repentance, a person different from what he was when he did the wrong, and then concludes that he does not deserves any retaliatory action, and therefore forgives him. If genuine repentance washes off the guilt of the guilty, genuine forgiveness granted by the victim amounts to admitting, or certifying, that it has been washed off. Therefore, it lifts up the status of the guilty by enabling him to extricate himself from his own sense of having become unworthy or lowly by wronging an innocent person. It thus helps him to emotionally rehabilitate himself. It does not humiliate him, or humble him down. To forgive is not to pity. The forgiver must forget, sooner or later, the guilt of the forgiven. Not to feel repentant after realising that one has done a moral wrong is a sign of moral deficiency. And, so is not to forgive the wrongdoer after being convinced that he is genuinely repentant, or not to forget his guilt after having forgiven him. If *B* forgives *A*, he gives us not a mere hope, but rather a conceptual right to believe, that he is going to forget *A*'s wrongdoing. It is because of some such feature of the act of forgiving that the saying 'forgive and forget' is contentually, and not merely phonetically, so cohesive, and reassuring too.

Speaking from the side of the forgiver, to forgive is not to show his cowardice, or inability to retaliate. His act of forgiving makes him feel not how weak he is, but how elevated he is, or has become, by not retaliating against the wrong, by exemplifying liberality instead of revengefulness. If repentance is a sign of one's underlying, basic, moral purity, granting forgiveness is an ornament of the morally brave. They are consistent with the self-respect of the forgiven as well as of the forgiver.

Both repentance and forgiveness involve, as has been already said, change of attitudes. When *A* repents for having done *W* to *B*, he changes his attitudes towards *W*, towards himself and towards *B*. He now considers himself a wrongdoer, *W* a wrong action, and *B* a person who has been undeservedly harmed, or more harmed than he deserved. For example, (a) at the time of rebuking *B*, *A* may think that he is justified in rebuking him because he deserves the rebuke.

But a post-rebuke reflection may convince him that *B* was innocent and therefore it was mean of him to have rebuked him. Here his attitudes towards both, himself and *B*, have changed from what they were at the time he rebuked *B*. Or (b) it may also happen that at the time of rebuking *B*, *A* realises that it is in principle bad, or mean, to rebuke anyone and he would be demeaning himself by rebuking *B*. But still he rebukes *B* because he thinks that what *B* has done to him (or even to someone else, say, an innocent, helpless, widow) demands that he should give to *B* a harsh rebuke. Then, a post-rebuke reflection makes him change his mind: He now thinks that even a milder rebuke, or reprimand, would have done, or would have been more appropriate, or that *B* was mean but not as mean as he thought him to be. Here his attitudes towards both, himself and *B*, have changed in their rigour or tone, though not in kind. Again (c) there is another possibility. Assume that *A* is a wicked person who believes that *B* is, and *B* really is, an innocent person. Still *A* rebukes *B*, and takes delight in doing that. But a little later, he undergoes a sea change, realises his wickedness, and repents for having rebuked the innocent *B*. Here *A*'s attitude towards himself changes: He condemns his own wickedness, but his understanding of *B* remains unchanged. He feels sorry for having wronged him, not because he perceives anything new in *B*, but because he has now developed an attitude of aversion towards his own wickedness.

What I intend to emphasise is that a repentant person develops towards himself an attitude different from the one he had when he wronged the victim. Generally he develops a different attitude towards, or a different understanding of, the victim too, though it need not always happen. But the former has to happen in the case of every genuine repentance.

Sometimes we say that there must occur a change of heart in the offender to deserve forgiveness. But a change of attitude, as explained above, is enough. Morever, it is not very clear what the phrase 'change of heart' exactly means. Speaking common-sensically, it is nothing but a change of attitude in a deeper and extensive manner. But it must not be taken to denote a change of personality. The offender must remain the same person when he becomes repentant, and is forgiven. It is the same person, who did the offense, who is forgiven when he is repentant. We forgive the repenting offender. If, in becoming repentant, he undergoes a change of heart in the sense of becoming a different person, then he would no longer remain the original offender, and therefore the question of forgiving him would not arise. If only such a repentant is to be forgiven, then, since he is a person different from the offender, the concept of forgiveness would become infected with the paradox that one person does the offence and another person is forgiven. When *B* forgives him, his attitude towards *A* changes: he does not consider him as bad as he did before forgiving him in response to his repentance. Although he still considers *W* a wrongdoing, his attitude towards his own harm or hurt, resulting out of *W*, is now different: his sense of hurt is now balmed, or has become less hurtful. He does not consider himself so much injusticed as he did before. If *A* repents to *B* and obtains his forgiveness, the attitudinal change so effected in him may become so pervasive that he may not do in future a similar wrong not only to *B* but to any person whatsoever. Something similar may happen to *B*. He may develop a forgiving attitude towards anyone like *A* and forgive almost spontaneously anyone who does him a wrong but then sincerely repents. Granting forgiveness is overcoming one's moral anger. Therefore, one may have to make efforts with himself in order to be able to forgive even a repenting wrongdoer. That is why sometimes one forgives an offender only when someone else argues with him and convinces him that the offender really deserves to be forgiven. He forgives when he finds the arguments convincing. But in course of time, he may not need to struggle hard with himself, or someone else's persuasion, to do that. He may become a fluent forgiver. As experience goes, some people are, by nature or nurture, more forgiving than some others. It is possible, therefore, that one person is a spontaneous, or almost spontaneous, forgiver while another is always unforgiving, or vary rarely forgiving. In between the two poles are the normal run of people who grant forgiveness to an offender only after having argued the matter with themselves, or after someone else's having argued it with them.

Because forgiveness involves the victim's overcoming moral anger for the wrong done to him, only he can forgive the wrongdoer. Only Draupadī can forgive Duryodhana for the insult he does to her. Bhīma can avenge her insult because he is one of her five husbands, but he cannot forgive Duryodhana for his having insulted her. Another person can help the wronged to overcome his anger, but he cannot overcome it. It is a logical truism that only he who feels an emotion can overcome it. The wronged may not be able to punish the offender, or he may not be allowed to punish him. In fact, to preserve the social order, this is generally the normal social arrangement that the authority to punish the wrongdoer vests with some other agency, and not with the wronged. Sometimes the wronged person himself is considered to be punishable by the empowered agency for having inflicted an injury on his wrongdoer.

Another person, say, *C* may feel moral anger for the wrong done to *B* by *A*. But this will be *his* moral anger, and not *B*'s which *B* has to overcome in order to forgave *A*. The more remote is *B* to him, the more moral would be *C*'s anger at *A*'s wrongdoing to him. But normally we would not consider *C* to be the right person to forgive *A*. If he per chance thinks that *A* is forgivable and forgives him, he would be overcoming his moral anger, and not *B*'s. It is *B*'s forgiveness which *A* really seeks, and needs, in order to be forgiven. It is also *B*'s forgiveness which, when granted, would make him feel relieved from his sense of guilt.

The view, maintained above, that only the victim of a wrongdoing can really forgive the wrongdoer should be taken in a liberal way. Taking it in a literal, or absolutist, manner would not be fair because it would go against some of our normal moral intuitions and therefore would not be able to take care of certain difficulties which its absolutist interpretation would give rise to.

There may be a case in which the victim is not available to the genuinely repentant wrongdoer to whom he may apologise for the wrong he has done. The victim may be dead because he has been killed by the offender when killing him is the crime he has committed and is repenting for. Or, the victim has met his natural death. The victim may even be alive and still the wrongdoer may not have any chance of meeting him: *A* and *B* meet in an aircraft in which the unfortunate incident takes place and, by the time *A* realises his fault, *B* has left. An important feature of being sincerely repentant is that the repentant has a strong desire that the person he has wronged take, or accept, him as sincerely repentant. When he receives his forgiveness, he treats it as a sign of this acceptance. Receiving forgiveness is like receiving a certification from the appropriate authority that his repentance has been accepted and therefore his guilt has ceased to be looked at in the way it was looked at earlier.

If the victim is not available, then, if he alone has the authority to forgive, it may seem that, in spite of his satisfying the conditions for being forgiven, the wrongdoer would remain always unforgiven. But this is not an insuperable difficulty for the theory. By satisfying the conditions, *A* has made his fault forgivable: he has now become a wrongdoer who deserves to be forgiven, and is not being forgiven because of the contingent fact that *B* is unavailable. The realisation of this truth would itself give *A* a lot of satisfaction, or moral boosting up, and would help him to rehabilitate himself. The same thing would be the case when *B* is available, but being inordinately obdurate and vindictive, refuses to forgive him, in spite of his genuine repentance, etc. Even when the guilt has not been forgiven, genuine repentance for having done it would take away a large part of its guilthood, if it does not wash it off.

Another thing which can happen in such cases is that there is a person *C*, other than the victim *B*, who, because of his close affinity with *B*, has identified himself so much with *B* that he has taken the wrong done to the latter as a wrong done to himself. This person can also forgive *A*. For example, if *C* is *B*'s son and *B* is dead, *A* may seek and get *C*'s forgiveness. This would also work as the certificate *A* needs. Perhaps it would not carry as much of certification as one from *B* himself would have carried. But *C*'s forgiving *A* does not go against the theory because *C* is doing it because of his having identified himself with *B* as far as *A*'s having wronged *B* is concerned. This would be a case of *C*'s vicarious feeling of having been hurt by *A*'s wronging *B*, and therefore *C*'s forgiving *A* may be called vicarious forgiving, or surrogate forgiving. In the case of a wrong done to a corporation, or organisation, someone has to be delegated the authority to forgive, or punish, the offender. Or, if A insults the national flag of *B*'s country, a wrong is done to the entire nation to which *B* belongs. A nation, not being an entity, cannot forgive the repentant *A*. That can be done only by an individual, or a group, say, the president, or parliament, of the country, to whom, or to which, this authority has been given.

But does not considering god as the supreme forgiver go against the theory presented here? It does not, because of a variety of reasons. In ordinary human transactions one seeks god's forgiveness when he is not able to secure the victim's, or, a surrogate's, forgiveness because of their being unavailable, or being too vindictive. A believer considers god to be the ultimate, unfailing, and unerring giver of what is his due to every person. Therefore, when *A* thinks that he deserves to be forgiven and is not forgiven by *B*, or his surrogate, he may appeal to god. God is said to be angry with anyone who does any wrong to anyone, including himself. A wrong done to any innocent person, for the believer, is a wrong done to god. Therefore, neither appeal to god for forgiveness, nor the belief in his authority to forgive, is out of order. When Christ appeals to god to forgive his tormentors because they do not know that what they are doing is wrong, he not only appeals but gives a ground for their being forgiven. The ground is their ignorance, and ignorance is, even in day-to-day affairs taken to be a ground for forgiveness, or for not taking the fault seriously, no matter whether it is taken to be an excuse or a reason for doing that. The appeal amounts to saying the following to god: Any wrong done to anyone is a wrong done to you because you are in everyone. What the tormentors have done is a wrong done to someone. But it is a wrong done by them because of their ignorance, and a wrong done out of ignorance is forgivable (or excusable). Therefore, I request you to forgive (or excuse) them for their wrongdoing.

Christ's appeal to god also illustrates the possibility of one's seeking forgiveness for another person, or for a group of persons, though he himself has no share in the wrongdoing. This may happen when, for example, *C* identifies himself with *A*, wants to protect *A* from *B*'s anger, out of self-interest, or benevolence, and finds that *A* does not have the mental and moral maturity to realise his fault and seek *B*'s forgiveness. Christ seeks god's forgiveness for the tormentors out of benevolence. Similarly, the father of a teenager may apologise to a teacher of his son's school for the son's misbehaviour. Such requests have their point only when the wrong-doer is not himself capable of seeking forgiveness and there exists some excuse or reason for his being forgiven. Otherwise, forgiveness would be a proper response only to the wrongdoer's sincere repentance, and not to anyone else's entreaties, and it has to be the response of the wronged person himself, or of the delegated person, or persons, in the case of an organisation.

In order to be fogiven, it is not necessary that *A* explicitly makes a request for it. If a morally sensitive *B* is convinced that *A* has done a moral wrong to him, it would be natural and appropriate for him to respond by feeling moral anger towards *A*. Equally natural and appropriate it would be for *B* to respond to *A* by forgiving him if he gets convinced that *A* is sincerely repentant for the wrong he has done to him, whether or not *A* openly requests to be forgiven. Forgiveness is a moral, reactive, response of the wronged mainly to the wrongdoer's sincere repentance and his suffering arising therefrom. If *A* is really repentant for the wrongful harm he has done to *B*, and *B* is convinced that he is, forgiveness would be *B*'s natural response to him, unless he is in some sense an unusual person, or a person of no, or of a very low, moral sensitivity, a person devoid of what Shakespeare calls the milk of human kindness.

The way Mrs. Erlynne gets not only Lady Windermere's forgiveness but her admiration and gratitude, in Oscar Wilde's play *Lady Windermere's Fan*,[4] very ably illustrates what has been said above. Mrs. Windermere is, without knowing that she is, Mrs. Erlynne's daughter. Mrs. Erlynne abandons her and her father who is also her husband, when Lady Windermere is a child in the cradle, and runs away with her lover. The latter abandons her. Since then Mrs. Erlynne is leading an unhappy, socially infamous, life. Somehow she enters into the life of Lord Windermere, her son-in-law. Lady Windermere hears of it and suspects her husband's having an affair with her. When she feels convinced of it, she runs away from her house and comes to that of Lord Darlington, carrying with herself the fan her husband had presented to her on a birthday of hers. While leaving her house, she leaves there a letter for Lord Windermere, telling him that she has come to know of his infidelity and affairs with Mrs. Erlynne, and therefore frees him of the marriage bond, and is going to the house of Lord Darlington whom

4. Oxford University Press.

she would now marry. Lord Darlington has, for sometime in the past, been expressing his love for her, and persuading her to leave Lord Windermere and marry him. But so far she had not been moved by his entreties. Now she thinks of taking this step more out of grief caused by Lord Windermere's suspected infidelity than out of her love for Lord Darlington. Mrs. Erlynne happens to get her letter, reads it, and then realises the great moral wrong and calamity she is about to do to her daughter. She is not willing to reveal herself as her mother, fearing that her infamy would ruin the respectable status her daughter and her family have in the then English society. She feels extremely repentant and suffers a lot for what she has done. Her suffering is made many times greater because of her handicap in openly owning her guilt and expressing her genuine repentance. She then does several deceptions to expiate and save her daughter: She burns Lady Windermere's letter so that Lord Windermere may not know what its contents are, convinces Lady Windermere that there is nothing between her and her husband, as she is really going to marry Lord Augustus. She proves it to be true by actually marrying him which amounts to making a great sacrifice because she is not really in love with him, though he is in love with her. She tells another lie to Lord Windermere that she had inadvertently carried with her Lady Windermere's fan to Lord Darlington's drawing room when Lord Windermere finds the fan there, though the truth is that the fan had been brought there by Lady Windermere hereself. She does all this to atone for her guilt and compensate for the wrong she has done to her daughter, but without openly owning to her daughter her fault, repenting for it, and asking for her forgiveness. She cannot do anyone of these three things because of the delicate situation she is placed in. The way Mrs. Erlynne does all this makes Lady Windermere believe that she has done them out of her nobility and benevolence. Therefore, she ignores all of the infamies she has heard so many of her acquaintances attributing to her. She does not hesitate to tell her husband, who has by now developed great hatred for Mrs. Erlynne: 'She is better than I am', which makes the latter forgiven without her asking for forgiveness.

In the ideal case, when the wrongdoer is unqualifiedly repentant and the wronged fully convinced of his sincerity, the latter unqualifiedly forgives him, and then his moral anger towards the former goes away. This is conceptual, or almost conceptual. We would not call his forgiveness complete or unqualified if he still retains a part of his anger or feeling of estrangement with him. But ideal kind of repentance, or of forgiveness, is only occasionally exemplified. In most of the cases when one repents for having wronged someone else, seeks his forgiveness, and gets it, he takes sometime to mould his future attitudes and behaviour towards the forgiver in the light of his past experiences of wronging, repenting, and having been forgiven. Similar is the case with the forgiver. In most of the cases, after having forgiven the offender, the forgiver takes some-time to think of him, or behave with him, as he used to before his doing the offence. He may no longer have a hostile attitude towards him, but he may remain for some-time a little in different towards him, or cautious in associating with him, giving him full credibility only after finding him true to his promises. But it is none the less true that his forgiveness has definitely begun the process of normalising the disturbed social relationship between them.

Now I shall dilate upon some of the features of the conceptual context outlined above.

(a) If *W* is not morally wrong, nor is it taken to be morally wrong by *B*, the anger which it arouses in *B*, if it does, would not be a moral anger. *A* morally neutral, or even a morally right action of *A* may arouse *B*'s anger. But that would not be a moral, i.e., morally justified, anger, even though *A*'s action which has aroused it, has caused great unhappiness to *B*. Suppose *A* is a judge and *B* an accused for having committed a murder, and *A* awards life imprisonment to *B* when his crime has been proven and this is the punishment prescribed for such a crime by the relevant laws of the land. Then *B*'s anger aroused by the judge's action would not be a moral anger because it has not been aroused by a moral wrong.

(b) If on the other hand, *B* believes that his imprisonment is morally wrong, though it is not, his anger against *A* would only be subjectively, and not objectively, justified. Though

> it would look a little odd, still we could say that he is justified in feeling angry but his anger is not justified. In neither of the cases (a) and (b), *A* would be expected to feel repentant and to ask for forgiveness because what he has done is not morally wrong. In such cases, it is not the mechanism of repentance and forgiveness but something else which is needed to restore good social relationship, or social understanding, between *A* and *B*.

In (a) and (b) different types of measures would be required. In (a), *A* himself, or someone else, would have to effect a moral change in *B* by convincing him that, though his imprisonment has made him unhappy, it is the demand of morality that, for such a crime as his, the punishment that has been given to him ought to have been given to him. Therefore, in giving him the punishment *A* has not done anything wrong. Meeting the demand of morality is, for *B* as well, more ennobling, or morally dignified, than flouting it, escaping from it, or nursing anger against it. Such a reflection on his punishment and consequent unhappiness and anger, *B* himself may have on his own, without anybody else's prompting. If on account of his own reflection, or on that of someone else's moral persuasion, he changes his way of looking at his punishment and takes it to be one he really deserves and therefore should be undergone without malice against the judge, or anyone else, it would really be a great moral change in him, an admirable moral elevation of his personality. The change from being resentful of a morally justified punishment to considering it well-deserved and therefore worth undergoing is a big moral change. It is a change of attitude, or the acquisition of a proper attitude towards what is morally right, and therefore a morally right attitude. Its acquisition amounts to having the right attitude towards morality as such.

In (b), *B* has to be convinced that in awarding him the punishment *A* has not done anything morally (or even legally) wrong and therefore *B*'s belief that he has is false. This may be done by *A*, someone other than *A* and *B*, or even by *B* himself in his self-critical moments. Assuming that *B* admits now that an anger aroused only by something morally wrong can rightfully be called moral anger, if he is made convinced of the falsity of his belief that his punishment is morally wrong, he would have no genuine ground to feel moral anger against the judge and therefore no ground for any grudge against the punishment. To accept that his punishment is appropriate and that *A* has done nothing wrong in inflicting it on him, though it has caused a lot of unhappiness to him, would make him cease to have any hostile attitude, or ill-will, against *A*. He still may not like or love him, but he would definitely not wish to wound him. And, this too is a moral change, and not an insignificant one.

In both (a) and (b), to change *B*'s attitude towards *A* what is needed is moral reasoning. In (a), it has to be shown that anger aroused by a morally wrong action alone is moral anger, and only the experiencer of a moral anger can rightfully expect the wrong-doer, i.e., the doer of the morally wrong action that has caused his moral anger, to repent and ask for forgiveness, or consider him punishable if he does not repent, or is not forgiven. It is both ethical and conceptual that a moral anger can be given rise to only by a moral wrong. In (b), *B*'s belief that his punishment is morally wrong has to be shown to be false, if it is false. To show that a moral belief is true or false is also to indulge in moral reasoning, which may involve both normative and metaethical reasoning, depending on the facts of the case. In both the cases, (a) and (b), if the reasonings succeed in changing *B*'s attitude towards *A*, the resulting change would, in all likelihood, be both moral and conceptual. He would now be more cautious in giving to his anger the status of moral anger because he would have first to ascertain that the action of *A* which has caused it is morally wrong, and he would also realise that his belief that it is morally wrong must be true and not a hurriedly acquired false one.

Like the concept of moral anger, the concept of repentance, as well as that of asking, or granting, forgiveness, is also conceptually linked with that of a moral wrong. And, the link is not just conceptual, but much more than that. It is conceptually completely in order for a person to repent, on moral grounds, for having done a moral wrong, or to ask for it forgiveness. It is conceptually odd, on the other hand, to repent, or ask for forgiveness, for having done a morally right thing. But in neither of the two cases, the matter is only conceptual. In the former, we can very well say that repentance, and praying for forgiveness, are the appropriate responses of a morally sensitive person after realising that he has done a moral wrong. He would, or should, not have done it, in the first instance, but when he has fallen to do it, the morally correct way to get up from the fall is to repent for what he has done and to pray for forgiveness; if he does not, or cannot, or is not forgiven, he should bear the appropriate punishment meted out to him without any grudge or resentment. It is unresented punishment, besides repentance and forgiveness, which washes off the black spots on the wrongdoer's character left by his wrongdoing.

But human nature does not always function in accordance with purely logical or conceptual, or even moral, considerations. However, when it does not, it may recognise that it does not. One instance of such a functioning of it is visible in a person's repenting for having done a morally right thing. This sort of repentance is nothing but the exhibition of a weak moral character, or akrasia. It is a post-performance akratic reaction. The standardly mentioned akratic behaviour is said to be that of a person who knows that *X*-ing is right and *Y*-ing is wrong in the situation *S*, but, because of weak moral will, or being strongly motivated by the non-moral, or immoral, desire to achieve what *Y*-ing is likely to yield and which *X*-ing is not likely to yield, he does not *X* by *Y*-es instead. But one can also be akratic in a retrospective manner. For example, *A X*-es because he considers it morally right, but after *X*-ing, finds that an important self-interest of his, which has become frustrated by his *X*-ing, would, in all likelihood, have been promoted, had he *Y*-ed and not *X*-ed. Thereupon, he repents for having *X*-ed, which he considered at the time of *X*-ing, and even now considers, to be morally right. This kind of repentance is not rare, but I have called it non-standard because it is repentance for having done something right, and not for having done something wrong. Even here there may occur the appearance of forgiveness. He may ask himself to forgive himself, and we shall see a little later that self-forgiveness is possible. He may even ask his wife to forgive him if she also is a sufferer on account of the frustration of his self-interest caused by his *X*-ing. But, as in the case of repentance, this forgiveness also is of the non-standard type.

There is a variety of the standard type of repentance, as well as of forgiveness, which, if looked at superficially, appears to be similar to the above, non-standard type. Suppose *A*, with no evil intention, tells *B* the truth that his father has been arrested for smuggling so that he may take necessary steps to get him released on bail. This information hurts the self-respect of *B* and makes him very unhappy. Knowing that his telling the truth with a good intention, a morally right action, has made *B* very unhappy, *A* repents and even asks for *B*'s forgiveness because he holds the moral belief that anybody's unhappiness is a morally bad thing. This case is different from the standard case because *A* is not repenting and asking forgiveness for having done a morally wrong thing. It is different from the above non-standard case because he is neither repenting, nor asking forgiveness, for having done a morally right thing. He is repenting for what his morally right action has produced which he considers to be an evil. But still it is a non-standard case. If *B* is a morally mature and sensitive person, he would not straightaway say 'I forgive you', as he would have done in case *A* had done something morally wrong. Rather, he may say something like this: 'You need not feel sorry, you have done your duty. The information itself was so ominous that it broke me.' This would not be exactly the same as forgiving him, because it does not convey that *B* considers him a wrongdoer. A forgiver, on the other hand, in forgiving a person's guilt, does convey to him, by the very act of forgiving, that he is a wrongdoer but is forgiven because of such and such reasons. If one is not guilty, not a wrongdoer, then he is neither to be forgiven, not to be punished, nor is he to repent for what he has done, or missed to have done.

What *B*'s words to *A*, in the above example, do is to tell him that he need not feel guilty because he has done no wrong. If the grant of forgiveness to a wrongdoer is *intended* to free him of the guilt-feeling weighing heavily on his head, then what *B* has told *A* can be said to be very much like the latter because it also is intended to have the same kind of effect on *A*. But it is clear that it is not a standard case of forgiving because there is no guilt here to be forgiven.

It has been said that *B*'s anger with *A* for doing *W* would not be morally justified if the facts of the case are such that *A* cannot be held responsible for doing it. This would obviously be so if he has done it under someone else's coercion, or under the influence of a drug deceptively administered to him by someone else. It would not be any different if it has been caused by something, physical or mental, which has happened to him as a natural disorder. For example, he may drop on the floor the cup of tea he is carrying because of a sudden arthritic pain in his knee-joint, or hand over the cup to a wrong person because of a sudden loss of memory about the identity of the person to whom he has been asked to give it.

But suppose *A* intends to do one thing and another thing is done because of something accidental or unforeseen. Karṇa's arrow kills a *brāhmaṇa*'s calf when he is practising archery. There is no animal in the path of his arrow when he releases it from his bow. But all on a sudden the calf comes in its way, is hit by it and killed. Karṇa explains to the *brāhmaṇa* that he did not mean or intend to kill the calf. He still expresses to the *brāhmaṇa* his sorrow for what has happened, promises to give him one thousand ordinary cows, fifteen thousand black cows with calves, six thousand oxen, seven hundred elephants, hundreds of male and female servants, a well-furnished house with all luxuries, and begs him for forgiveness. But the angry *brāhmaṇa* does not melt and punishes him by cursing that, while fighting in war, when he will experience great fear, at that critical moment, the wheels of his chariot will fall into a ditch.[5] This does happen in his encounter with Arjuna in the *Mahābhārata* war. When he is trying to lift the wheels up and therefore is not in a position to defend himself, Arjuna, under Kṛṣṇa's instigation, attacks and kills him.

It is just bad luck for the calf that it strays into the area under the range of Karṇa's arrow and therefore gets killed. It is bad luck for Karṇa that he shoots his arrow in that direction and thereby causes the death of the calf and incurs its owner's curse. It is the latter which leads to his defeat and death at the hands of the enemy he himself has been preparing since long to defeat and kill. I call it luck because, right from the accident of the calf getting killed, his receiving the *brāhmaṇa*'s curse, the wheels of his chariot falling in a ditch, his remaining unarmed while trying to lift the wheels up, to his defeat and death at the hands of Arjuna, nothing is the result of any lapse on his part. Circumstances so contrive that a valiant warrior is killed for no fault or weakness of his. What is Karṇa's bad luck is Arjuna's good luck. It would not be unfair to say that it is his

5. *The Mahābhārata*, Vol. 4, (Gita Press) pp. 3887-91.

sheer good luck that there occurs a moment in his fight with Karṇa when he finds the latter unarmed.

Actions unknowingly or inadvertently done are very much like things accidentally done insofar as they too are unintentional, done without any thought-out plan or purpose. Therefore they also do not conceptually qualify to be called culpable. If *A* unknowingly pours salt, in place of sugar, into *B*'s cup of coffee, thinking it is sugar, or inadvertently pours, while talking to *C*, more sugar than *B* takes, we would not consider him culpable. We would not call *B*'s anger, if aroused, in either case, moral anger, nor would we expect *A* to feel guilty, be repentent, etc., and ask to be forgiven. After realising what has really been done by him, *A* may say to *B* 'I am sorry', or even 'Forgive me'. But this would be more a matter of etiquette than of apologising for a fault, more a matter of observing a social ritual or practice than of pleading guilty. It would be something like what one does when he utters 'Beg your pardon' when he really means 'Please say it again', if he has not properly heard or understood what the speaker has said.

When the result of an unintentional action is conspicuously evil, as it is in the case of Karṇa, it may naturally arouse anger in the victim, or in the owner of the victim if the victim is an animal, or an inanimate object. The latter is the case with Karṇa. The calf's getting killed is conspicuously evil and therefore its arousing the owner's, i.e., the *brāhmaṇa*'s, anger is natural. The question is whether or not we can call it moral anger. An anger can properly be called moral anger only if there is a moral reason for its arousal. In a sense any death is an evil, and so is the calf's when it got killed. But it would be morally wrong only if it has been caused by an intentional action of Karṇa, i.e., only if he has intentionally killed the calf. But that is not the fact. It is an accident that the calf gets hit by his arrow and killed because the arrow is aimed at something else. Therefore, it is not fair to blame him for the killing, or to call the *brāhmaṇa*'s anger moral anger. Here is a good example of a sin without the person associated with it as its (alleged) doer being a sinner. In the strict sense of the term, he is not its doer. This means that he is not culpable or punishable for it. Therefore, he should have been, one may say, forgiven for it. Such a view is held by philosophers who hold that an untoward action's being accidental, or unintentional, is a sufficient reason for forgiving it. But it is based on a serious confusion which I will soon clarify.

That Karṇa should not have been punished is true. But to say this is not the same as saying that he should have been forgiven. The question of granting, or refusing, forgiveness to a person arises only if he is assumed to be responsible for a wrongdoing, i.e., for having intentionally done something wrong. To forgive *A* for having done *W* is to presuppose that he has done it intentionally and that it is morally wrong. So is it, rather more obviously, in refusing to forgive him. Only if *A* admits that he has *done W* to *B*, i.e., done it intentionally, and that it is wrong, he can, properly speaking, request *B* to forgive him for having done it. And, only if *B* knows, or believes, that he has (intentionally) done it and that it is wrong, he can, properly speaking, forgive, or refuse to forgive, him for having done it. Therefore, to consider an untoward action's being accidental a sufficient reason, or any sort of reason, for forgiving its (alleged) doer, is to hold that the latter is responsible for it, i.e., has intentionally done it, and therefore is culpable. But this is not true; he is not responsible for it and therefore not culpable for having done it, simply because, to repeat, it is unintentional, or accidental. An accidental action, or the person associated with it as its alleged doer, belong to a category to which the concept of forgiveness is inapplicable.

The reverse of what has been said of an untoward, or a wrong, accidental action and its alleged doer can be said of a favourable, or right, accidental one and its alleged doer. We do not give moral credit to the alleged doer of an accidental action which turns out to be right or commendable. Suppose a tiger, rushing to pounce on the *brāhmaṇa*, accidentally comes in the path of Karṇa's arrow, is hit and consequently killed. The *brāhmaṇa* is thus saved. A morally right thing has been done because saving the life of an innocent person from being killed by a ferocious tiger is morally right. But for this right thing, or for killing the tiger, which also is in this context morally right, no moral credit can be given to Karṇa. He does not intentionally kill the tiger, or save the brāhmaṇa. The tiger gets accidentally killed, and therefore the *brāhmaṇa* gets accidentally saved. The *brāhmaṇa* may thank Karṇa and even give him his choicest blessings, but Karṇa cannot lay any moral claim to them.

Being the kind of person he is, as protrayed in the epic, it seems sure that he would have said he deserved no credit for what had happened and declined to accept, with respect, of course, any of the *brāhmaṇa*'s gifts.

A blameworthy action, after having been forgiven, becomes unculpable. *B* cannot both forgive *A* for his fault and also punish him for it. An unintentional action is also, we have seen, unculpable. Therefore, since both the actions, a forgiven and an unintentional one, are unculpable, one may think that an unintentional action can also be taken as forgiven. But it would be a wrong inference, as would be clear from the argument mentioned below, which formally expresses it:

If an action is forgiven, it is unculpable.
If an action is unintentional, it is unculpable.
Therefore, if an action is unintentional, it is forgiven.

This argument is invalid because it is possible to consistently assign truth-values to its premises and conclusion in such a manner that the premises are true and the conclusion false.

However, sometimes to console a person who is grieving over an action he has unintentionally done, say, inadvertently spilled curry on his friend's dinning table, we may say 'Don't feel guilty. Such things are 'forgivable' (or forgiven). In such uses the term 'forgivable', or 'forgiven', is used to indicate that what has happened is not a fault, or, one which is automatically forgiven, a fault too trivial to be required, for being forgiven, to meet the normal conditions for the grant of forgiveness, etc. The upshot of this mode of speaking is to tell the agent that what he has done and its ilk are not culpable, that they are not treated as offences in our social ethos.

It is not being maintained here that unintentional actions are not in fact punished. They do arouse, quite often, their victim's anger and their doers, or persons associated with them as their doers, are sometimes punished by their victims, as Karṇa was by the *brāhmaṇa*. When a victim considers such a doer punishable, or the doer himself considers himself to be guilty, he may repent, etc., and pray to be forgiven. This happens in Karṇa's case. What I have been maintaining is that in the case of an unintentional doer of an untoward action, there is no moral reason for punishing him, nor for the arousal of moral anger in the victim. I admit that in such a case the victim requires a great moral maturity not to feel angry with the agent, and a great rational maturity to distinguish between moral and non-moral anger and to call his non-moral if, per chance, he feels angry. Not to act out of anger, again, requires a still greater moral balance and stability. Morever, in a good number of cases, it is not at all easy to decide whether or not an action is unintentional.

To forgive an action is to exempt it from punishment. This means that only a punishable action can be forgiven because there would be no point in exempting from punishment an action which is not punishable. Therefore, there would be no point in forgiving an unintentional action because it is not punishable. Nor would there be a point in refusing to forgive it because forgiveness can be refused only of a punishable action. Moreover, not to punish an agent for an action of his does not imply that the action has been forgiven. It does not when the action is unpunishable, as an unintentional action is. The latter is not punished not because it is forgiven but because it is unpunishable. It may not also imply, when the action is punishable, because the victim may neither forgive nor punish its agent for it. It is possible for a punishable action to be neither forgiven nor punished. *B* may not forgive *A* for having done *W* if *A* does not fulfil the conditions required for being forgiven. He may not punish *A* if he himself is lazy, or too busy in getting his daughter's marriage settled, or too timid, or afraid of *A*'s superior might, or keen to keep his mental peace undisturbed, or eager to look great in social estimation, or hopeful to get some favour from *A* in future if he does not retaliate now, etc., etc.

An unintentional action, with a conspicuously evil consequence, may not only arouse anger in the victim, but also some feeling of sorrow or pain in its (alleged) agent, i.e., the person associated with its casuation or happening. The reason is that although he did not intend to do it, it has occurred in a context with which he is intimately, or rather causatively, associated. A morally sensitive person, while realising that he is not culpable for it, may feel sad and pained for it. We feel sad or pained not only for things we intentionally do, but also for things which happen (or which others do). But this feeling of sadness, or pain, is different from that of repentance for having intentionally done a moral wrong. The former is due to one's general moral sensitivity and the latter due to his sense of guilt. To restore his mental peace when he feels sad for something unintentionally done by him, a proper response of the victim would be saying to him something like this: 'Don't feel sad: you did not do it intentionally. It is just unfortunate that such a thing has happened, etc.' A similar response would be proper even from an outsider. In the case of a repentant person, a proper response from the victim would be different. It would be saying to him, something like 'I know you are really sorry for what you have done. Don't chastise yourself any more. Take it as already forgiven', etc. Such a response cannot be appropriate from an outsider because he cannot forgive the offender. Only the victim can.

We have seen that a wrongdoer can legitimately ask for forgiveness only if he sincerely repents, etc., and that his sincere repentance is born out of his realisation that he has done a moral wrong to the victim. For a normal person to acknowledge that a certain action is wrong is, as has been already said, to have, if he has not yet done it, an attitude of disaprobation, a con-attitude, towards doing it, and feeling of repentance, if he has already done it, for having done it. His feeling towards any actual, or possible, doer of it, including himself, would correspondingly be one ranging from moral aversion to moral anger, depending on the circumstances and the depth of the action's wrongness. All this would be true, almost analytically, of him only if he possesses, at least, what may be called, average rationality and moral sensitivity. This is not to lay down too stiff a condition for experiencing repentance. The possession of average rationality and moral sensitivity is a necessary condition of being a normal person, or a normal, adult, human, being. We would not call one a normal person, or even a *person*, if he does not fulfil it.

The repentant person finds himself fallen in his own estimation. He feels that some sort of a lowering, or devaluing, of his personhood has been caused by the wrong he has done. Whether this feeling is due to his own reflection on what he has done, to his own conscience's calling him guilty, or to his confabulation, or interaction, with another, morally mature, person, his resultant mood is one of unhappiness, or agony. And, for this moral tragedy of his he would consider his own action, or rather himself, responsible. For any person to repent for having done a wrong is to hold himself responsible for having done it and for all that it has led to. This is nothing more than the obvious denotic truth that to blame anyone, including oneself, for having done *W* and for its consequences, is to hold him responsible for what he is blamed for. Repentance is a child, or form, of self-blame for having done a wrong, just as self-satisfaction is a child, or form, of self-appreciation for having done a right. The repentant, or penitant, thus suffers, and his suffering is self-inflicted since it has been born out of his own realisation of having done a wrong. It can therefore be called a righteous punishment, one which he deserves to be inflicted on. Like any other punishment, its rigour, or paining, capacity, may differ in different cases.

One who has done no wrong, or who is morally so perfect that he cannot do any thing wrong, therefore, cannot, in point of logic, be expected, or required, to experience any kind of moral repentance. Even he, who believes, or whom we believe, that he cannot do any thing wrong, cannot be expected to have this experience. In order to have the right to expect, or require, him to have it, his belief, or our belief, that he cannot do any thing wrong, would have to be proven false.

Forgiveness has been presented here as a fitting response to the repentance, etc., of the offender. But may not it be granted even when the offender does not repent for the offence he has done and therefore does not seek for it? Yudhiṣṭhira thinks it may be granted, while Draupadī thinks that it cannot, or should not, be granted indiscriminately to every offender.

Yudhiṣṭhira tells Virāṭa, the king of Matsya, who requests Yudhisthira to kindly forgive him for his insulting and hurting him, that he (Virāṭa) need not repent or pray for forgiveness. His wrong-doing has already been forgiven by Yudhiṣṭhira because he has taken a vow, since long, to forgive everyone who does any kind of

6. अभयन्तं तु राजानं पाण्डवः प्रत्यभाषत ।
चिरं क्षान्तमिदं राजन् न मन्युर्व्रिद्यते मम ।। ६३।।

Seeing the king apologising (the Pāṇḍava) Yudhiṣṭhira said: O king, I have taken the vow of forgiveness since long. Therefore, this guilt of yours has already been forgiven. I do not have even the least anger towards you. — The *Mahābhārata*, Vol. II, pp. 2028:63

offence to him.[6] The context of his making this statement is this: He, as Kaṅka, is playing a game of dice with Virāṭa, and praising repeatedly the combating abilities of Bṛhannalā who is really Arjuna. Virāṭa gets exasperated at his praising Bṛhannalā and hits him by throwing a dice piece at his face. His nose gets hurt and starts bleeding. In the mean time, Bṛhannalā returns victorious from the battle-field after defeating the Kauravas who had attacked Matsya. Virāṭa comes to know that Kaṅka is really Yudhiṣṭhira and Bṛhannalā Arjuna. He feels extremely repentant and prays to Yudhiṣṭhira that he be forgiven.

Draupadī is against forgiving every offender, and she requests Yudhiṣṭhira to have moral anger for Duryodhana and use his military might to take back his share of the kingdom the latter has usurped. Her stand is that a king, or rather any sensible person, must feel moral anger towards the man who has done an injustice to him, as Duryodhana has done to Yudhiṣṭhira. She tells him that the very meaning of the word *kṣatriya* is one who experiences anger towards evil-doers. He, being a *kṣatriya*, has no reason at all to adopt a forgiving attitude towards Duryodhana. It is as wrong to forgive a wrongdoer, as it is to punish an innocent person. She mentions, *via* narrating a dialogue between Bali and his grandfather Prahlāda, the conditions in which a wrong-doer can justifiably be forgiven. He can be, (a) even if his crime is serious, if he has sometime done some good to the victim, or (b) if he has wronged the victim unkowingly or inadvertently. But if he calls a crime unknowingly done which he has knowingly done, he should be severely punished even if his crime is a minor one. (c) The first crime of everyone should be forgiven, but if a person forgiven for this reason commits a second crime, he should be punished even if the latter is trivial.

She mentions these conditions with Duryodhana's wrongs to her family in mind. Her request to Yudhiṣṭhira is to inflict on Duryodhana the punishment he deserves and not to forgive him, because he satisfies none of the above three conditions. Instead of repenting for any of the large number of wrongs he has done, and requesting forgiveness, he has gone on doing one injustice after another in an extremely agressive and unrepentant manner. Yudhiṣṭhira does not reply to her point-wise. He does not discriminate between different types of anger, even between moral and non-moral, or immoral, anger, nor between justified and unjustified forgiveness. On the other hand, he condemns all types of anger and advises her to keep them under control and never to yield to anyone of them. Forgiveness he considers to be an absolute, unconditional, virtue, the exemplification of which is never unjustified. One should be forgiving even in adverse circumstances. It is the forgiving person who safequards the life of all living beings.[7] He speaks of it in a highly extolatory manner. He calls it *dharma* (virtue), *yajña* (sacrifice), Veda, and Śruti (revealed wisdom). One who knows what it is becomes competent to forgive every crime. Forgiveness is, he continues, *Brahman*, *satya* (truth), *bhūta* (the past), *bhaviṣya* (the future), *tapa* (penance), and *śauca* (cleanliness).[8]

The dialogue between Draupadī and Yudhiṣṭhira brings to the surface the issue whether any crime whatsoever can justifiably be forgiven, or only that which satisfies certain conditions. Draupadī's stand is nearer than Yudhiṣṭhira's to the common man's intuitions about the use of forgiveness, though the set of conditions she has listed for granting forgiveness is incomplete and unsatisfactory in many respects, as is evident from the analysis of repentance given here. But she has put her finger at the right spot when she says that moral anger is not only desirable but could sometimes be necessary, and that every offence cannot be justifiably forgiven.

7. क्षन्तव्यं पुरुषेणेह सर्वापत्सु सुशोभने ।
क्षमावतो ही भूतानां जन्म चैव प्रकीर्तितम् ।। ३२।।

O elegant lady, one should retain his sense of forgiveness in all adverse situations. It has been said that the life of all living beings is protected only by a forgiving person. — *The Mahābhārata*, Vol. II, p. 1026:32.

8. क्षमा धर्मः क्षमा यज्ञः क्षमा वेदाः क्षमा श्रुतम् ।
य एतदेवं जानाति स सर्वं क्षन्तुमहति ।। ३६।।

क्षमा ब्रह्म क्ष्मा सत्यं क्षमा भूतं च भावि च ।
क्षमा तपः क्षमा शौचं क्षमयेदं धृतं जगत् ।। ३७।।

Forgiveness is morality, forgiveness is sacrifice, forgiveness is Veda, forgiveness is revealed truth. One who knows all this becomes capable of forgiving everything.

Forgiveness is the highest reality, forgiveness is the truth, forgiveness is the past, and the future too. Forgiveness is penance and forgiveness is cleanliness. Forgiveness alone has been sustaining the entire universe. — *Ibid.*, p. 1027:36-37.

The fact of the matter is that when we forgive, we forgive a criminal for the crime he has committed and not merely the crime, disassociated from its doer. It is the criminal who repents for the crime he has committed, promises not to repeat it, etc., or offers excuses by saying that it was accidentally, unknowingly, or inadvertently, done, etc. It is the criminal, again, who exhibits a change of attitude when he genuinely repents, and who, after having been forgiven, experiences a restoration of his own damaged personhood caused by the crime, and of the pre-crime social relationship between him and his victim. The crime, after having been committed, becomes an object of the past and therefore nothing can be done to it; it cannot be undone, or obliterated. But the criminal can be changed, purified, or washed clean. This is what repentance does, or is supposed to do, and when it moves the victim to forgive him, the criminal gets the satisfaction of having been re-accepted by the victim.

Draupadī quotes Prahlāda's saying to Bali that he who always forgives suffers in many ways. His servents, enemies, and non-attached people, disrespect him. No one behaves with him with humility. Therefore, forgiving every offender is prohibited even for wise people.[9] What Prahlāda means to say is that a habitual forgiver becomes socially ineffective.

To forgive an offender is not just to forbear punishing him, but to do that on moral grounds. Forgiveness is a reactive response of the victim to the offender which would be a morally fitting response only if it is made on moral grounds, i.e., only if the offender repents, etc., for the wrong he has done. A blanket type of forgiveness granted to every offender cannot called justified. To say all this is to

9. यो नित्यं क्षमते तात बहून् दोषान् स बिन्दति ।
भृत्याः परिभवन्त्येनमुदासीनस्तथारयः ।। ७।।
सर्वभूतानि चाप्यस्य न नमन्ति कदाचन ।
तस्मान्नित्यं क्षमा तात पण्तैरपि बर्जिता ।। ८।।

My child, he who always forgives acquires many defects. His sevants, enemies, and those who are unrelated to him, all disrespect him.

No one behaves with him in a humble manner. Therefore, my dear one, forgiving in all conditions is not allowed even for wise people. *The Mahābhārata*, Vol. II, p. 1022: 7-8.

reaffirm that forgiveness is a conditional virtue, as Draupadī says, even if she has not described its conditions exhaustively or correctly, and not an unconditional one as Yudhiṣṭhira claims it to be.

It is obvious by now that the grant of forgiveness benefits both the offender and the offended. When the offender is convinced that he has been forgiven, he gets relieved of the pricks of his sense of guilt. When the offended is convinced of the offender's genuine repentance, etc., and therefore forgives him, he gets relieved of his moral anger and the feeling of having been wronged. The victim's desire to punish the offender is a natural child of his moral anger, and it has the support of his conscience, or retributive moral sense; he feels that the wrongdoer deserves, or, ought to be, punished. The experience of moral anger, like that of a non-moral anger, is itself quite disquieting. It may even be extremely painful. It is his moral anger which provides the motivational force to his feeling of having been hurt which moves him to take steps to punish the offender, leading sometimes to great clashes between the two when the offender resists. Therefore, his getting rid of his moral anger is very important because it not only conduces to restoring his mental peace but also to that of social peace by normalising the relationship between him and his offender.

The belief that a moral wrong has been done to one may not be true, and when it is not, the anger it has aroused in him, as has already been said, would not be justified. But it would still be subjectively justified because it has been aroused by a moral belief, namely, the belief that he has been morally wronged, though the belief is false. Since it is this sort of belief that causes moral anger, before entertaining the belief, one should take enough care to ascertain that it is true. This is not only an epistemic duty, as in the case of non-moral beliefs, but also a moral duty of his. If he believes that someone has *X*-ed him, he must ascertain that the former has *X*-ed him and that *X*-ing him is morally wrong. If to wrong a person is morally wrong, to entertain irresponsibly, or without proper assessing its truth-claims, the belief that he has been wronged is also morally wrong.

Not feeling morally angry when a moral wrong has been done is, in a normal person, a sign of moral insensitivity, or of low moral sensitivity. Not granting forgiveness, and thereby overcoming his moral anger, is, in a normal person, a sign of low morality, or of low moral development. Contrarywise, granting forgiveness, when its required conditions have been fulfilled, is a sign of high morality, or high moral development. However, there is a view, attributed to some classical Indian thinkers, according to which it is possible for a normal person to attain a state in which he would have no feeling, desire, etc., and therefore no feeling of anger against anybody, no desire to retaliate any wrongdoer, etc. This state is said to be the highest which he can and ought to attain. A person who has attained it is called *sthitaprajña*, *jīvanmukta*, *samadarśī*, etc.

The *sthitaprajña*, the man of steady wisdom, is one who has realised himself, has no desires to fulfil, and is satisfied in just being the self he is. No sorrow disturbs him, no delight elates him, no wrongdoing hurts him, no praise pleases him. He has no attachment for anything, no anger and fear, or rather no feeling or passion.[10] Such a person would feel no moral anger against any wrongdoer because he would feel no anger. Nothing makes him feel hurt or pleased, because he has a neutral attitude towards everything, towards things which may be likeable, or, dislikeable, for others. He has the same non-discriminative feeling or attitude towards everyone, no matter whether he is a well-wisher, a friend, or enemy, an indifferent person, an arbiter, a hateful person, a relative, a saint, or a sinner.[11] He cannot, therefore, feel morally wronged, or wronged, by anyone because that would mean treating the latter as a wrongdoer, and reacting to him by feeling resentment, or moral anger, towards him. But this he cannot do. If he cannot feel moral anger towards anyone for having done a wrong to him, he cannot feel it for a similar thing done to anybody else. To forgive anyone is to forgive him who is a wrongdoer and towards whom the forgiver feels moral anger which has been aroused by his wrongdoing. But the *sthitaprajña* cannot feel moral anger also because he cannot feel any sort of anger, or rather any sort of feeling. This means that he cannot be said to forgive anyone. But the *Gītā* says that he is an unfailing forgiver (*kṣamī*). He does not hate anyone, is friendly and

10. *The Gītā*, chapter II.55-7.
11. *Ibid.*, chapter VI.9.

compassionate to all, is free from the sense of 'mine' or ego, is the same in sorrow or happiness, and is forgiving.[12]

But since the *sthitaprajña* does not take anything done to him as a wrong, and anybody as a wrongdoer or a foe, there would be none for him to forgive, or to deny forgiveness. In fact, there cannot be any occasion for him to forgive anybody. He can neither be wronged by anyone, nor can he wrong anyone. Therefore the grant of forgiveness by him to anyone, including himself, i.e., even the grant of self-forgiveness, would be uncalled for, or impossible. And, the question of his doing a wrong to someone and seeking his forgiveness would not arise. He can neither be a wrongdoer, nor a forgiver. For any person to be a forgiver there must be a wrongdoer whom he forgives. Since the *sthitaprajña* does not consider anybody a wrongdoer, there would be none whom he needs to forgive. To say all this is only to unfold what is contained in the *Gītā* concept of a *sthitaprajña*. If the *sthitaprajña* is what the *Gītā* says he is, then he cannot be called a forgiver in spite of the *Gitā*'s calling him a forgiver.

The above line of thinking may be extended even to his being kind or compassionate to all creatures. Since he has the same attitude towards all, whether one is a learned *brāhmaṇa*, a cow, an elephant, a dog, or an eater of dog's meat,[13] he cannot have one attitude towards a sorrowful man and another towards a happy one. Kindness, or compassion, like forgiveness, is not a virtue which one can exemplify, i.e., feel or express, for everyone. To have it would be a fitting response only towards those who are unhappy or sorrowful. This would mean that only he can have compassion who has different attitudes towards sorrowful and happy persons, just as only he can have forgiveness who has different attitudes towards wrongdoers and right-doers. Therefore, the *sthitaprajña* can neither have compassion for a sorrowing person, nor non-compassion for a non-sorrowing one because he cannot have different attitudes for the sorrowing and the non-sorrowing, since he would not see them differently, as he is *samadarsī*. But if the *stithaprajña* cannot have virtues like forgiveness, compassion, etc., he cannot be said to be

12. *The Gītā,* chapter XII.13.
13. *Ibid*., chapter.V.18.

morally perfect, as the classical Indian tradition claims him to be. In ordinary discourse when we praise someone as being non-partisan, or egalitarian, in being kind, or forgiving, etc., what we mean is that he has the same attitude towards all unhappy, or wrongdoing people. That is, if he is kind to his unhappy, widowed sister, he would be kind to all other unhappy widows. Similarly, if he forgives *A* for having done *W*, he would forgive all others who are like *A* in having done wrongs like *W*. We do not mean that he would be kind, forgiving, etc., to all creatures whether or not they are sorrowing, or wrongdoing, people. Therefore, it would be incongruous to call the *sthitaprajña* a *samadarśī*, i.e., a person who has the same attitude towards all creatures, and at the same time to attribute to him such virtues as kindness, forgiveness, etc. It is appropriate to be kind to some but not to everyone; it is appropriate to be forgiving to some but, again, not to everyone. Perhaps because the classical thinkers did not try to unfold what is involved in the attribution of virtues like kindness, forgiveness, etc., to anyone, they did not realise the difficulties in attributing to the *stithaprajña* the virtues of being kind, or forgiving, etc., to all creatures.

To be kind to a person is a fitting reactive response to his sorrowfulness, just as granting forgiveness is to the repentance of a wrongdoer. It is extremely odd to express one's kindness for a friend's having been declared the winner in a hard competitive game, or to grant forgiveness to him for having done the right thing. To be kind, or forgiving, to everyone would be a sign of being virtuous only if it is assumed that everyone is sorrowful, or a wrongdoer. It is true that it is difficult to be kind, or forgiving, even to some. But to conclude from this that it would be a sign of being perfectly virtuous, if one is kind, or forgiving, to all, would be a wrong inference.

But suppose it is said that it may be true of an ordinary person that a moral wrongdone to him arouses in him moral anger and he forgives a wrongdoer, and only a wrongdoer, when the latter genuinely repents, etc. A *sthitaprajña* is not bound to behave like an ordinary person. He may not perceive anybody as a wrongdoer, any action as a wrongdoing, and may not feel any moral anger towards anybody, and still be forgiving towards everyone. But this is not possible because of certain logical or conceptual constraints.

That only a wrongdoer can be forgiven is a conceptual, and not just an empirical, truth. Therefore, none, not even a *sthitaprajña*, can forgive one who is not a wrongdoer, or whom he does not perceive as a wrongdoer. Similarly, it is conceptual that unless a doing by someone is cognised to be a wrong-doing, he cannot be called a wrongdoer. But is it possible that the *sthitaprajña* cognises a doing as a wrongdoing and does not react by feeling moral anger, or resentment? Certainly not. Not to feel resentment against a wrongdoing is to be morally insensitive, and moral insensitivity, or even subdued moral sensitivity, would be a sign of moral imperfection. This would not be the case only if cognising a moral wrongdoing is taken to be like cognising a (factual) state of affairs, or happening, which has no impact on our feelings, or attitudes, which leaves us completely unmoved. But that would be untrue to the logic of conceiving, or cognising, a doing as a wrongdoing. A *sthitaprajña* cannot say that he cognises *X*-ing as a wrongdoing without feeling any resentment, or any reaction, against it, and forgives its doer without feeling any disapprobation for what he has done. If he says all this, it would mean that he does not understand the logic of the concept of wrongdoing and therefore suffers from some sort of conceptual or logical deficiency. This deficiency would also tell on his claim to perfection.

One who believes that some doings are really, i.e., objectively, morally right and some others morally wrong, would say that if the *sthitaprajña* does not discriminate between them, or is not moved by them, i.e., does not have a pro-attitude towards the former and a con-attitude towards the latter, then he is morally inferior to those who have a pro-attitude towards the former and a con-attitude towards the latter. Not to cognise, say, the morally wrong as morally wrong, and not to feel repulsion against it, is a sign of moral imperfection. But the tradition considers him morally perfect, though it does not give a convincing solution to the problems raised here. Perhaps to make these problems irrelevant to its conception of a *sthitaprajña*, it sometimes says that the *sthitaprajña* is outside the zone of morality and therefore exempt from the application of all moral predicates. But this would not defend the claim of his being morally perfect. It would imply that he can neither be called morally perfect, nor morally imperfect, because both 'morally perfect' and 'morally imperfect' are moral predicates.

The statements, made above, that the *sthitaprajña* cannot be called either forgiving or non-forgiving, compassionate or non-compassionate, morally perfect or imperfect, etc., should not cause any offence to the admirer of the ideal of the *sthitaprajña*. They are not substantive, or normative, statements about the *sthitaprajña*. They are only conceptual corrolaries of the classical Indian conception of the *sthitaprajña*.

To feel morally angry with a wrongdoer is, I have said, a sign of moral sensitivity. Moral sensitivity, as well as moral insensitivity, admits of degrees. One person may be more sensitive, or insensitive, than another, and the same person may be more, or less, sensitive, at one time, or in one part of his life, than at another time, or in another part of his life. Again, the same person may be more sensitive to some kind of immoralities than to some other kind of them, and different individuals may have different degrees of sensitivity or insensitivity for different kinds of moralities or immoralities. We lable a person as morally insensitive when we find him generally, and not only occasionally, insensitive, that is, when we find that, in general, neither the sight of a morally commendable action arouses his admiration, nor that of a palpable wrongdoing arouses his moral anger. We call a person morally hyper-sensitive if he neither misses to cognise even the slightest wrongdoing, nor fails to feel resentment against it. He cannot even try to get all the wrongs he meets with corrected because their number would be too large, nor would the doers of all of them beg his forgiveness. All of the wrongs would not even be worth resenting against and their doers too would not think it necessary to apologise for them. Therefore, the hyper-sensitive moralist is bound to make himself miserable by constantly feeling angry towards this or that offender. If he becomes a hyper-activist, trying to take retributive action against every wrongdoer, he would not only make himself miserable, but may look like a laughing stock to his companions. The Hindi moovie *Albert Pīnṭo ko Gussā Kyoṅ Ātā Hai*? (Why is Albert Pinto Angry?) very well illustrates this truth.

The hyper-active moralist would fail not only because his powers are too limited to cope with the gigantic task, but also because hyper-activism is very likely to be counter-productive. Too much interference in the life-style of an individual, even with the intention of making him morally better by remonstrating with, or persuading, him to mend his morals, or to apologise for every lapse of his howsoever small it may be, is very likely to develop in him a resistance, or unwillingness, to change the way the hyper-activist wants him to.

There are two devices in the phenomenology of our moral life which help us to cope with the problems thrown up by hyper-sensitivism or hyper-activism. They are (a) condoning and (b) making peace with ourselves.

(a) To condone a fault is to consider it not very serious, not worthy of resenting against. To forgive a fault is to free the guilty of the complaint one has against him, and that is what the victim does by forgiving him when he repents, etc. But to condone a fault we do not require its doer to repent, etc., nor do we free him of the complaint we have against him for having done it. We only take the fault lightly. We consider it a fault because we think that it would have been better if it would not have been done, though we do not think its having been done too bad. Its doer continues to be the doer of a fault, though he is not punished, or not considered to be punishable. If we put at the end of the line representing forgivability a fault which is too serious to be forgiven, say a fault like raping a child, at its other end we can put a fault too small to merit punishment, say, a fault like using the office gum to paste a private envelop. We save ourselves from worrying about, or resenting against, a fault by condoning it even if we realise that we cannot stop its commission, punish its doer, or forgive him because of his not fulfilling the conditions of meriting forgiveness. But to decide which action is, and which one is not, condonable is not always easy because it itself is a moral decision. But that it is not always impossible to decide is clear from the fact that in every moral community there are faults it considers condonable.

(b) When one finds that a serious wrong has been done to him but he is not in a position to punish the guilty, nor is the latter going to repent, etc., in order to free himself of his moral anger, or to calm it down, he may argue with himself on the following lines: 'Nothing can be done in the circumstances. The wisest thing would be not to think of what has happened, or to think of it as something unfortunate or sad which has to be borne with.' If he succeeds, he softens the anger aroused by the wrongdoing and in course of time it may cease to disturb his mental peace. I call it making peace with oneself because in adopting this device, the victim restores his peace of mind only by working on his mind or mental resources.

It is not easy, however, to subdue or pacify one's moral anger which making peace with oneself is intended to do. It costs a lot of mental energy, and makes one feel that he is a helpless creature with no alternative but to silently drink in his victimisation. The hyper-sensitive moral agent is more likely to meet this kind of fate than one who is less sensitive. The latter can keep up his morale, — and one has to keep up his morale even in moral matters — by convincing himself that keeping peace with himself, as he is presently doing, is the best possible way to keep himself mentally and therefore morally fit. This is so because he would be able to take right moral decisions and regulate his moral anger in accordance with the offences done to him and their contextual conditions only if he is at peace with himself.

The conceptual matrix of wrongdoing and forgiving outlined and elaborated in the foregoing pages is the normal one in which one individual does a moral wrong to another, the latter feels morally angry with the former, but on his fulfilling certain conditions he forgives him, and as a result of his forgiving him, the rupture in the social relationship between the two, caused by the wrongdoing, is, wholly or largely, repaired. But, because of the peculier structure of a society, the guilt accruing from a wrongdoing may be assignable not only to the individual wrongdoer but also to the group he belongs to. This is very much true of the Indian Hindu society in which every individual, by birth, belongs to a cetain caste, and cetain things are done by, and to him, not as an idividual but as a member of the caste he belongs to. For example, *A*, being of caste *B*, does not allow *C* of caste *S* to touch the earthen piture containing his drinking water because he believes that the water would be defiled if the piture is touched by any member of *S*. By not allowing him to touch the piture *A* does moral wrong to *C* because thereby he insults *C*'s personhood, thinking of him as a lowly creature *because* of his belonging to *S*. *A* thus thinks that *C*'s touch would defile his drinking water *because* *C* is of the caste *S* and he of cast *B*. Had he disallowed him on the ground that *C*'s hands were dirty, or suffering from some contagious desease, the matter would have been different. In the present case, although *C* is wronged, he is wronged not as the individual *C* but as an *S*, and although *A* does the wrong, he does it not as the individual *A* but as a *B*.

Being caste-oriented, this situation prompts *C* to generalise that ordinarily all *B*'s look dawn upon all *S*'s and therefore to make not only *A* but the entire caste of *B*'s the object of his moral anger. This can happen with any C_i and the result is that the caste-group *S*, as a body, feels morally angry with the caste-group *B*, treating the latter as another body. Both the bodies may be more or less well-knit depending on how closely, or loosely, structured the two castes, or caste-groups, are. All this may happen even when it is a fact that all *B*'s do not consider all *S*'s defilers and all *S*'s do not believe that all *B*'s look down upon all of them. In this way the unfortunate phenomenon of one caste feeling wronged by, and therefore morally angry with, another caste has become a social reality. Even moral anger of such an individual, or a group, towards another individual, or a group, when no moral means for its alleviation or elimination seems to be in sight, turns into enemity. The feeling of enemity grown out of moral anger is likely to be deeper or more ruthless than the one which has grown out of some non-moral anger. The reason is that the former has the backing of a sense of righteousness. One would feel that his feeling of enemity for the person or group concerned is morally justified, that he has the moral right to feel anemetic towards the latter, because of the moral wrong the letter has done to him (or to someone else of his group). Even an outsider may not consider it condemnable or uncalled for.

When the wronged and the wrongdoer are individuals, we have seen, the situation can be retrived and the ruptured social relationship restored if the wrongdoer repents, etc., and the wronged, being satisfied with his sincerity, forgives him. But a caste is a class with an indefinite number of members and therefore it is not possible for a whole caste to repent to another caste for some wrongdoing. Some members of it may do that, but the wronged can think that the number of unrepentants is still quite large. And, the process of convincing the wronged caste of a change of attitude in the wrongdoer caste is made more difficult by politicians fanning the latter's anger in the interest of their petty political ends. Gandhi tried to prepare the wrongdoer castes to develop self-repentant, self-corrective attitudes which should have been helpful in convincing the wronged ones that there was a change in the latter's attitudes towards them. But he could not be let to live long enough to fulfil his mission. A governmental legislative action may compensate for some of the damage caused by the wrongs done to the wronged castes, and therefore it is in order. But it may not restore the ruptured social relationship between the wronged and wrongdoer castes. Very often the way the damages are compensated for is likely to make the wronged group feel friendly with, or even obliged to, some politicians, and not likely to make them friendly with those towards whom they have their moral anger. It may even widen the gap between the two groups if the wronged group is led to believe that it is some politically influential members of their own group who are instrumental in their having been given the compensatory benefits, and not anyone of the wrongdoer group.

Repentance and consequential forgiveness are the most effective means to repair ruptured social relations, to get moral anger, or any anger as a matter of that, replaced by good will. This is so because they are accompanied with the hope of, and belief in, having a worthwhile existence as a result of living together in a cohesive way. This work can be facilitated more meaningfully by individuals from the wrongdoing class coming forward to exemplify that they really treat the people of the wronged class with respect and fairness. They may not apologise, or repent, in explicit terms because the wrongs might have been done not by them but by their forefathers, or by their kith and kin. But they must express their disapprobation of the wrongs done whosoever be their doers. Education, properly attuned to help change of attitudes in the right direction, would very greatly be needed to make all this possible.

Conceptual analysis, as an important component of education, would play a very important role. It can be done primarily by able philosophers. It should distinguish between moral anger and non-moral anger, hammer at the point that only anger aroused by a moral wrong is moral, i.e., justified, anger, show that any harm done to a person is not a moral wrong, etc., etc. For example, to demote an employee on account of incompetence is to harm him but it is not doing him a moral wrong. This is true irrespective of the castes to which the harmed and harm-doer belong. A detailed programme of conceptual analysis of the very many issues involved in such a venture cannot be given here.

Moral anger or resentment has been maintained here to be not only a natural but also a fitting response to a moral wrongdoing, and that is why a person who does not resent a wrongdoing has been said to be morally insensitive, or less sensitive than what he should be. But, one may ask, does not this view smack of moral intolerance? If one is to resent every wrongdoing, then where is the place for tolerance in his moral life? To see that it does not imply moral intolerance we have only to properly understand what moral tolerance, or, intolerance, means.

To tolerate a view, or an action, is obviously not to oppose, or resent it. It is to adopt a not-to-brother-about attitude towards it. In theoretical matters one is tolerant of a view opposed to his when he does not oppose it, or call it false. This sort of tolerance would be worthwhile when he is not absolutely sure (a) of the truth of his view, or (b) of the falsity of the opposed view, or (c) of there being possible one and only one true view about the subject concerned, or (d) of there being a foolproof method of proving the truth, or falsity, of a view about it, etc. This is the case with almost all of the religious views we hold. Either one of (a), (b), (c), or (d) can be said to be true of almost every religious view or opinion we hold. Therefore, to be tolerant in religious matters is considered to be the most rational thing to do. In ethical matters, too, things similar to what have been mentioned above about theoretical matters may sometimes happen. If *B* is *X*-ed by *A*, *B* may not be absolutely sure (a′) that his having been *X*-ed is morally wrong, or (b′) that there was another alternative, say, *Y*-ing him, available to *A*, which was better (e.g., less painful than *X*-ing) than *X*-ing and equally permissible, or (c′) that of the various permissible alternatives available to *B*, *X*-ing alone is morally wrong, or (d′) that there is a foolproof method of proving that *X*-ing him is morally wrong, etc. If either one of (a′), (b′), (c′), or (d′) is the case, then it would be unjustified for *B* to be morally angry with *A*. That is, it would be proper, or rational, for him to be tolerant of his having been *X*-ed by *A*. But when none of them holds good, i.e., when *B* is convinced that *X*-ing him by *B* is unqualitiedly a moral wrong-doing, then his moral anger is a fitting response. This would mean that, then, his not feeling morally angry, i.e., being tolerant of what has been done to him, would be unjustified or morally wrong. Tolerating a morally wrong thing is itself morally wrong. Therefore, if to be morally tolerant means to be tolerant of immoralities, then there is no place for tolerance in moral matters.

It is true that if one is morally angry on account of every wrong-doing, he would be miserable. Because of his limited resources, mental, moral, or physical, he cannot fight against all immoralities. Therefore some immoralities have to be rated as trivial, or not worth bothering about. It is these, we have seen, which are called condonable. Therefore, one meaning of being tolerant could be condoning those of wrongdoings which are of very little importance. It seems to me that this is the ordinary, or normal meaning of being tolerant in moral matters. In other words, to be tolerant is not to be fussy about every immorality. We have to exercise economy even in moral matters because we cannot afford to be serious about each and every moral wrongdoing. Therefore, to conclude, tolerance in morals is desirable when either one of the conditions (a´), (b´), (c´), (d´), already mentioned, hold good, or when an immorality, we are confronted with, is condonable. Condonable immoralities are of very little importance, and generally the importance of immoralities is utilitarianly decided. But one may use a different method of grading them. What I want to assert is that only such wrongdoings, or immoralities, can be called condonable, or tolerable, which are graded to be of very little importance, in whichever way one decides to grade them. It is possible that one society is tolerant of one's extorting money from hand-to-mouth foot-path vendors to contest an election, but intolerant of one's making pleasantries with another man's young wife, whereas the *vice versa* may be true of another society.

Linguistically not to be tolerant should be considered synonymous with being intolerant. But since 'intolerant' has acquired a pejorative emotive meaning, I will use 'non-tolerant', in place of 'intolerant', as the opposite of 'tolerant'.

When one is non-tolerant of a wrongdoing done to him, he

obviously has the right to take appropriate action against the offender if the latter does not repent and seek forgiveness. But if he is morally angry for a wrong done to another person, or a group, he may or may not be the right person to take action against the offender. Suppose *A* is trying to molest a helpless girl in a roadside, small, tea shop in which *B* is taking tea, and society has not assigned to any special set of people the duty to protect such victims, or to act against such offenders. Then, any citizen, any human being, if he comes forward to help the girl, would not be doing anything he is not authorised to do. Here the wrong is about to be done to the girl, and not to *B*, but *B* also feels angry with the offender. He takes the wrong as vicariously done to him, and therefore resents and fights with the offender to stop him from molesting the girl. Vicarious feeling of having been wronged is as much in order in morals as it is elsewhere. If the offender appologises, he has, though, primarily to apologise to the girl, he must apoligise to *B* as well. Or again, vicariously, *B* may take the offender's apologising to the girl as apologising to him as well.

But suppose *A* is a teacher whose assignment is to teach arithmatic to the childern of class III in a primary school. But in every session he has with the children, he tells to the children funny stories and never talks of arithmatic. Certainly he is doing a wrong to the children who are too small to take the wrong as a wrong, or to do anything in the matter. *B*, who is the contractor of their mess, comes to know of it. *B* feels morally angry with the teacher but he is not authorised to take any action against him. That responsibility has been given to the headmaster of the school. Teaching the scheduled subject in the classroom is the only right thing for *A* to do. But if he does not do it, or does anything else, it is the headmaster who has to see that he does what he is supposed to and does not do anything else. *B* has nothing, one may say, to do with the derelict *A*, even if he is morally angry with him.

In a sense it is right to say that *B* has nothing to do with the teaching in the classroom, and the headmaster, on the other hand, has it as his duty to see that it is properly done. This is the standard, orthodox, position about the division of labour in respect of the assignment, fulfilment and supervision of duties in an institutional sphere. But this would mean the adoption of too narrow a view about taking steps against wrongdoings. A wrongdoing is a wrongdoing for everyone, though it would cause some damage only to a particular person or group of persons. Therefore, anybody, even one unconnected with the wronged, or with the person legally assigned the duty of stopping it, or of punishing the offender, and not only the wronged, or the latter, may take steps to stop it from being done, or to get retributive action taken against the wrong-doer by the appropriate agency. *B* can take morally permissible steps to stop the class-teacher from telling stories in the classroom, and even steps to get him punished by the headmaster. And, in doing all this, he would not be doing anything wrong. He may not enter the classroom and request or order the teacher to teach airthmatic. But he can report that matter to the headmaster and pursue it till the wrong is righted.

It is in the nature of the moral concern that none can say that he is not concerned with this or that kind of immorality which is being perpetrated in front of him. He may not have the power to stop its perpetration and for getting the perpetrater properly punished. For all this he may have to refer to some assigned authority. Assuming that giving a threat to report the matter to the punishing authority, or condemning the wrong, is also some kind of a punitive step, in quite a few cases, anybody can take such punitive steps and, in quite a few cases, he may succeed in stopping the wrongdoing. If *B* keeps himself off by saying that, although he knows what *A* does in the classroom and that is wrong, he is not concerned with it, he is shirking from doing a public duty of his. In fact, when *B* is told by the children of what *A* does, if he has a developed moral sensitivity, he would feel unhappy. That would imply that he himself has begun to feel wronged by *A*'s wrongdoing to the children. When *A* realises his guilt, he would consider *B* as one to whom also he should apologise and seek his forgiveness. The children he is teaching, *B*, the initiator of the process of taking action against *A*, and the headmaster, the institutionally assigned authority, all from a group to which *A* would need to repent and apologise, of course, if he repents and therefore wants to be forgiven. He may not apologise to the children for strategic, social, reasons. But that would be another matter. What I want to bring out is that, if there is a viable place for the public litigation scheme in judicial matters, there is an equally viable place for there being a public initiation of the process of taking action against a moral wrongdoing. Rather, it seems to me that it is the latter which is the basis, or justification, of the former.

It has been said that to grant forgiveness to a repentant wrong-doer does not go against the retributive intuition that the wrongdoer ought to be punished. It does not, because in experiencing the pangs of repentance the wrongdoer does experience some sort of a self-inflicted punishment. But since the retributive intuition in some circle enjoys the status of almost an ethical *a priori*, it is better to discuss the relationship between forgiveness and retribution in some detail.

The relation between forgiveness and retribution is not too straight because that between wrongdoing and the punishment it deserves (or is said to deserve) is not too straight. When these relations are properly understood, it will become completely clear that there is nothing self-inconsistent in granting forgiveness to a repentant offender while continuing to be a retributivist.

After a wrongdoing has been forgiven, the question of giving to the wrongdoer any punishment on account of that wrongdoing does not obviously arise. Forgiving a wrong is to close the matter of the wrongdoer's getting, or being given, the punishment deserved by him in virtue of his having done that wrong. The fact of the matter is that forgiveness is not granted gratis but because the wrongdoer repents, etc. When he repents, he suffers the pangs of his repentance. This self-inflicted suffering can be taken as the moral equivalent of the suffering which might have resulted from an external agency's infliction on him of the punishment his wrong-doing has made him deserve. Therefore, he can be said to have got the punishment he deserves, or its equivalent, and therefore to have satisfied the requirement of retribution. It is this suffering of his, i.e., the suffering resulting from his repentance, etc., which enables him to get the victim's forgiveness.

It is possible, however, that even after *B*'s having forgiven *A*, another agency may think that the latter still deserves to be punished. This would happen, for example, when the authority to punish the wrongdoer vests in someone, or some agency, other than *B*, i.e., the wronged person. Suppose *A* is a professional medical practitioner who has done the moral wrong of giving, out of wilful negligence, a wrong medical treatment to *B*, on account of which *B* develops an irremovable physical deformity, say, paralysis of the little finger of his left hand. Suppose, *A* fulfils, to the satisfaction of *B*, the normal conditions which justify a wronged person's forgiving his wrongdoer, i.e., sincerely repents for his guilt, does his best to make the finger function as it did earlier, though he fails, and genuinely promises not to be negligent in future and look after *B*'s future ailments, etc. *B* then forgives him. But the state's legal agency, entrusted with the work of ensuring that its medical personnel do not do any negligence in the treatment of patients under their care, may still punish the guilty physician, say, by cancelling his professional licence to practice medicine. This would be an example of a retributive legal moral action. But it does not go against the analysis of forgiveness presented here. It neither shows that the retributive action is taken even after the guilty has been forgiven, nor that the retributive punishment given to the guilty is uncalled for because he has already been forgiven by the wronged. What has happened here is that the authority to forgive, or punish, does not vest, as per the state's prescribed code of medical ethics, in the patient but in a legal agency established for that purpose. Therefore, the guilty has not really been forgiven in being 'forgiven' by the wronged person because the latter is not authorised to forgive.

Therefore, the claim that no retributive action can be taken against the guilty by the forgiver after he has been forgiven by the latter remains unaffected. In the present case, *B* did forfeit *his* right to punish *A* in any way, after forgiving him, and even his right to file a complaint to the competent authority to punish him. *A* is still punished by the state because the real right to punish belongs to the legal agency. In such cases there are likely to be variations depending on the state's, or public, arrangement for taking care of professional wrongdoings. It is possible that the legal agency takes into account the wronged person's changed attitude towards the wrongdoer and drops the case, or reduces the deserved punishment, after knowing that the wronged person has forgiven him. But it is also possible that there is no such provision and the state's agency takes, what it considers, appropriate action against the wrongdoer irrespective of the attitude of the wronged towards the wrongdoer.

Since a wrongdoer's repentance is a consequence of his realisation of his guilt, an execution of the verdict of his own conscience, or moral reason, it is very likely to purify, or cleanse his heart. This is reflected in the popular saying that the tears of repentance wash off the sin. Genuine repentance does mean some moral improvement in the repentant. This may not happen in the case of the guilty convicted and punished by an external agency, formal or informal. It may not, because the convict may think that he is not guilty, and that he has been punished simply because he did not have the resources to prove his innocence. After completing his term of imprisonment, therefore, he may become a real criminal if before the conviction, he was not, or become more callous than what, before the conviction, he was. Most of the current Hindi movies very ably illustrate these possibilities.

In a retributive handling of an offence, the offence concerned occupies a central place. The punishment awarded has to be appropriate to its status as an offence. But the centrality of the offence is not denied, or belittled, even in forgiving, or in considering the forgivability of, the offence. To forgive an offence is not to annul, or cancel, its existence. Rather, it is to admit, or presuppose, that the forgiven person has done something wrong. One can be forgiven only if he is at least assumed, or believed, to be a wrongdoer. The act of forgiveness may, or rather would, in all likelihood, make him feel a bit better, or relieved, making his guilt-feeling cease to be tortuous, or become less tourtuous than what it was before his receiving the forgiveness. But he would not forget that he has been forgiven because he has done the wrong thing. That he has done it is a past fact and a past fact cannot be erased or obliterated. Punishing the wrongdoer is to take note of the fact that he did the crime, but so is to forgive him.

Forgiving is not like eating. If one eats a cake, the eaten cake ceases to exist. A forgiven wrongdoing, on the other hand, does not cease to exist, not does it cease to be a wrongdoing. What happens is that it ceases to arouse resentment in the victim, and thereby ceases to cause social discord between the two. However, some trace of the victim's memory of the offender's having wronged him may remain alive in his mind for some-time even after his having forgiven him, though he may not do to him anything which an unforgiving, resentful, person is likely to do.

Speaking from the side of the wrongdoer, it can be said that he too, after being forgiven, does not start disbelieving that he did the wrong, or believing that he is completely innocent. What happens is that his sense of guilt and the consequent repentance and agonising self-tourture cease to exist, or begin to fade out. All this depends, of course, on his belief that the forgiveness given to him is whole-hearted, or genuine, because, as it has been shown, forgiveness, as well as repentance, could be non-genuine, lukewarm, or merely strategic.

In an ideal retributive situation, when the wrongdoer receives the punishment he deserves, he would be expected to realise that he has received what he ought, that it would have been wrong even for him if he had not received it. He would not then have any grudge, or complaint, against the agency which has given him the punishment, no matter whether it is the person to whom he has done the moral wrong, or an external body authorised to attend to such offences. In such a situation, the social relation which existed between the wrongdoer and the wronged before the wrongdoing, and which got ruptured by the wrongdoing, is very likely to be restored. If the wrongdoer realises that something morally right has been done by giving him the punishment, — since it is morally right to appropriately punish one who has done something morally wrong, — he would have no reason to have strained relationship with the person he had wronged because of the latter's having been instrumental in getting him punished. Nor would the victim of the wrongdoing have any reason to continue having a strained relationship with the wrongdoer.

But the above kind of understanding even of an extremely fair retributive handling of a wrongdoing by the agency, or agencies, concerned is not always had by the offender, or by the victim. Sometimes the offender thinks he has been given a harsher, or the victim that he has been given a lighter, punishment than what he deserved. When either of the two things happen, there is no chance, or there is only a very bleak one, for the restoration of the pre-offence relationship between the two.

But sometimes it happens that a retributively conscientious

offender, even after having undergone his well-deserved punishment, retains a part of his sense of guilt, or moral deficiency, caused in him by his wrongdoing. Suppose *A* has returned home after completing his full term of imprisonment for having stolen the jewellery *B* had bought with the money he got by selling the only house he had. *B* bought the jewellery to be given as dowry for his daughter on the occasion of her marriage, and the theft of the jewellery not only led to the breaking of the marriage negotiation but forced him to get the daughter married to a much less desirable groom and that too after a lapse of some years. *A* realises his fault, considers his imprisonment his comeuppance, but still feels morally deficient or fallen whenever he thinks of what he did, and finds it difficult to stop thinking of it. Similarly, *B* too feels morally angry, even after having succeeded in getting *A* convicted, whenever he thinks of him, and he too cannot stop thinking of the past fact that because of the theft committed by *A* his daughter got ill-married. In such a case, the social relation between *A* and *B*, which got fractured as a result of *A*'s act of theft, would remain fractured even after *A* has been appropriately punished. But, if *A* is really sorry and repentant, and requests *B* to forgive him, saying he has been punished but still his sense of guilt is weighing heavily on his heart, and *B* being convinced of the sincerity of his feeling repentant, forgives him, his forgiveness can act as social and moral cement in rejoining their fractured relationship. What the punishment could not do, genuine forgiveness in all likelihood would.

This is what I meant by saying that, even after the wrongdoer has been properly punished, forgiveness may be called for to restore the pre-offence social relationship. Forgiveness can achieve this result because forgiving an offence implies that both the offended and the offender would henceforth cease to be hostile to, or estranged from, each other. The real point of forgiveness is not in being a substitute of punishment but in being some sort of a social as well as a moral cement. It works as a social cement because it repairs the fractured social relationship between the offender and the offended. It works as a moral cement because it makes both of them feel morally rehabilitated: the offender by freeing him of his sense of guilt and thereby establishing peace between the guilty and the guilt-condemning components of his being, the offended by freeing him .of his feeling of having been wronged and thereby making peace between the morally injured and the injury-resenting, i.e., the self-respecting, components of his being.

Forgiveness is thus a moral virtue because of its role as a social and moral cement. But not only for its being that. It does several other things besides. The offender, after being forgiven, may develop a sense of moral regard for the offended and not only a wish that he may not commit any offence in future, but also another wish that if anybody else offends him as he has done in the present case, he may also forgive his offender as his victim has forgiven him. If there is nothing else in their circumstances, or surroundings, which prompts them to think otherwise, both of them may realise, in an authentic way, that what has happend between them illustrates not only the truth that to err is human but also the other truth that to reactify an error is equally human.

In being forgiven the repentant wrongdoer gets what he deserves, since he deserves the forgiveness he is given in virtue of his being repentant, etc. The grant of forgiveness also meets the Kantian requirement of universalisability without self-contradiction. The forgiver's experiment in universalisation 'Let everyone like me forgive an offender, like the present one, who repents, etc.', would lead to no self-contradiction. Forgiveness is definitely a morally better way of dealing with a wrongdoing, or of overcoming moral anger, than the way of avenging the wrong by punishing the wrongdoer. The latter may prolong the enemity between the two parties. Forgiveness would definitely not do that.

One may not forgive his offender, or may even punish him, even when he meets all the conditions of being forgiven. Like any other virtue, forgiveness too is, what Kant calls, "moral strength of will".[14] Only he who has a certain amount of moral strength can forgive his offender. Therefore, one cannot be called a morally good person if he is always, or generally, unforgiving. This is illustrated in the ordinary use of 'unforgiving'. To call a man unforgiving is ordinarily to judge him to be morally deficient. That forgiveness may be

14. Quoted by J.B. Schneewind in his paper "Autonomy, Obligation, and Virtue: An Overview of Kant's Moral Philosophy", in Paul Guyer (ed.), *The Cambridge Companion to Kant*, (Cambridge University Press, 1993), p. 310.

misused, i.e., one may forgive an offender who does not deserve to be forgiven, is also possible. But this possibility holds good of any moral virtue whatsoever, e.g., of kindness, generosity, benevolence, etc. Therefore, it does not go against calling forgiveness a virtue. It is an obligatory, and not merely a supererogatory, virtue, as I have shown above, because it is wrong not to forgive an offender when he meets all the required conditions for being forgiven.

All along uptil now I have been discussing the use of forgiveness only in an inter-personal context. But we also have such phrases as 'You may forgive me for not paying attention to you when you came to my house to bless my newly born grandson, but I cannot forgive myself for this lapse', 'His father has forgiven him but he himself has not', 'Nobody else but I myself am responsible for tarnishing my reputation and for this I cannot forgive myself', 'For such a lapse you would surely have forgiven anybody else, that is why I say, forgive yourself and don't keep cursing yourself', etc. The use of the phrases 'forgiving myself', 'forgiving himself', 'forgiving yourself', etc., indicates that we do have a concept of self-forgiveness. It seems to me that it is a valid concept because there do occur situations in which we can correctly apply it, and that it can be explicated by using, with some adjustments, the conceptual structure of inter-personal forgiveness presented in this chapter.

An occasion for the use of self-forgiveness can arise when one wrongs somebody else, as well as when he wrongs himself. If *B* is not available to forgive *A* who has wronged him and *A* is repentant, etc., he may argue with himself as follows: 'Had *B* been available, seeing me so repentant and remorseful, he would have forgive me. Even I would have forgiven anybody else if he had done a similar wrong to me, and been repentant, etc., as I am. Why can't, or shouldn't, I then forgive myself, when I have made myself suffer a lot by sincerely repenting for what I have done?' An outsider also can argue with him on similar lines: 'The way you have made yourself miserable for having done *W* to *B* would surely have procured his forgiveness had he been alive. Rather, anybody, even you, would forgive a person so repentant as you are. Therefore, back up, forgive yourself'.

When one does something hurtful to his own self-interest, some damage to his own image of himself, or to his moral reputation, involving no wrongdoing to anybody else, a similar drama may be enacted in his mind. Suppose he has taken pains to build an image of himself as a morally upright person. He sits on a committee in which the case of the Chairman's wife for a prestigious award is being considered. In his view she does not deserve it. But all other members are in favour of giving her the award. Even if he declines to sign the award sheet, or gives a dissenting note, she will get it because the majority is in her favour. He too then signs the sheet, but later on repents and feels guilty for having been a party to a wrong decision. He feels that by this act of his he has wronged himself by damaging his own moral reputation, has made himself a corrupt person like other members of the committee who never had the reputation of being morally upright. There is no way now to get the decision changed, or even to add a dissenting note. He thus keeps brooding over the lapse, repents a lot, looses his sleep, feels no appetite, etc. In this situation he can assume the role of an observer looking at his own case as if it were somebody else's, as the Vedāntin's *sākṣī caitanya* (wittnessing consciousness) is supposed to do with regard to the performances of the empirical self (*jīva*). He may then decide that his lapse is not so great as to be unforgivable, or that his repentance, etc., and the consequential agonies he has suffered entitle him to be forgiven by himself because he himself is the victim of his offence. He then forgives himself which means making peace with himself. The guilty and the guilt-condemning aspects of his being make friends with each other, as the victim and the offender do, or are supposed to do, in a successful grant of forgiveness in an inter-personal situation. The self-introspective argument 'when I myself would forgive another person who has done a similar wrong to me and is repentant, etc., why can't I forgive myself?' is as sound as its corresponding one would be when the offender and the victim of his offence are two different persons.

It happens sometimes that one breaks a rule he has legislated for himself and considers it a serious moral lapse, a moral wrong done to himself by himself. Suppose the rule relates to sex: I will not indulge in any kind of sexual activity. But he fails, and then experiences feelings of shame and guilt and remorse, and repents very intensely for his failure. No wrong has been done to anybody else. But he thinks he has done to himself something very mean, and therefore falls in his own estimation. On self-argumention, he may conclude that his repentance, determination not to repent the act in future, etc., make him deserve forgiveness. Since he himself is the victim, the accuser of the fault, and the accused, forgiveness has to come from himself. Self-forgiveness is very much necessary in such cases because, if the repentant person does not forgive himself and none else can, he may do something extremely drastic and damaging to his own being. As the story goes, the famous Hindi poet Sūradāsa, originally Bilva Mangala, had prescribed for himself the rule 'No sex, not even a sexual desire'. But he did have the desire when he saw one day a charming village woman. The woman, or anybody else, knew nothing of what had happened to him, but he felt extremely guilty, ashamed, and repentant. He considered his guilt unforgivable, blamed his eyes, which saw the beautiful woman, for causing in him the attraction for her, and therefore made himself blind by piercing an iron rod into both of his eyes. It was since then that he was called Sūradāsa.

Self-forgiveness is possible because self-punishment, infliction of suffering on oneself by oneself, is possible. Self-punishment may even be physical, as in the case of Sūradāsa. Mental punishment is very common; one may keep brooding over his lapse and condemning himself for having done it for days and nights, causing very intense suffering to himself. Man has the capacity to do self-reflection, or self-criticism, and both, self-punishment and self-forgiveness, are born thereof, or are expressions of self-reflection, or of self-criticism. They are mechanisms bestowed by nature on us which help us in keeping ourselves on the right track and in having a unified being. Self-forgiveness too, like other-forgiveness, works as a cement, more precisely as a psychological cement. It unifies the wrongdoer self with the repenting self and enables the person concerned to live and move as an undivided moral agent, as an individual which really means an indivisible being.

8

Ethics in Professional Practice

Being a Good Professional, a Morally Good Professional, and a Morally Good Person

IMAGINE a dental surgeon *A* who is conveniently located for a patient *P*, is a nice gentleman, very courteous and considerate, in general, to his patients. But *P* does not consult him because he cannot take out the last of his upper molars without doing some surgery. It is not possible, he says, to catch it with pliers with the required grip to pull it out; therefore, some surgery is unavoidable. The other dentist *B*, on the other hand, does this work in a minute without even mentioning the word 'surgery'. But he looks only at the ailing tooth, and not at the person whom it ails. He pulls it out as smoothly, and also as impersonally, as a carpenter pulls out a pricking nail from the seat of a chair. *P* goes to him, though he has to wait, on some days, for hours to get his turn.

Imagine another dentist *C*, who is as conveniently located for *P* as is *A*, and has the reputation of being very competent and friendly with his patients. He also gives an advance appointment on telephone to a patient who does not want to wait for his chance in his clinic. But he is too commercial. The work, which B does in one sitting, he does in three sittings and charges three fees for it. *P* does not go to him. Mostly those go to him who are entitled to get their medical expenses reimbursed by their employers. They like him also because he is willing to give a (false) certificate of fees received without having done any treatment on payment of 10 per cent of the amount an employee gets reimbursed. Both are happy as *C* gets some money without rendering any service and the employee makes a saving of 90 per cent of the amount reimbursed.

A patient *R* goes to *D* who, in his watch-repairing shop, has a cubicle in which, as a side business, he provides dental treatment to the patients who come to him. *R* considers him a good doctor because his charges are nominal, and he behaves with a patient very cordially. Therefore, a good number of poor, and even some not very poor, people, use his services, but *P* does not, though he finds it not so easy to consider *R*'s going to *C* totally unjustified.

What has emerged from the above narrative is as follows:

A is a *morally good man* but not a good professional because he lacks the expertise which the dental profession requires of a dental surgeon. *B* is a *good professional* because he has the expertise but is not as good a person as a patient would wish him to be; he has a completely objective attitude towards his patients in the sense that he treats them as objects, or things, and not as persons. But patients go to him because he is affordable. *C* too is a *good professional* because he is really competent, and amiable too, but is not a *morally good professional* because he is not professionally honest; to earn more money he does in three sittings what can be done in one and gives false certificates of fees received. *D* is not professionally qualified but still he attracts patients who cannot afford to consult a professionally qualified one. It is obvious how greatly a patient would wish that there was a dentist who was professionally competent and honest, not too expensive, and not too selfish to treat his patients simply as sources of income.

Three interrelated things, or sets of things, are, thus, the prominent components of a professional: (a) expertise in his profession, (b) some sort of relationship between him and the recipient of his services, and (c) his right to charge some remuneration for his services to their recipient. If these items are explicated, they would go a great way to unpack at least a large part of the contents of the concept of a professional person. This is what I intend to do in this chapter. Since the three items are interrelated, a discussion of anyone of them would criss-cross with that of one or both of the remaining two.

A professional man is obviously one who has acquired expertise in some area of human concern or importance in virtue of which he can render some services to those who need them. These services are considered to be useful and people needing and willing to utilise them are available in the society. But every expert need not be a professional. He would be one if he charges some fee for the service he renders. His fee does not have to be paid by the recipient of his service. It may as well be paid by some other agency, for example, by a government, a cooperative, a charitable institution, or a friend, *et al*. It may even be nominal, but some fee he must charge for his expertise if he is to be called a professional of any sort. A singer may have been trained like a professional and may even sing as well as, or better than, a professional singer. But if he sings only for pleasure, his own or his beloved's, and never charges any fee from anybody for his singing, we would not call him a professional singer. If we anytime call him a professional singer, we simply mean that he has the professional, i.e., technical qualification or expertise which is required of a professional singer.

What is normally done by a professional may sometimes be done, and done tolerably well, by a non-professional. For example, homoeopathy is generally practised by professionally trained homoeopaths, but sometimes even by some non-professionals. A professor of philosophy may prescribe, and even distribute, homoeopathic medicines every Sunday morning, or even every morning, to those who come to him for treatment. It may even be true that his homoeopathy is better than his philosophy. Similarly, what is generally done as something non-professional may be taken up by some as a profession. Very many young people play football as non-professional players; they play it for pleasure, or as it is commonly said, for fun. But some of them become professional football players. Here again, a non-professional footballer may be as competent as, or even more competent than, a professional one. Normally a professional *X* is taken to be more competent than a non-professional *Y*, though it does not always have to be the case.

What makes one a good professional is very largely his expertise. He may have very good manners, may even be a good person, but if he is not an expert in his area, he cannot be called a good professional, as is the case with the dentist *A*. Being well-mannered, being a decent person, has got its own importance. In fact, everyone ought to be decent, and therefore one cannot take any special pride in being decent, no matter whether he is, or is not, a professional.

On the relevant expertise of a professional we cannot, therefore, compromise. And, other things being equal, or sometimes even being a little unequal, we prefer an expert to a non-expert, or to a lesser expert. That is why *P* goes to *B* who is a better expert than *A*, even though he is inconvenient and too impersonal. He is inconvenient because he does not give prior appointment on telephone, and is too impersonal because he seems to treat his tooth, and him too, like a thing; he does not seem to consider his decayed tooth as a source of human suffering, or him as a human being. But he prefers him also because he is an expert who suits his pocket. It is his economy which deters him from going to *C*. One whose economy is better than his, or who does not have to pay from his own pocket, may not do what he does. He whose economy is worse than *P*'s, and who has neither the time to wait for hours, nor the ability to distinguish between a professional expert and a quack, may not think of going to anybody other than *D*, the watch-repairer with a dental cubicle. One may also choose the latter because of his carelessness, laziness, or sheer thoughtlessness. But that would be another matter.

Ordinarily when we talk of professional services rendered by, or expected from, professional experts, we mean useful or desirable services, sevices which are, in a moral sense, worth having, or at least those which it is not wrong to have. Gewirth considers it a defining characteristic of a professional person "that he or she uses this expertise to provide valued services to other persons"[1] and on the next page of the same paper he makes it clear that the ends of professional activities and roles are "admittedly desirable". Bassford too avers that

> Professions exist in order to provide human services, to help make the quality of human life better. This is the context in which its role-specific norms are developed, and

1. Alan Gewirth, "Professional Ethics : The Separatist Thesis", *Ethics*, Vol. 96, pp. 282-300.

> it is the context which must be kept in mind whenever they are applied.[2]

But it seems to me that having a desirable end cannot be called a defining characteristic of a profession, nor can it be said that professional norms are always, in fact, developed to make the quality of human life better. We can, of course, and I think we should, make it a normative requirement that a professional expertise, or service, ought to be used to achieve a desirable end. The snag in it is that this requirement can be made of every human enterprise and therefore, one may say, there is not much of a point in making it one of professions. But since some professions have been specifically developed to make human life better, for example, the medical profession, it is worth reiterating, when one notices a medical professional behaving callously with a sick man under his care and thereby adding to his suffering, that the objective of the noble profession he belongs to is to reduce human suffering and not to increase it.

I am not in favour of including having a desirable end in the very definition, or concept, of a professional. If we do that, we would not be able to distinguish between a desirable, morally oriented and an undesirable, immorally oriented profession. The latter would then not be a profession and therefore not an immoral or ignoble profession, because we would be making, by definition, its occurrence impossible. It may be suggested that no profession has a morally undesirable end; only some member, or members, of it may have it. It is true that most of the professions are morally oriented, in the sense that their members are expected or required to provide morally desirable, or premissible, services to their clients. And, this also is true that some members of them, for some monetary or political gain, provide morally undesirable, or forbidden, services to their clients. For example, though the aim of the teaching profession is quite noble, because it is to impart knowledge to students, some college teachers do form an intra-state, or inter-state, group and arrange for the award of doctorate degrees to aspirants who do no research, by getting their dissertations compiled from some others,

2. H.A. Bassford, 'The Basis of Medical Ethics' in Macniven, Don (ed.), *Moral Expertize : Studies in Practical and Professional Ethics,* (Routledge), 1990. p. 140.

or from some books, and charge heavy amounts for their sevices.

But it is not only empirically possible that a profession has intentionally been developed with an immoral objective, but there do exist such professions. It is common knowlede that there are professional *thugs*, pickpocketers, dacoits, booth-capturers, sex-touts, bribe-managers, sometimes called contact-men or middlemen, etc. Some of these professionals make very well-organised groups and operate on national or international levels. Some of these groups have a rigid code of conduct which each one of their members has to follow. For example, I am told that booth-capturers are strictly forbidden by their organisation to overdrink in the night in which the actual operation is to be carried out because, if they do, they may oversleep, or lose control over their weapon-manipulating muscles, leading to their failure in achieving their objective. Even such professionals acquire the requisitic kind of skill and expertise to achieve their goals. They charge fees for their services, and their services are valued by those who hire them. Their fees vary, like other professionals', in accordance with their reputation and the risk involved in the execution of the intended work. All such people can quite correctly be called professionals. There is nothing in the concept of a profession which restricts the application of the term to an enterprise with a morally, or non-morally, noble aim. But since I am concerned in this chapter with professional ethics, or moral issues relevant to professional life, I shall take my examples from, or refer to, only such professions which avowedly have morally desirable goals.

The agency to which a professional is responsible can very even among professionals belonging to the same profession. A private professional medical practitioner is obligated to attend to the patients he has received his fee from and is responsible, or accountable, to them for providing the services he has been paid for. A doctor in the employment of a private, or public, agency is primarily responsible to his employer for providing services to those for attending to whose ailments he has been appointed and is being paid.

The non-charging, philanthropic, physician, on the other hand, one may say, is not responsible to anyone for providing to him, or to someone else, his services; he has no obligation to the patients he treats, nor to any other agency for treating them, because he charges no fee from any source. In a sense it may be true, but it is not wholly true.

Quite obviously an expert can choose to charge, or not to charge, fee for his expert service. But has he the right to do with his expertise *whatever* he wants to do? Certainly he has no right to use it to do something morally (or even socially, or legally) wrong as nobody has that right. But has he the right to let it remain completely unused? One can do that if (a) he leads a completely idle, unproductive, life, or (b) engages himself in a pursuit in which its use is not called for. Anyone's leading a completely unproductive life is a very remote possibility, but obviously it is not impossible. One who has enough to eat and drink may decide to do nothing productive after graduating, say, as a lawyer. He does not need to earn anything and therefore may not want to be a professional lawyer, or to do anything else; he has no philanthropic motivation to provide legal aid to those who are too poor to pay for it, or even to provide some other sort of help to anybody. Therefore, he may decide not to join the bar. And, since he has no other interest, he may not engage himself in any productive occupation.

The possibility of a completely unproductive life raises the general moral question (a) 'Has anybody, who can lead a productive professional life, the moral right to lead a completely unproductive one?' Related to it is the context-specific moral question: (b) 'Has one, who has an expertise, say, as an engineer, to provide useful services to some needy people, the moral right to decide not to use that expertise, and do something else, say, to become a magistrate, in which occupation its use is not required?'

(a) As regards the general moral question, we can straightaway give a negative answer to it: Nobody who *can* engage himself in some productive enterprise has the moral right to remain totally idle. If one has the talent to acquire a certain capability, developing his talent and thereby acquiring the capability is, slightly adapting Kant, his duty to himself. If he acquires the capability and the capability can be used to provide some useful services to the society, it is his duty to the society to provide them to some members of it, with, or without, some appropriate remuneration, depending upon certain conditions relevant to his providing the services. It is his social duty, i.e., duty to others, because, in the development of his talents and in the consequent acquisition of his capabilities, society makes some sort of an investment by making available to him some of its resources, human as well as non-human, without utilising which he could not have developed his talents, and acquired the consequential capabilities. Therefore, the skilled professional owes a debt to his society, which he should, or ought to, repay by providing his services to those members of the latter who need them. It may be that he does not provide the services he can in virtue of his expertise, but some other ones. To discuss how far it is justified to do that naturally takes us to (b), the context-specific question.

(b) When an engineer competes in the reequired test and beccomes a district magistrate, he does provide some services to his society. Is it morally right for him to become a magistrate when his society has invested a lot in his education as an engineer? Since he serves his society as a magistrate, he is not like the idle affluent, and can claim to be doing his social duty by the work he does as a magistrate. His position can be defended on the ground that it is morally permissible to change one's profession when his interest changes. The skilled person has to repay to his society for what the society has invested in his acquisition of the skill. But he can repay even in terms of services which do not involve the use of that skill if, because of a change of interest, he has taken a job, or profession, which does not involve the use of that skill. Not to permit him to change his profession would amount to curtailing his freedom to choose his style of life. It may also be counter-productive. To force anyone to do what he is not interested in is not likely to deliver the goods.

A change of interest may take place in a natural way, or it may be deliberately acquired because of certain circumstantial factors. Suppose a doctor, holding the position of a civil surgeon, has to deal with a large number of medico-legal cases. In course of time he gets more and more interested, in a natural way, in the legal aspects of these cases, and then changes his profession from medicine to law. Or, noticing the power and authority wielded by a magistrate, he may deliberately acquire the motivation to become an Indian administrative officer, and may ultimately become one, giving up his job of a civil surgeon. Both of these possiblities are open to a professional and neither of them can be called morally impermissible. Sometimes when professionals of a sort start giving up that profession and opting for some other, a law may be enacted to ban the change if the profession concerned is considered socially useful; or, it may be made so lucrative that competent candidates get attracted by it and those who are already in it do not like to give it up for joining any other. Banning professional mobility is in general wrong because (a) it stultifies growth of talents by not allowing one to leave his present profession in which he is no more interested, and (b) it forecloses the possibility of a profession being enriched by the entry into it of an alien professional who has some different sort of talents from those of its own professionals.

To say that one ought to serve his society because he can, or has the ability to, do that may seem like deducing 'ought' from 'can', and therefore contravening Hume's law. But that is not the case. The argument already informally stated above, when made explicit, would have the following form:

> Everyone who is capable of doing something useful has a social duty, i.e., a duty to his society (because the acquisition or development of the capability has been made possible by using some societal resources made available to him by the society).
>
> A professional is capable of providing some useful professional services to the society. Therefore, he has a social duty to provide those services to the society, i.e., to the needy members of it.

The major premise of the argument enables it to fully conform to Hume's law.

A professional is, thus, obligated to repay, by means of his services, his debt to the society which he owes to the latter because of the latter's investment in his acquisition of the skill he possesses. This is true of that professional also who is professionally qualified, but works like a non-professional insofar as he does not charge any fee for his services. He is not directly obligated to his clients because he does not charge any fee from them, or from any other agency. But he has the general obligation to his society, like the fee-charging one, for the society's investment in his training. Anybody who does some free social service does not do it completely on gratis: he repays to his society for what he has received from it. But since he does not charge any payment, his service is of a higher moral order than that of fee-charging one. If the latter thinks that he can charge any exorbitant amount as his fee because the expertise he is using is his, he forgets that he has not acquired the skill single-handedly but with the cooperation of the society he belongs to. Therefore, the society too has a claim on the use of his expertise which he can satisfy by rendering his services in a socially desirable, or beneficial, manner. This he would not be doing when he would be charging exorbitant fees. All those professionals who do that are more or less guilty of being *ungrateful* to the society which has contributed to their being what they are, and of being *exploitative* with their clients who come to them for their expert or specialised services.

A professional plays the role of an obliger to his clients. Even after paying his fee, when a patient gets himself treated, or even examined, by his doctor to his satisfaction, he feels obliged to the latter. This happens in professional-client relationships. In a sense the client buys the professional's sevices, but still he says 'Thank you' to him and the professional takes it as a courtesy he deserves. The reason for the client's feeling obliged is that the professional has an expertise which he does not have, and therefore he has to take the help of the professional. In the majority of cases, particularly in India and in other developing countries like India, the client does not have the ability to understand what the professional does to help him. He does not understand the nature of the disease he suffers from, the composition of the medicines he is asked to take, the reports of the pathological, or other sort of , tests, etc. He may not understand even if his doctor is kind enough to explain these things to him. Similarly, an accused in a criminal case does not understand the legal strategies and procedures which his lawyer adopts, or the way he conducts his case. He too has to have faith in his lawyer, just as the patient has to have in his doctor. The professional, therefore, occupies a superior position *vis-a-vis* his client who is dependent on him. Although he pays for his services, he cannot ask him to give such and such sort of services, and not of some other sorts, because he does not know which sort of services he really needs to be out of the muddle he is in.

The superiority of the professional's position gives him the power to exploit the client if he wants to and he can exploit him, i.e., extract money from him, for doing, or getting done by some others, things which are not necessary. The doctor may ask him to get some tests done by his wife who runs a pathological-radiological laboratory, by prescribing costlier medicines in place of their cheaper equivalents, and asking him indirectly to buy from his son's drug store because they are not available in any other medical shop, etc. The lawyer may prolong the peroid of brief and argumentation. Instead of arguing the case for two days which would have been enough, he may prolong it for five days and charge five days' fees, etc. All this shows that in a professional life there is a large scope for the professional to adopt immoral practices to extract money from his client, without letting him know that he is being cheated. Therefore, the lawyer may receive from the client he has cheated, at the conclusion of the case in his favour, not only some gift, in kind or cash, over and above his regular fees, but also a really grateful 'Thank you'.

Because of easily available opportunities of adopting immoral practices in professional transactions, it is necessary that professionals have a very high general morality. Only he whose general morality, i.e., morality as an individual, is very high would not adopt direct or indirect methods of extracting money from his clents. This is only to assert the obvious truth that only an individual of high morality would not (or, very rarely would) succumb to using immoral strategies to increase his income.

There is another way in which an unscrupulous professional may improve his status, social as well as financial, by using immoral means. For example, being in an obliging position, a lawyer may help a minister out of some legal proceedings he has been very rightly caught in. For example, although he has really been guilty of getting a political rival killed and therefore made an accused, a clever laywer by discovering, or cooking up, some lacunae here and there in the complaint, or in the police report, may get the minister acquitted, and thereby is made by the latter, or because of his influence, the chairman of the city's Board For the Grant of Loan for Constructing New Houses. He then may contribute, in collaboration with the acquitted minister, to spreading immoral practices in the functioning of the Board too, and thereby add to his as well as to the minister's coffer.

A professional, we have seen, has to have the expertise required by the nature of his profession and to use it in a manner which accords with the ethics of the latter. But the standard of expertise is relative to what may be called the state of the craft, in the sense that what is considered to be adequate expertise today may not be so considered after a few years because of new findings, or advancements, in the subject, or area, of specialisation concerned. This means that he ought to keep his expertise updated. If his expertise is not up to date, he may do some irreparable harm to his client by trying to identify, or solve, his probelm on the basis of his outdated knowledge, or by using methods or techniques which have been discarded since long because of their damage-causing long-range effects. In the case of some professions the damage done is palpable, for example, when the prolonged use of a medicine, which has been de-recommended because of its carcinogenic effects discovered by recent researches, is prescribed by an unupdated physician to a patient and damages the retina of the latter's right eye. But in some others, the damage is quite serious but is not easily noticeable even to the victim of the outdated expertise of a professional. For example, a professor of philosophy, who has not read any work in ethics published after the Second World War, by teaching a course on recent ethics, in all likelihood would cause a serious damage to the mental habits of his students (unless they distrust him and work on their own, which is very unlikely to happen). This sort of damage may not be noticed by his students and may even remain unnoticed by them all their life. It would not be less difficult to disabuse such a student's mind of the not-worthy-to-be-learnt things his unupdated professor's teaching has put into his mind than to undo the harmful effects caused to the patient's retina by faulty medication.

We can, therefore, say that a professional's keeping abreast of recent advances in the field of his specialisation is not a luxury, but a requirement of professional ethics. He can absolve himself from meeting it only if he is well aware of the limits of his expertise *and* has the moral good sense of not taking up an assignment he cannot properly handle even if it is highly lucrative, or socially prestigious. But he cannot absolve himself from the obligation of acquiring or developing the expertise required by the performance of duties he has himself chosen to fulfil, or of those he has to fulfil in virtue of the office or position he holds. If he has chosen to teach modern logic, or has been appointed to teach it, he cannot justify his remaining unacquainted with modern developments in logic. If he makes no effort to update his study of logic, he is not simply incompetent but a moral defaulter.

There are two other important ways in which a professional may default. One of them consists in (a) the non-use of his expertise and the other in (b) an injudicious use of it.

(a) By the non-use of expertise I mean not using it with the commitment and seriousness with which it should be used. For example, an academician may have the required expertise or competence to write a good paper, as per the standards of his subject, on the theme of a seminar he has consented to participate in. But he presents a lousy one, written only in a couple of days, in a cavalier spirit, though he knows that for making his participation possible the organisers of the seminar have to spend a sum consisting of some thousands of rupees which ultimately belongs to the public exchequer. The academician himself does not take any part of the money spent on him but he is the *cause* of the wasteful expenditure and therefore as much guilty as he would have been if he had swindled it. In addition, he is guilty of betraying the trust his co-professional organisers had put in him: they believed and expected that he would present a good piece since they knew that he had the competence to do that. If, on the other hand, the organisers invited him knowing that he would not do a good job, it would mean that they too are guilty of professional immorality. There can be several varieties of such immoralities in any professional practice.

(b) A professional makes an injudicious use of his expertise if he uses it for purposes which go against the accredited norms of his profession. One of the academic goals of a professional academician, say, a professor of philosophy, is to help, by his teaching and/or writing, his students, or those who read his work, develop and improve their creative talents. But if he writes materials which provide to students a short-cut to passing their examination, without reading the standard books prescribed, without developing and exercising their talents, he would be making an injudicious, professionally undesirable, use of his expertise. By producing such writings he would be causing to the mental health of their readers a harm in no way less serious than what a professional pharmaceutical manufacturer would be causing to the physical health of those who take the stimulant produced by him which works as an instant energiser but damages some of the cells of their brain.

What I want to emphasise here is that acquiring and keeping updated his professional expertise is not only necessary for enabling a professional to earn his fee, but it is also his moral duty. And, so is his honest use of the expertise in the best interest of his client. This means that its non-use, non-serious or irresponsible use, and injudicious use, all would be morally wrong, as much according to his professional, as according to general, ethics.

One joins a profession, i.e., becomes a professional, to earn his living. Therefore, his charging the recipient of his services some fee is reasonable. Whether he charges a moderate, or an exorbitant, amount depends on his general moral culture, or on how much in demand his services are. Normally when one pays for a service, he may feel that he has no reason to be grateful or obliged to the person who has provided him the service because he has bought it. And, in a sense, the supplier of the service may be expected to feel grateful to its recipient because he has given him an opportunity to sell his service. But in the case of some professions, for example in the medical profession, the client very greatly values the sevice he expects and gets from the professional. The sick man is very greatly concerned about his illness, does not know how to get rid of it, and the physician has the expertise to help him out of his malaise. He, therefore, approaches the physician with trust not only in his expertise but also in his good will. This is a situation in which the professional may, if his general moral culture is not of a high order, treat his patient as a thing, or an object, a means or source of income, and not as a person. The Kantian principle 'Do not treat any person only as a means' is very relevant to a professional situation in which one person seeks the help of another.

To treat a patient as a person does not mean getting personally involved in his sick condition. A physician cannot work as a professional if he takes the death of a patient under his treatment as a personal loss or tragedy. It only means to treat the patient as a reactive or responsive being who, or whose being, responds not only to the medicine he takes as prescribed by the physician, but also to the latter's behaviour, his words addressed to him, his attitudes towards him, his manners and ways of dealing with him and his ailments, his overall concern for his recovery, etc. When he satisfies our normal expectations in these respects, we say that he takes personal interest in his patient, which is the same as saying that he treats his patient as a person. The physician's treating him as a person, i.e., respecting his personhood, is not a favour done to him but a fitting reactive response which he deserves because of reposing his trust in the physician's ability and sincerity. To repose this sort of trust in him is to do him honour both as a professional and as a person. To expect, or even demand, in return, that he treat the patient as a person, and not as an object, is nothing but fully fair. To come up to this expectation the professional needs to have a mature and well-developed moral sense, i.e., comprehension of his general as well as professional obligations and a strong moral will to fulfil them.

To treat his client as a person, which he is, is a moral requirement a professional cannot flout without demeaning his moral status as a professional. That is, to be a morally good professional it is necessary that he treats the recipients of his professional services as persons, as ends in themselves, deserving respect in virtue of just being persons, irrespective of their social, religious, political, or economic status. This means that expertise may make one a good professional, but alone it does not make him a morally good professional. To qualify for being the latter, he has to treat his clients not as means, or objects, but as persons. To be a morally good person he does not have to be a professional. But if one is a professional, then, if he is not a morally good professional, he would not be a morally good person. His moral deficiency in his professional performance would adversely affect his general status as a moral agent (or person). If a professional is unaware of his professional deficiency, or is aware of it but still undertakes responsibilities to fulfil which he does not have the required competence, he would be a poor, even morally poor, professional. On the other had, a weak professional would be a good moral agent if he is morally good in other respects and takes up only such cases which he can competently handle.

There are, however, some contextual, or empirical factors in the case of some professions which make it difficult for the professionals to qualify to be called morally good professionals. I have in mind, in this connection, particularly the legal profession. The moral norm of the judge is obviously to award to both the parties of a case the fairest possible judgement in terms of the relevant laws. The aim of each one of the parties is to get the most favourable judgement no matter whether or not it also is the fairest judgement. Even if *M* has committed the murder of *N*'s brother, his aim would be to get acquitted, or get the minimum punishment, and *N*'s to get *M* most severely punished. Both *M* and *N* would hire lawyers with their respective aims in view. What should be, in such cases, the moral norm of the lawyers, the legal professionals? If a lawyer's norm is to present, say, *M*'s case in such a manner that he gets the fairest possible judgement from the court, which may even be a death-sentence, then *M* would feel that he has been cheated by his lawyer. Such a lawyer is not likely to get clients who have been charged of having done some crimes. Rather, he may not get any client if it becomes widely known that he does not present his client's case with the intention to get the case decided in the most favourable way for the client. But if he does the latter, his professional norm, in at least a few cases, would be morally indefensible, or immoral. For example, he may be trying his best to get *M*, a murderer, honourably acquitted. Lawyers may say that their aim is to help the court in giving to their clients the fairest possible judgement, but in practice it turns out that they aim at helping their clients to get the most favourable judgement. This situation can improve only if all, or the majority of, lawyers have as their professional norm the award, to their clients, of the fairest possible judgement, which may, or may not, be a favourable judgement. It would also improve if all, or the majority of the litigants, have acquired the moral maturity to wish for the fairest possible judgement, and not necessarily, for a favourable one. The chances of either one of the two possibilities becoming real are very bleak. There may be some other professions with a similar handicap in keeping their norms morally high. But what I have said here does not mean that no legal professional or practitioner is, or can be, a good moral professional.

Professional ethics seems to be an ethics of compromise. The professional has to serve his client. Some clients would not seek his services if he is not willing to provide them the required services on the ground that they involve the adoption of some immoral, or morally impermissible, measures. Therefore, he may make a compromise, and accept even such clients in serving whom he has to do what appear to him some minor immoralities. But once he starts to make compromises, it is difficult to say that he would not take up cases which involve doing some major immoralities. It is this which litigants say in their own way when they say that, whatever be the nature of one's crime, he would surely get a lawyer to defend him in the court.

Some legal experts even think that the professional norm of a lawyer is not to help the judge in giving a fair judgement but to use his legal expertise to procure for his client a favourable judgement. If we accept this view, we would have also to accept that sometimes something may be professionally right, e.g., trying to get a murderer acquitted by using legal loopholds in the complaint, which is palpably wrong as per ordinary, or general, morality. I have denied this position. It seems to me that the right thing to say of such cases would be that defending a murderer may be prudentially right, i.e., right from the point of view of the lawyer's self-interest to earn money. But it is wrong not only according to ordinary, but also, professional, morality, i.e., the morality of the legal profession. To make what is ordinarily wrong professionally right seems to be revolting to our moral common sense. Nobody can have the (moral) permission to do what is morally wrong, or even to do what he thinks or believes to be morally worng. This means that a lawyer's advising his client to tell a lie in the court, after his taking the oath that he would tell the truth and only the truth, in order to get him acquitted, or to get his opponent convicted, should be considered wrong not only according to ordinary ethics, but also according to the ethics of his profession.

It is possible, however, that the internal rules of a socially accepted profession make an action right which, according to ordinary ethics, is wrong. Take, for example, the profession of priesthood. Suppose a religion prescribes animal sacrifice to attain a specific end, say, the recovery of one's son from a serious illness. Its priest advises a sick youngman's father to perform the ceremony of sacrificing a goat to please a deity, and supervises the ceremony of killing the animal as per the required set of rituals. This action is obviously morally wrong because it is the killing of an innocent animal. But the priest and his client would say it is right. It is professionally right for the priest, one may say, to have given the advice and supervised its implementation. But the root of this alleged rightness lies in the religion which prescribes animal sacrifice, and not in the profession of priesthood. A religious fundamentalist, who holds that a religious consideration can override an ethical consideration, would call it right. A secularist, who may even be a religious person, say in the Buddhist way,* who considers an ethical consideration overriding all other, non-ethical, considerations, would say that it is wrong in spite of its being prescribed by the religion concerned. It can also be said that, if the rules of a profession make an action right (or wrong) which is, as per ordinary ethics, morally wrong (or right), it would imply that there is something wrong also with the rules of the profession, or with the preofession itself.

There is a moral risk in conceiving a professional norm as permitting doing something which is otherwise, i.e., in non-professional life, morally wrong, or morally not right. For example, if we say that the professional norm of a lawyer is to try to get for his client the most favourable judgement by using any means he considers appropriate, then we are conceiving the norm as permitting the use of even immoral means. The only reason for conceiving it this way is that the lawyer has made a contract, or entrered into an agreement, with his client to give him legal help in the case he is

* See chapter 6 above.

involved in. But if a contract to provide legal help authorises the lawyer to use any means, even an immoral means like advising him to tell a lie, then we cannot forbid, in any profession, the use of an immoral means, even one of the vilest kind. Moreover, such a conception of a professional norm can be held only if one holds the view that a means does not affect the moral character of the end it is used to attain. This is a wrong conception of the means-end relationship. A victory of any sort, even a legal one, attained with the use of immoral means is of an inferior moral quality in comparison to one attained with the use of moral means.* A norm or goal which in immoral, or infected with immorality through the means used, cannot be the norm or goal of any professional, as it cannot be the norm or goal of anybody.

Some professional groups have prepared their pofessional codes of conduct which their members have to follow. Let us call such a code of conduct the professional praxis of the group concerned. For example, it is one of the principles, or conventions, of the medical profession that a pathologist, who examines the blood of a patient under the treatment of a physician, should not comment on the line of treatment adopted by the latter, or suggest medicines in the light of his blood report. Normally a pathologist follows this convention, but largely because of the fear that, if he comments on the line of treatment the physician has adopted, sooner or later the latter would know of it and then would not send any patient of his to him for any pathological test. The pathologist's motive is purely prudential, and not moral, and therefore it may not operate when there is no danger of his comment's being known to the attending physician. It was an ethical convention among university teachers that one, who was to conduct the *viva voce* examination of a doctoral candidate, would not accept any gift, even a tea, or dinner, from the examinee before the examination or on the day of the examination even after the examination had been held. But no punitive action was to result if this convention was not observed by an examiner. It was left to the professional conscience of the examiner. Nowadays, when professional conscience of the university teacher has become highly anaemic, if not completely dead, this convention is generally

* See my *Karma, Causation, and Retributive Morality* (ICPR), chapter 18.

flouted and its flouting is not even noticed by many as something morally wrong. Only a few, whose general morality is very high, do not flout it, or see its flouting as flouting a professional principle.

A professional code of conduct is limited in its application because it is applicable only to the members of the profession concerned. For example, the principle about the pathologist's not commenting on the physician's prescription applicable only to the members of the medical profession. So is the one about an examiner's not enjoying the examinee's hospitality applicable only to university teachers, or to those who can be examiners of doctoral dissertations. It is not impossible that a professional observes his professional code but is pretty loose in observing some rules or principles of general morality. But the fact of the matter is that one who is strict about observing the rules of general morality would also, in all likelihood, be strict about observing those of his professional code. If one's general morality is strong, he would, in all likelihood, observe his professional code even when it hurts his self-interest; if it is weak, he may flout it when it suits him. A professional code is formulated to ensure that the members of the profession may do their professional work without interference or obstruction, direct or indirect, from other co-professionals. This is nothing but to protect the liberty of a professional to function as a professional; i.e., to protect it from direct or indirect onslaught from other co-professionals. The principle of letting an individual function as a free agent, as long as he is not tending to function in a morally undesirable way, is a principle of general morality. In fact, every principle or rule of a professional code of conduct can be shown to be grounded in some principle or rule of general morality.

To be a professional is to voluntarily assume or occupy a social role. It is not necessary that some special ceremony is done to mark an individual's assumption of his professional role. By deciding to be a private practitioner and opening a clinic, or by joining a private or government hospital, a medical graduate assumes the role of a medical professional. By joining a college as a lecturer in philosophy one assumes the role of a teacher of philosophy. To assume a role is to own or admit that one has incurred a set of rights and duties. To do that one does not have to make a public declaration, or sign a formal document. To be a medical professional is to have the right to ask his patient some questions about his ailment which a non-medical may not have, and to be obligated to attend to his ailments, no matter whether his remuneration comes from the patient, or from some other agency. Similarly, for one to be a teacher of philosophy is to have the right to examine his students' performance and to be obligated to teach philosophy to them. To be a morally good professional is to play one's role morally well, i.e., to use his rights judiciously and to fulfil his obligations conscientiously.

A distinction is generally made between assumed or acquired roles and the roles one is born into. For example, one acquires the role of a lawyer and is born into the role of a son. It is his biological relation with his parents which makes him their son. He cannot cease to be their son, but if he wants to, he can cease to function as a lawyer and assume some other social role. But he may not do what a son, in his society, is expected or required to do, in a normative sense, for his parents, and then we may say that he does not play the role of a son. This is so because, with every role, whether it is, or it is not, rooted in a biological relation, there is associated what Downie calls "a cluster of rights and duties with some sort of social function"[3]. One can cease to occupy, in a full-fledged sense, a role by ceasing to perform the relevant duties, or disowning them as his duties, as well as by being divested of the relevant rights. One does not play his role as a son if he does not do his duties, or disowns to have any duty, towards his parents because of something done by them. In case his parents divest him of his right to inherit their property because of his having married against their wish, even if he does his duties towards them, he would not be said to be having, in a full-fledged sense, his role of being their son. Similarly, one would not be having, in a full-fledged sense, his role as a college teacher if he is divested of his right to examine his students' answer papers, or if he does not do his duty of teaching them the subject assigned to him.

One can, thus, be said to be playing his role as a professional only if he enjoys the rights and performs the duties which go with his profession. He may also have some other role, or roles to

3. R.S. Downie, *Roles and Values : An Introduction to Social Ethics*, (Methuen, 1970), p. 128.

perform, and they may be acquired, or natural. By and large, every individual has to perform a number of roles, for example, those of being a neighbour, a spouse, a section-head in his office, a member of his area's welfare committee, etc. But what would make him a good professional is his justified use of his rights and fulfilment of his obligations. His performance of his other roles, along with that of his professional role, would count in our overall rating of him as an individual, but the former would not make him a good professional if his performance of his professional role is not up to the mark. It may seem, then, that if an individual performs all his roles well, we cannot refuse to call him, in the moral sense of the term, a good person. But this need not always be the case because there are certain things which are not covered by role-performance and which count in the overall rating of one's personhood. For example, having politeness, courteousness, amiable manners, etc., do not come under the duties of any specific role, but they count in our grading of a person.

Because of the nature of his specific job, a professional may have a right to do something which others may not have. For example, a doctor has the right to examine the naked body of a patient if the nature of the latter's ailment requires him to do that. Nobody else has this right. If one asks anyone else to stand naked before him, we would call it wrong, even morally wrong, while admitting that it is morally right for the doctor to do that. Such cases make some philosophers hold that something which is wrong in ordinary, or general, ethics, may be right in professional ethics. But this is not really the case, not even in the above example. This example is one of means-end relationship. The doctor's end is to properly diagnose the patient's ailment. That is a bonafide professional end, and one in the interest of the patient. To achieve that end the doctor needs to examine the naked body of the patient. In fact, the patient has come to him for getting his ailment properly diagnosed and treated. And, the means, wanting to see the patient's naked body, in itself is neither morally right nor wrong. What makes it right or wrong is the motive or intention of the person concerned. This is as true in ordinary ethics, or in non-professional life, as it is in professional life. Gāndhārī wanted to see Duryodhana, her eldest son, naked to make his whole body invulnerable to any kind of assault, and that was as noble a desire as a desire could be.

A professional person is not just a professional person; he is an ordinary individual too. Professional life is a part of ordinary life, and a professional works under the general cover of ordinary ethical practice. Whatever he does is as much subject to general moral supervision as what a non-professional does. The only difference between the professional and the non-professional life is that the kind of things a professional has to do may not be required of, or relevant to, what a non-professional does, or is required to do. Every person is a moral agent under the governance of general morality. In this sense every person has his ethical identity, as every citizen of a country has his national identity. On adopting a profession and in practicing it he develops his professional identity. But in doing that he does not lose his general, ordinary, ethical identity. That is why professional practice, or ethics, cannot make morally right what is morally wrong in ordinary, general ethics, or ethical practice.

For anyone to adopt a profession is *ipso facto* to acknowledge that the obligations accruing from the adoption are binding on him. This means that it would be irrational, or wrong, for him not to fulfil any of these obligations. But since, even after adopting the profession, the professional as a person retains his general ethical identity, he may reflect back on these obligations. If the profession he has adopted is morally undesirable, he may find that a professional obligation conflicts with a general moral obligation. In such a case, if his general ethical identity asserts itself, he may relinquish that obligation and in doing that he would not be doing anything wrong because its parent, the profession which had yielded it, is itself morally undesirable. Suppose a taxation lawyer, working as a middleman between tax-evaders and tax-collecting officers, promises to his client to get his case cleared by bribing the taxation officer concerned. Since he has adopted the profession of middlemanship, and has made the promise, he may feel obligated to bribe and to get the client's case cleared. But if his ethical identity asserts and he realises that the promise is morally wrong because the profession of middlemanship which houses it is itself morally wrong, he may break the promise without being guilty of professional impropriety. This is so because a professional obligation yielded by a morally undesirable profession is morally void.

But sometimes even a morally desirable profession may give rise to an obligation conflicting with a general moral obligation. Doctors and lawyers are expected to keep confidential, i.e., to themselves, what their clients tell them in confidence. Confidentiality is an important component of both medical and legal ethics. Suppose a client tells his lawyer that he did commit the murder for which he has been accused and requests him to try his best to get him acquitted. His professional ethics, one may say, requires him to keep this truth to himself and his general ethics requires him to reveal it if he is asked by anyone whether or not his client has committed the murder he has been accused of. This conflict is more apparent than real. It would be real if general ethics accords to the principle of truth-telling the status of an absolute principle, i.e., that of a principle inviolable in all situations, admitting of no exception at all. But that is not the case. Even general ethics to which the principle belongs, considers it violable in some conditions, for example, in a situation in which telling the truth is going to cost the life of an innocent man. Our moral common sense would not approve of anyone's telling a truth and thereby helping a dacoit to kill an innocent person.

I do not mean to minimise the complexity of the lawyer's dilemma. I only want to say that his case is not an instance of professional ethics making an action right (or wrong) which general ethics considers wrong (or right). His case is one in which two principles conflict with each other and he has to decide which one of the two should override the other. The two principles are the principle of confidentiality and that of telling the truth. His client has told him the truth which he has consented, or implicitly promised, to keep confidential as is the practice in the profession. The dilemma is this: If he tells the truth his client has admitted to him, namely, that he has committed the murder, he would be violating the principle of confidentiality by making public what he has promised to keep confidential; if he keeps the client's admission confidential by not revealing the truth to anybody, either by saying that he does not know whether or not the client has committed the murder, or that the client has not told him anything about it, or even that as a lawyer he is obligated not to answer such a question, he would be violating the principle of truth-telling. Such a situation can arise even in one's general, non-professional, ethical practice. The problem to be solved here is one about deciding whether or not confidentiality is a good enough reason to justify making an exception to the principle of truth-telling. One who decides that it is would decide in favour of not telling the truth. For him the principle of truth-telling would mean that a truth ought to be told but not when one has promised or consented to keep it confidential. One, who decides that it is not, would decide in favour of telling the truth as known to him. For him the principle of truth-telling would mean that truth ought to be told even when one has promised or consented to keep it confidential. Whether or not confidentiality is really, i.e., objectively speaking, a good enough reason for not telling a truth is an independent ethical question which cannot be discussed here. The other question, whether or not there is any non-ethical consideration for the lawyer's not telling, or telling, the truth as known to him, — and there may exist more than one such consideration — also need not be discussed because it is not an ethical question, i.e., a question relevant to professional ethics or general ethics. It is obvious that a non-ethical consideration cannot in principle override an ethical consideration, though it may in fact sometimes do.

Suppose the lawyer reflects back on the nature of the legal profession, on what he and his other colleagues have been doing, decides to give up legal practice, and to do something else. He then would ask his client to hire another lawyer. He is now a non-professional, an ordinary person, and not a lawyer, but the dilemma whether or not he should reveal to anyone what his client has told him would remain alive if he has not decided whether or not confidentiality is a good moral, not just prudential, reason for making an exception to the principle of truth-telling. This fact makes it amply clear that what seemed to be a conflict between professional ethics and general ethics is really a domestic conflict (between two principles) in general ethics.

The scope of a professional obligation is much more limited than that of a general obligation. A doctor's obligations are to those sick people who are under his treatment, and not to others, not even to all sick people. But his general obligation to abstain from hurting an innocent person holds good of all innocent persons. A professional obligation cannot, in principle, as has been maintained earlier, override a general one. But it may appear that we do sometimes morally approve of its overriding the latter. Let us imagine that the patient *P* comes to the clinic of the doctor *D*, complaining of excruciating headache. In course of examining him *D* discovers that he is the man who fatally assaulted his neighbour a few days ago and the police were trying to catch hold of the assailant. But still *D* gives him the required treatment, and holding as a doctor the view that he is too sick to be immediately handed over to the police, he does not inform the police, but admits him in his nursing home.

We may say that *D*'s behaviour as a doctor is admirable and that the reason for its being admirable is that he has let his professional obligation as a doctor override his general obligation to inform the police of the criminal's being present in his house, an obligation which every citizen has. But that is not really the case. We admire *D*'s behaviour not because it is a case of his professional obligation's overriding his general obligation, the one he has as a citizen, but because it is an exemplification by *D* of the general virtue of kindness towards a sick, suffering, human being. It is this trait of his character which is a general, and not just a professional, trait which is the reason for our admiration. It becomes more conspicuous in his case because it has been exhibited by him towards a person towards whom he has a good moral reason to exhibit an attitutde of hatred or animosity. The virtue of kindness can as well be expressed in the form of a general obligation as 'You ought to be kind to the sufferer'. But even if it cannot be so expressed, *D*'s case continues to be a case in which a general virtue, or a general virtue along with the fulfilment of a professional obligation, and not the latter alone, overrides the general obligation of a citizen. It should also be noted that even the general virtue of kindness has to function under the overall supervision of general morality because it may sometimes be misused. If the doctor sheilds the sick criminal and never hands him over to the police, even after he has been cured, he would be misusing his kindness. It is such misuses of kindness on account of which to call someone too kind, in an evaluatively derogatory sense, is in order.

Benjamin Freedman[4] has argued that professional morality does not have to conform to ordinary morality. Taking the example of the confidentiality of an information given by a patient to his doctor, or discovered by the doctor in course of his examination of the patient's ailment, he says that it is right for the doctor, as per his professional ethics, not to divulge it to a third party, though as per ordinary or general ethics, it may be wrong not to divulge it. For example, the patient may reveal to the doctor his intention to kill somebody. Ordinary morality would require that the doctor divulge it to some third relevant party in order that the patient may be prevented from killing the person concerned if he actually tries to kill him. But medical ethics would consider the doctor's divulging the information wrong. A doctor is morally committed to keep confidential, i.e., to himself, the information conveyed to him, directly or indirectly, by the patient. His deviation from ordinary morality is justified, according to Freedman,[5] because, since society has approved of the medical profession and its goal, which is the patient's health care, it has to approve of the principle of confidentiality and other such principles which are essential for the medical profession in the sense that, without observing them, the doctor cannot fulfil his responsibility of properly treating the patient.

The principle of confidentiality is a tenet of medical ethics. Society does approve of the medical profession and of health care which is its goal, and consequently it also approves of a doctor's observance of confidentiality. But, like any other moral principle, the principle of confidentiality too cannot be called absolutely inviolable. Secondly, the doctor, like any other professional as has been pointed out earlier, is not only a professional, he is also an ordinary person who is committed to observing the principles of ordinary morality. Therefore, there may occur a situation in which it may be morally right for him to violate the principle of confidentiality.

4. Benjamin Freedman, "A Meta-Ethics for Professional Morality", *Ethics*, Vol. 89, pp. 1-19.

5. Benjamin Freedman, "What Really Makes Professional Morality Different: Response to Martin", *Ethics* Vol. 91, pp. 626-30.

Suppose the doctor *D* was treating the patient Nathuram Godse for severe pain in the wrist of his right hand. Somehow, from Godse's telling him, or from some other source, *D* came to know that Godse was very keen to get rid of the pain in the shortest possible time because he was planning to fire shots next day evening, in his prayer meeting, at Mahatma Gandhi to kill him. *D*, being committed to the principle of confidentiality, did not divulge this information to anybody, and next day, as planned, Godse killed Gandhi. Freedman would have to say that *D* did not do, as a professional, anything wrong in not divulging Godse's intention to a third party, and that even society would have to approve of his not violating the principle of confidentiality. But I do not think he would really say that. Perhaps he would like to say that the non-professional, the sensible person, in *D* should have overruled the professional in him and communicated the information to the police, or to anyone else he considered relevant. But this would amount to admitting that ordinary ethics can override professional ethics in some circumstances, or that the principle of confidentiality can sometimes be justifiably violated by a medical professional if it conflicts with ordinary morality. This would go against his position, and this is what I have been maintaining.

Alan Gewirth has maintained that, if we accept his ethical theory, as propounded in his *Reason and Morality*, we would find a good reason to say that the separatist thesis of Freedman does not hold good. But it seems to me, as I have shown in the preceding discussion, that common sense, or ordinary ethics by itself can refute Freedman. We do not need a sophisticated theory like Gewirth's to do that, nor do we need to buttress common sense ethics with the latter. Mike Martin[6] tries to refute Freedman by showing what he considers to be the faults in Freedman's argument to which Freedman replies and Martin responds to him again[7] by pointing to some loopholes in his defence. Both of them remain entangled in a cobweb of technicalities and their debate does not

6. Mike Martin, "Rights and the Meta-ethics of Professional Morality," *Ethics*, Vol. 91, pp. 619-25.

7. Mike Martin "Pofessional and Ordinary Morality: A Reply to Freedman", *Ethics*, Vol. 91, pp. 631-3.

show any clear way out. The most effective way to refute Freedman is not the way of Gewirth, or of Martin, but to look closely into ordinary, common-sense, ethics, because professional ethics flourishes under its overall supervision and protection. The latter cannot survive, if it conflicts with the former, or at the cost of the former. Therefore, if any time professional ethics seems to contradict or go against ordinary ethics, it is extremely likely that the discordance between the two is apparent and not real, and that it can be shown, or ascertained, that it is not real by looking into both as they actually function in real, human situations.

A conflict between professional and ordinary morality aries only in extraordinary, or unusual, circumstances. Ordinarily the doctor (or the lawyer) does not find it difficult to observe confidentiality. If a dying patient tells him he wants to kill his wife whom he considers adulterous, there is no problem for his doctor in keeping it confidential. But if a patient suffering from a mild attack of malaria says that, the doctor, if he really believes that the patient would try to kill her and that even killing an adulterous wife by her husband is morally wrong, he would have to decide whether he should observe the principle of confidentiality binding on him as a medical professional, or break it to observe the general moral principle of saving the life of another person. He would face no such problem if he were only a professional, or a non-professional, ordinary, individual. But he is both, as every professional is, and therefore he would face the moral problem of decision. And, he can solve it only by looking closely into the scope and rigour of his professional, and of his general ethical, views. It is obvious that his society would not, nor does it have to, approve of his observing confidentiality and letting the patient kill his wife because it has approved of the medical profession as a socially desirable institution. Rather, it also seems obvious that it would grade saving a life morally superior to observing confidentiality.

A professional is guilty of a professional misconduct when he does anything contrary to a moral, or even to a conventional, norm of his profession. A teacher is guilty of misconduct if he awards more marks to an examinee of his caste than he awards to one of a different caste even when the latter's answers are better than the former's. This would be a general moral lapse on his part, a lapse which would go against the principle of distributive justice. It would not be a case of professional misconduct. He would be guilty of professional misconduct if he charges some fee from a research scholar whose research work he supervises. The rules of his university do not provide for his charging any fee from the research student, or even from the university he, or the student, belongs to. He may argue that, since he gives a lot of time and academic help to the latter, he must be paid some appropriate fee by him. But since it would go against the existing convention or norm of the teaching profession, it would be counted as professional misconduct. The reason behind the convention or norm is that guiding research of his research students is considered to be one of his normal duties for which he gets his salary. That is why if he accepts any payment from a research student, whether in cash, or in kind, that would be taken to be an illegal gratification.

A professional misconduct spoils the image of the profession and erodes people's faith in the integrity of the concerned professional group. But sometimes when a convention is more often flouted than observed, an impression is created that there is no point in being a stickler for it. But it is a deceptive impression. If the convention concerned is a desirable one, its frequent violation does not make it unimportant. Rather, it makes people feel that the present-day concerned professionals are not as strict, or keen, to observe the norms of their profession as those of earlier times used to be. This means an overall downgrading of the profession by its professionals. This is what seems to have happened with the convention that an examiner should not accept even a cup of tea from the examinee before he has examined him. Its frequent non-observance, instead of making the old convention look pointless, has very much lowered down the image of the teaching professional in the public eye, and definitely in the eyes of the examinees who offer the hospitality to their examiners. A convention may be culture-relative. For example, in India a teacher's drinking alcoholic drinks with his students, or even sharing a packet of cigarettes with them, would lower down his image in the public eye and even in his students's eyes, though it may not have such an effect in a Western society. What I want to emphasise is that when a convention has a normative force, even if it is culture-relative, its flouting by a professional would be a professional misconduct.

Professionals also hold important bureacratic positions which sometimes make it difficult for them to stick to the ethics of their professions. Suppose a minister wants a bridge to be constructed on the river *R* at *P* because the areas around *P* come under his constituency. Therefore, the construction of the bridge is expected to ensure his victory in the next election. The chief engineer of the state's Bridge Corporation, on assessment of the various factors involved, comes to the conclusion, as a professional expert, that if the bridge is constructed at *S* it would cost less, take less time, and be more useful because on both sides of the river at *S* there are big commercial and industrial centres. But *S* falls in the constituency of the leader of the opposition in the state assembly. The minister, therefore, tells the chief engineer to manoeuvre with the data and make a proposal for the construction of a bridge at *P*. If the chief engineer does that, he would be going against his professional ethics. But if he does not, the minister would transfer him to some unimportant office, put some other engineer in his place, and the latter would make the proposal as per the minster's wish. This would mean that even then he would not be able to stop the construction of a bridge at *P* and, in addition, would lose his present position. Therefore, he does as desired by the minister; the bridge is constructed, a lot of money is spent, because of its inconvenient location the bridge is very occasionally used, people's transportation problems remain unsolved, etc., but the minister wins the next election and retains his ministerial position.

Any neutral person would say that the engineer's execution of the proposal for the construction of the bridge, as per the minister's wish, is not only professionally unethical but it has also caused a lot of expenditure to the state exchequer without doing any appreciable good to the people for whom the bridge has been constructed. Such things happen in professional life, and sometimes they cause a lot of miseries to the people concerned when they should have contributed to making their life better. Professionals too have a point here; if one engineer says 'no', another would say 'yes', to the minister; then why should one suffer by sying 'no'? The situation can improve only if the concerned professional's general moral calibre is of a very high level which makes him feel great even after having been placed in an insignificant office for having refused to do something professionally wrong, or unethical. Professionals play very important roles in maintaining the health and happiness of the society they belong to. They can perform their roles well only by sticking to their professional morality for which they have to have a strong base in general morality. This is why I have been insiting that professional morality can flourish only under the protection of, or with the support of, general morality.

9

A Problem Area

Business Ethics and the Limits of Applied Ethics

In Mokṣadharmaparva (of Śāntiparva) of the *Mahābhārata*[1] there occurs a dialogue between a saint named Jājali and a businessman named Tulādhāra. Tulādhāra is a householder who runs a grocery shop, sells several kinds of goods needed by the people of his locality, and maintains his family by the income he gets from his business. Jājali is a recluse who has acquired scriptural wisdom, leads a highly religious life and practices extremely difficult penances. He remains in a standing position, without taking any food or drink, for such a long time that the hairs of his head grow very long and, due to rain waters dust falling on them, become thickly matted. A pair of sparrows start sitting on his head and, by stocking on it some pieces of straw and some other stuff, they make a nest in his thick, bushy, jungle of hairs. In course of time they lay eggs in the nest and out of the eggs come their children. Jājali all along keeps his body in the standing position, completely static, without moving any limb of his, so that the dwellers in his hairs' nest may eat their food without letting even a tiny part of it fall down on the earth, and sleep undisturbed during the nights. After enjoying their sojourn on his head for some months, the parent birds leave, handing over the charge of the nest to their children. After a few months of stay there, they too, one day, do not return from their routine, daily, flying trips. Jājali waits for them for a number of days, still standing motionless. When they do not come back, he concludes that they have found

1. Vol.5, (Gita Press), pp. 5093-5105.

some other place to live and therefore makes his body mobile.

Recollecting his mastery of scriptural knowledge, his practice of religious rituals and penances, his remaining standing static for years to provide to the birds a comfortable habitat on his head, etc., Jājali now thinks that he has attained the state of moral perfection. Jubilating over and feeling proud of his achievements, he declares 'I have realised the *dharma*'. But to his utter dismay, immediately after his declaration, he hears a divine voice (*ākāśavāṇī*), saying 'In respect of morality (*dharma*) you, Jājali, come nowhere near Tulādhāra, the reputed, wise, businessman of Vārāṇasī. The kind of pride you feel has not been felt even by him.'[2] He feels greatly humiliated and hurt. He takes all the trouble to travel to Vārāṇasī to meet Tulādhāra to find out the secret of his attainments. On reaching the doorsteps of his house, he finds him busy weighing on his balance and selling to customers various kinds of goods they have come to buy from his shop. By means of the powers his high moral living has equipped him with, Tulādhāra has already come to know of Jājali's visit and its purpose. Jājali requests him to tell him what he has done to achieve the moral greatness which has been so highly applauded by the divine voice. The sum and substance of what Tulādhāra says to him in response is as follows:[3]

(a) He does his business to earn his livelihood. (b) In doing it he tries his best to avoid harming anybody's interest, and when it is not possible to avoid that, he tries his best to reduce the harm to the minimum. (c) He has a small hut, as his and his family's residence, which he has built out of materials locally available to, and affordable by, him. (d) He is satisfied with the kind of life his earning enables him to lead. (d) He fulfils the obligations the ethics of his profession, i.e., business (*vaṇikdharma*), requires him to by (d1) not selling things, like alchoholic drinks (*madirā*), which are harmful to their users, (d2) selling only things which are useful or beneficial to their buyers, (d3) abstaining from using any kind of deceit in selling any commodity to anybody, (d4) making no discrimination between one customer and another, i.e., not having a pro-attitude towards one and a con-attitude towards another, his balance weighing things in

2. *Mahābhārata*, Vol.5, (Gita Press), p. 5095: 41-3.
3. *Ibid.*, p. 5096.

the same manner to all buyers, and (d5) not misusing, or being callous in the use of, anything, non-living or living, in any work connected with his business, for example, never overloading the oxen driving the bullock-cart carrying the goods he brings to his shop for sale.

There is another important anecdote in Mārkaṇḍeya-samasyāparva of the *Mahābhārata*[4] about a great *brāhmaṇa* saint Kauśika's going to Dharmavyādha, who does the business of selling meat, for receiving lessons about *dharma*. Kauśika is a great scholar of Vedic and Upaniṣadic wisdom and a man of very high religious and spiritual attainments. He is advised by a woman, who is extremely devoted to her husband and fulfils all of her familial and social duties and obligations, to go to Dharmavyādha in Mithilā and learn from him the secrets of *dharma*. Dharmavyādha is, like Tulādhāra, a businessman who, besides fulfilling his other obligations, conducts his business of selling meat of animals butchered by others. Although selling meat is not very laudable, he is considered to be a laudable person because he fulfils all the norms of business ethics relevant to his business. He gives instructions to Kauśika on various subjects of moral, societal, and religious-spiritual importance. It is in virtue of his faultless business morals that he is given the status of one to whom a great scholar and saint may be asked to go for instructions.

References to business ethics and to its importance may be found in many classical or ancient works, Indian or non-Indian, rather, in works all through the ages in all cultures. But this does not mean that the philosophical study of business ethics, or business ethics meaning the philosophical characterisation of the moral norms relevant to business, can also be found in a full-blooded form in those works. In this sense of the term, it is a fairly recent arrival in the history of philosophy. Perhaps it has not yet arrived in India, or Indian philosophers have not yet taken cognisance of its arrival in the West. So far I have not come across any writing on the subject by any Indian philosopher.

Norman E. Bowie[5] dates the birth of business ethics, as a

4. *The Mahābhārata*, Vol. 2, (Gita Press), pp. 1544-77.

5. Norman E. Bowie, "Business Ethics", in Joseph P. DeMarco and Richard M. Fox (ed.), *New Directions in Ethics*, pp. 158-72.

philosophical discipline in the above sense, or as an area of applied ethics, in November 1974 when the first conference on business ethics was held at the University of Kansas, USA, under the joint sponsorship of the University's Department of Philosophy and the College of Business, though he admits of the existence of some ideas pertaining to it in some writings of Plato and Aristotle. In what follows I shall make references only to the Tulādhāra-Jājali anecdote because it serve fairly well to illustrate the points I want to make in this chapter.

Jājali is satisfied with Tulādhāra's account and also with the oracle's on-the-whole rating of Tulādhāra as a better person than him. He requests him to enlighten him on many other issues of moral and religious-spiritual concern and hears him with attention and gratitude. Tulādhāra says he fulfils well even his other duties, i.e., duties which fall outside the zone of his business ethics, for example, such duties as familial, neighbourly, religious, etc. But Jājali too fulfils all of his duties. Besides, his practice of religious rituals and penances is obviously far superior to that of Tulādhāra. The only morally relevant respect in which the latter excels him is that of fulfilling the (moral) obligations which his being a businessman enjoins him to fulfil and gives him opportunities to do that. On the other hand, Jājali, being a recluse, does not have any such obligation to anybody, and therefore does not get any opportunity to fulfil it. It seems, then, that it is Tulādhāra's business ethics, his moral uprightness in the conduct of his business, which makes his total moral score higher than Jājali's, and that on account of it he is rated by the oracle as a higher, or better kind of human being than the latter, even though in some religious, or spiritual, respects, the latter may be superior, or at least not inferior, to him.

Is it fair to give, as this anecdote does, such a high premeium to business ethics, to make it more creditable than the performance of extremely difficult religious and spiritual practices? There may be a point in claiming that a moral consideration overrides any non-moral consideration. But rating Tulādhāra as a higher kind of person than Jājali is not just making morality override religion, or spirituality: It is making a particular species, or zone of morality, namely business morality, do that. And, one implication of doing that is to give the impression that, among the various zones, or spheres, of morality, business morality occupies the central place on the moral stage which worthwhile human life is very often said to be. Therefore, the question raised above is not trivial.

Whenever an anecdote is used to highlight a point, some amount of exaggeration is almost always there. One may accept that the Jājali-Tulādhāra story exaggerates the importance of business ethics, but also add that there is a good reason for its doing that. The practice of business provides ample opportunities which tempt the businessman to accumulate wealth and/or power by the use of immoral, or morally not very upright, means. He may not feel the temptation, or may not yield to it, even if it catches his eye, only if he is a man of strong moral will, or (b) if the law of his land is so expansive that it covers all of his business transactions and forbids all possible immoralities, and the land's law-enforcing agencies are so prompt and effective that they do not let any law to be anytime infringed. It is rare to find an individual satisfying (a), and rarer to find a land satisfying (b). Therefore, if an individual conducts his business in a morally impeccable manner, as Tulādhāra does, he is really very greatly admirable. To keep one's hands clean is really creditable, when dirtying them is likely to be tempting, pleasing, or even in the short-run, paying. Therefore, it is really great to be a Tulādhāra, and therefore pointful to attach, even exaggeratedly, as the anecdote does, the highest value to anyone's doing his business in a manner morally completely faultless, or as faultless as the context of business makes possible. The thrust of the anecdote is that it is more difficult, and therefore more creditable, for anyone to remain morally impeccable in the practice of his business than to remain in a standing position for years and let some birds build a nest in his hairs, etc. That is, it is more difficult and creditable to be a Tulādhāra than a Jājali.

Tulādhāra's account of his style of business life, from (a) to (d) gives, a good description of what we would normally call the main constituents of a sound business ethics. It is a realistic account because it admits the possibility of a situation in which the businessman may not avoid harming someone, and only advises him to try his best, in that situation, to keep the harm to the minimum. It also reveals that to keep himself within the limits of morality, the businessman has to have a morally sound picture of the good life, guiding him in his various business transactions, even in dealing with his environment of which his oxen and bullock-cart are a part. Some of the ideas in the account do need augmentation, elaboration and precisification. I hope to do, in what follows, some such thing, along with trying to locate the role of the philosopher, or of philosophy, particularly, of the applied ethicist, or applied ethics, in providing guidance to the businessman in keeping up the norms of business ethics.

Wherever any commerce, i.e., an activity or procedure of selling and buying anything, is involved, an occasion could be available on which the seller may feel tempted to overcharge, and the buyer to underpay. The same shopkeeper may feel tempted to overcharge a buyer if the latter badly needs the commodity he wants to buy and the commodity is not available elsewhere (or he has no time to go elsewhere), and to underpay his salesman if the latter badly needs the job he has and is not in a position to get a more paying one. This is true irrespective of the nature of the commodity involved in the (commercial) transaction. It may be a material good, say, a life-saving drug, an organ of the body, say, a kidney, a socially sensitive thing, say, a call girl's sexual service, an expertise, say, one involved in brokerage, etc., etc. What can prevent one from overcharging (or underpaying), in addition to unfavourable circumstances, is mainly his moral character. This is a truism because it amounts to saying the tautology that he who has a morally virtuous character, i.e., he who is not prone to do a morally wrong thing even if doing it is likely to be advantageous to him, would not be prone to such wrong-doings in his business as overcharging, underpaying, etc. But we would soon see that there is a point in saying, or even in emphasising, it.

In addition to the businessman's not-much-bothering-about attitude about morals in exploiting his commercial transactions to his advantage, even at the cost of his customers, there is another factor which, in a large number of cases, stands in the way of anyone's, an affected person's, or even a neutral person's, conclusively establishing that a wrong has been done in a deal. This factor is the obvious fact that some of the important concepts of business ethics are not properly bounded. This fact quite often makes it very difficult to determine in a definitive manner whether or not a certain norm of business ethics has been infringed. We have learnt to live with such cases, but the unhappiness, or social discord or tension, they sometimes produce cannot be denied. Rather, on some occasions the tension caused is so great that it leads to violence.

Let us take, for example, the concept of profit. It may be called an economic concept, but it is not a totally economic concept. It is also a moral concept quite central to business ethics. It is, because the businessman has the moral right to make some profit, for example, to sell the goods he deals in, or produces, with some profit. His profit is the positive balance obtained after deducting the good's cost price from its selling price. If its cost price is *N*, then he has the moral right to sell it for *N+M*, assuming that *N+M* is a larger sum that *N*, speaking in arithmetic terms as we ordinarily do in such transactions. It is possible that he may, in some special situation, make a 'profit' in some other way by selling it to somebody for only *N*, or even for a lesser sum than *N*. But that would be another story. Such a thing would happen, for example, if by selling his goods at a lower-than-cost prices to the muscleman of a politician he keeps at bay, because of the latter's good will, the police constable posted on the road in front of his shop who wants to take five bottles of limca everyday without making any payment.

Profit-making is, thus, morally permissible. Even Tulādhāra takes his profit, otherwise he cannot earn his livelihood by running his grocery shop. A businessman's profit is his only income from his business, and he does not have to feel shy in saying that he does it to earn some profit. There is a sense of moral propriety in earning some profit, but not in earning *any* amount as the profit. There has to be some arithmetic relationship between the cost price and the selling price, taking into account market mores, status of the country's, or the region's economy, value of money, etc. But there is also a moral dimension to fixing the selling price and thereby the amount of profit.

In a particular case, the purchaser may say that the selling price is unjustifiably high, and the seller that it yields him only marginal, or no profit. There are occasions when the seller may consider it reasonable to charge even four times of the cost price of a certain commodity on account of its scarcity, demand, or of such incidental expenses as losses incurred in storage, increased cost of transportation, etc. Therefore, a morally not very scrupulous businessman may take advantage of the unclarity or indefiniteness of the moral bounds of the norm of profit-making and overchrage his customer. The practice of higgling is a consequence of this sort of indefiniteness: It is used by the covetous businessman in trying to sell a good at the maximum price he can extract from the customer, and by the latter in trying to higgle down the selling price to its lowest possible limit. The indefiniteness of the norm emboldens both of them to think that neither one can conclusively prove that the other is wrong: The seller cannot prove that the customer is infringing the norm of letting the businessman earn his morally permissible profit by offering the price he offers, nor can the customer prove that the seller is infringing the profit-norm by charging the price he is actually charging.

When a law is enacted to the effect that the maximum selling price be printed on every saleable good, it registers the fact that business ethics, left to itself, lacks the conceptual resources to fix the bounds of the norm of profit-making, which is one of its central norms, and the other fact that most of businessman are neither likely to properly fix the moral bounds of profit-making, nor to keep the practice of their business well within those bounds. After the enactment of the law the moral norm of profit-making has got a legal limit, since the legal requirement of printing the maximum selling price prescribes the limit of the chargeable price: It makes charging more than the printed price legally punishable. That a seller may still overcharge a needy customer does not disprove what has been said here. It only shows that a legal law can be transgressed. But printing the maximum chargeable price does not mean that the seller cannot sell it at a lesser price if he considers the profit accruing therefrom quite reasonable or sufficient. A covetous one, on the other hand, may not do that even if the printed price yields him a profit higher than what would be morally reasonable to earn from the sale of the good concerned.

When a moral norm is not likely to be satisfied by the majority of people who ought to satisfy it, and their satisfying it is of great social importance, the moral norm is sometimes converted into a legal norm. Therefore, the presence of a large number of moral norms converted into legal norms in a society would be a clear sign of a general tendency among its members to infringe their moral norms. The existence of a powerful judiciary, or executive machinery which does the work of conversion is an indicator of the weak morality of the members of the society they are housed in.

We also move in the direction of getting a moral norm converted into a legal one when we find that a dispute involving it is not likely to be settled by moral talk, not always because of the willyness of the parties concerned, but quite often because of some indefiniteness, or vagueness, in the concept of the norm itself. Doing so is considered imperative if such disputes frequently occur and disturb social harmony, or cause tension. Conversion of the moral norm into a legal one removes the norm's indefiniteness or vagueness, lays down in clear terms the conditions determining its satisfaction and violation, the nature of punishment consequent on its violation, the nature of the agency responsible for the enforcement of relevant law or laws, etc.

The legal institution of the consumer court completes the work of the conversion of a moral norm of pricing into a legal norm. It treats, what could have been, before the enactment of the law about printing the maximum selling price (or the date of expiry, etc.), called a moral dispute, as a legal one, and it is empowered to do that by the enactment of the relevant laws or statutes.

The way to solve a moral dispute is to have an open-minded talk about the bone of contention, or the point of dispute, between the disputants, without, or with, the help of some equally open-minded friends, or neutral persons. But this talk would help to resolve the dispute only if the disputing parties are willing to obey the moral norm or principle which is relevant and which one party accuses the other to have transgressed, and the norm concerned is well-bounded. When the accused person gets convinced that he has transgressed, he would feel sorry or repentant and may seek forgiveness and even promise to compensate for the damage done to the other. But this he would do only if he is convinced that he has violated the moral norm, and he would get convinced only if he is, in the moral sense, a cooperative, sensitive, person, i.e., a moral agent. And, if he is not such a person, or, because of some other factors, does not get convinced of his moral lapse, he would not repent, ask for forgiveness, or promise to compensate for the damage done, etc.. To give moral punishment is only to morally condemn the guilty, consider him a morally fallen person, to disassociate from him, not to involve him in social transactions, to socially boycott him, etc. We may morally punish him in one or more than one of these ways, but it would pinch him only if he is morally sensitive.

Even in the case of the violation of a legal norm, the punishment inflicted on the accused would make him repent and feel remorseful only if he is, or is made, morally sensitive, i.e., only if the punishment, or his trial in the court, arouses his sense of virtue, his sense that what he has done he ought not to have done even if he had not been legally punished. With this sense in him, we can depend on his no more charging a customer more than the printed price. In the absence of this sense in him, we cannot. If he lacks it, he may do the cost-benefit analysis of violating the law. If he finds the benefit accruing from the violation greater than the cost incurred in litigation, etc., he may continue playing with the law. He may even try to find out some other, immoral, or illegal, way of playing safe with it, say, by bribing the court, of course, if the court is bribable.

Enactment of a law, or a set of laws, may go a great way to stop immoral practices in business transactions. But it cannot do all that the acquisition of a virtuous character can. And, what it can do, it can do with full success only if in some way the moral senstivity of the erring businessman is aroused if it is dulled or dormant, and the existing moral senstivity of a concientious one is kept fully operative by respecting him, protecting him from the machinations of corrupt ones, etc.

After having become a legal norm, the moral norm does not cease to be moral. It has been made a legal norm because it is a moral norm, and it continues to remain one even after having become a legal norm. For example, if considering the various factors relevant to pricing, it is considered morally fair that the seller can charge profit up to 15 per cent of the cost of a certain kind of goods, and the selling price of the goods is legally fixed according to this principle, it would be legally as well as morally wrong for the seller to charge more than the legally fixed price, and equally, morally as well as legally, wrong for the buyer to ask him to charge less than that. It would be morally commendable, not just right, if the seller charges less, if he thinks that charging less gives him his due profit, and equally commendable, not just right, for the buyer to insist that he must not incur a loss, or lose his reasonable profit, in selling it to him at a throw-away price. The logic behind the policy of fixing the maximum permissible price of a commodity is to set the moral as well legal limit of the seller's profit, implying thereby that if he crosses the limit, then he would be not only infringing the ethics of profit-making, but also the law controlling the practice of profit-making relevant to his business. He still has the freedom to sell it at less than the printed price if his conscience dictates him to do that. Its implication for the buyer too is obvious: he has now no moral, or legal, claim to ask the seller to give him at a lesser price.

To do any business is to do a sell-purchase transaction, or to get such a transaction done, as is the case with a broker, or a middleman. One has the moral/legal right to sell a thing only if he owns it, or has been authorised by its owner to sell it. One can sell anything he owns, for example, the house he owns, the goods he produces, or stocks for sale, etc. He can also sell his service, for example, his physical labour, his legal advice, his managerial skill, etc. There are also instances of some parents selling their daughters to rich customers for making them their wives, or concubines. This we resent and there is a good moral reason for doing that. Speaking from the moral point of view, one person cannot be said to own another person, or one who is capable of becoming, i.e., has the potentiality to become, a person, in the sense in which he can own a property, or commodity, for example, a house, or a car. Therefore, he cannot sell, again speaking from the moral point of view, a human being who is a person, or is capable of becoming a person, as is the case with a child; that is, he cannot sell even his daughter, or wife.

What distinguishes a person from a property, or commodity, is that a person is, and the latter is not, a free agent. A person is a free agent in the sense that he can take decisions. He may take a decision even about what is, or is not, in his interest, and given the fulfilment of certain conditions, he can act in accordance with any decision of his, concerning himself, some other person, or some object. To respect a person is to respect his freedom, his free agency. To sell him is to reify, or commodify, him, i.e., to treat him as a commodity, which amounts to doing him the greatest disrespect, or injustice. This is what the selling parent of a girl does to her when he sells her to someone. A commodity is a mere means to satisfy an interest of one, or of more than one, person. To treat a person as a commodity is, thus, to treat him as a mere means, which, in virtue of his personhood, i.e., his freedom, or free agency, he is not. It is to this feature of the concept of a person to which Kant draws our attention when he says that it is wrong for anyone to treat any person, including himself, as a mere means. The feudal landlord who treats his ploughman, who owes some money to him, as a bonded labour, the contractor who supplies, on the payment of a commission, a labourer to a builder and does not allow him to change his employer when he is very unhappy with him, and the builder who keeps him like a sheep under the physical control of a muscleman, all of the three treat the labourer, who is a person, as an object or commodity.

What about one's body, or rather, bodily parts? Can one sell a part, or an organ, of his body? But can we say that we own a bodily organ in the same sense in which we own a commodity, say, a pen? We do not produce, or purchase, our organs; we get then from nature. Even when we try to imporve the function of an organ, or get an organ transplanted, say, a kidney, with the help of medical technology, the technology works only if the existing body accepts, or receives, agreeably, the medication done, or the organ transplanted. Therefore, our ownership is only to a limited extent. Moreover, there are certain values attached to certain kinds of activities, or things, which make trading in them morally abhoring. Selling a bodily organ is one of such things. Our normal moral reaction to anyone's selling a bodily organ, say a kindney, to someone, is that he has done something wrong, or mean, for money. Donating, i.e., giving free on demand, or out of kindness, an organ to someone is, on the other hand, taken to be commendable because it is a sign of altruism, sacrifice, or heroism. We admire the altruism of a person donating one of his kidneys to save the life of another person, and we admire Ekalavya's heroism and reverence for Droṇa when he chops off his right thumb and hands it over to the latter as asked for by him. Similarly, we admire the honeste of a person who returns the purse of a fellow-passenger fallen on his seat. But if he demands a price for his act of honesty, our respect for his honesty, or attribution to him of the virtue of honesty, would very greatly dwindle. We would admire a woman who breast-feeds a motherless child, but the moment she asks for a price of her breast-milk, or agrees to sell it, our admiration would not remain unaffected. Similar is the case with a non-mercenary surrogate mother. If a woman who has more than one child, allows her childless neighbour to adopt one of her children, or agrees to be a surrogate mother for a child by him, we call her action altruistic and a great sacrifice. But if she, on the payment of an agreed amount, gives her child for adoption, or agrees to become a surrogate mother of his child, we do not call her altruistic, or sacrificing. In fact, to play the role of a mercenary surrogate mother is to sell the child born. The child is as much the surrogate mother's, as the male person's whose sperm, through artificial insemination, grows in her womb into the body she delivers. Therefore, to hand over the child in lieu of some money to the childless male (or couple) is to sell it to him (or them).[6] The surrogate mother would then be a partner in the trade of selling a child which is partly her own child.

Selling a bodily, or managerial, service is a morally and, therefore, socially, acceptable business. It becomes morally objectionable only if it involves the violation of a general ethical principle like that of sincerity, or that of one belonging to business ethics relevant to the service concerned, for example, the seller's violating the mutually agreed, contractual, principle of his paying 10 per cent of the selling price to the broker who has arranged the deal. But selling a bodily organ (or renting it out, as the surrogate mother rents out her uterus), it has been said, is not considered as morally acceptable as selling a bodily service is, say, that of working as a maid-servant in someone's house. But a prostitute's selling her sexual services, which also are bodily services, is not considered, in almost any society, morally or socially acceptable. Ericson argues that there is no good, conclusive, reason, nor even an empirically

6. For a detailed discussion of various issues connected with surrogacy, see Lenove Kuo's "The Morality of Surrogate Mothering", *The Southern Journal of Philosophy*, Vol. XXVII, No. 3, 1989, pp. 361-80.

defensible utilitarian consideration, to do that[7]. It is true when we find that a woman is forced by her circumstances, for which she is in no way responsible, to work as a whore, or that she becomes one to save herself and her family from starvation, we do not condemn her as much as we would have done if she would have chosen to be one just for fun, or for having political influence. We not only sympathise with Sonya (of Fyodor Dostoevsky's *Crime and Punishment*), but feel respectful towards her who, having no other alternative, becomes a whore to provide monetary help to her drunkard father, and after his death, to save from starvation her widowed, tubercular, step-mother and her several minor children. Raskolnikov bows down to her to honour her suffering.[8] We do not have such feelings for a woman selling some other kind of bodily services which are socially acceptable, say, the services involved in working as a sweeperess in a rich man's house, even when we know that she too does that to save her family from starvation. It is not that we do not sympathise with, or respect, the work of the sweeperess, but the feeling core, or the intensity of the feeling core, of our attitudes in the two cases is not the same. The reason for this difference, it seems to me, is located in our assessment of the whore's attitude towards her sex-business. We have a respectful attitude towards her only if we find that she is well aware of the moral/social disvalue of her business, only if she feels unhappy for being forced by her circumstances to have adopted this (so-called) dirty business; we would not have it if we find that she feels proud for being in it. Sacrificing what the woman considers morally commendable, and adopting what she considers morally condemnable though she does not want to do it, is making a great sacrifice, perhaps a greater sacrifice than any other. It is for doing this short of heroism that we admire Sonya. And, a similar sort of heroism we find in Mrs. Warren (of Bernard Shaw's *Mrs. Warren's Profession*). Finding no other way out, she prefers prostitution to starvation and exploitation. The most fitting admiration for what she has alone is expressed by her daughter, Vivie, who, after

7. For a good discussion of several moral problems posed by prostitution, see Lars O. Ericson's "Charges against Prostitution: An Attempt at a Philosophical Assessment", *Ethics*, Volume 90, No. 3, April 1980, pp. 335-66.

8. Oxford University Press.

knowing her mother's circumstances, calls her "stronger than all England".[9]

What has been said above about sexual services may also be said to be true of one's selling an organ of his body. Many poor people throng around blood banks to sell blood to make their both ends meet. If one sells one kidney of his to get some money to pay for the medical treatment of his ailing father, we would consider his doing it an act of sacrifice, or of moral heroism, even when he gets some money in the deal. It is true that a bodily organ, as well as a sexual service, is not considered to be a saleable commodity, and with both of them is associated a great moral value in every culture. Both of them are very dear to human beings. But in some circumstances one may have to sell anyone of them, while realising that he/she is going to lose something very dear and dignified. It is in such cases that the offer, in spite of the fact that it brings some money and is a sale, is considered to be a great sacrifice, a great loss, because nothing given in exchange is considered to be an adequate compensation for what has been given out and lost in the bargain, because what is given out is (considered to be) priceless. May be, all this is more true of the sale of a sexual service than of a bodily organ.

After the short aside to body-business, let us return to normal, regular business. Since doing business is not just selling something, but selling it on some profit, it is not doing charity, or philanthropy. A businessman may spend a part of his profit for some charitable purpose, but that would not make the business a charity. Nor can the primary purpose of doing it be said to do, or to be able to do, charity. One does it to earn his livelihood, as Tulādhāra frankly admits, and there is nothing morally wrong in doing that. The question of right or wrong, i.e., ethics, may enter from any one of the following sides of a business concern: its (a) owner, (b) customer, (c) managerial team, (d) community of other businessmen, and (e) environment. The owner, the customer, and the owner's manager (or managerial team or staff) have to be fair to each other. The owner of a business, i.e., a businessman, has also to observe the ethical

9. Quoted by John Allett in his "Bernard Shaw and Dirty Hands Politics: A Comparison of *Mrs Warren's Profession* and *Major Barbara*", *Journal of Social Philosophy*, Vol. 26, No. 2, Fall 1995, pp. 32-45.

code current among the members of his business community, i.e., among his co-businessmen or groups. And, he also has to see that he does not do, in the conduct of his business, any damage to his environment, for example, the kind of damage which would be done by piling up rotten fruits and vegetables, not fit for sale, on the common footpath of the road opposite his shop.

The owner of a business may be a single person, a single family, or a group of unrelated people forming a limited company, a cooperative society, etc. In a small business concern, like Tulādhāra's grocery business, the owner may also be his managerial team. He may not employ even a salesman because he does not need one. But he cannot be his only customer. The profit-making aspect of his business has two main, or terminal points: one touching his interest and the other the customer's. But to maintain moral equilibrium in the business he has to regulate profit-making in such a manner that it hurts neither his, nor his customer's, nor his manager's, nor his business community's interest, nor does it pollute the environment. That is what Tulādhāra means when he says that he tries to avoid causing any harm to anybody. What is being said here applies even to that owner who himself is his manager or helper. When the owner is *A* and his manager is *B*, it can easily be understood that *A* may ill-treat or ill-pay *B*. But a similar thing can happen when *A* is both the owner and manager. He may be so much interested in amassing money that he does not give enough of rest, or food, to himself to keep his body and mind in good health.

The ethics of management is held by many to consist in promoting the interest of the owner. But if doing that involves doing something unethical, then it cannot be the manager's duty. Doing anything unethical cannot be anybody's duty. Morever, the customer cannot be ignored. The customer is the profit-giver. If he is not to be done any charity, he is not also to be cheated, or overcharged. Neither is any other businessman to be cheated, though rivalry, or competitiveness, in business, is not to be ruled out. And, to promote the owner's interest, even the environment is not to be polluted; even the bullock-cart-carrying oxen are not to be overloaded. To say all this is to say what ought to be done by the manager, and this is a case in which 'ought' does not imply 'can'. As expected, the manager would say that he cannot do all this because then the owner's interest may be harmed. When there is even the least possibility of that, the owner would get rid of him, and would easily get another manager who would not do such ethical things.

The manager's fears are genuine. The owner generally wants one who would do all that would promote his interest. Several years ago a British association of chemical industrialists issued a statement about the kind of chemical engineers the chemical industries needed to man or manage them. A famous British daily commented in its editorial that the society might not need the kind which the industries needed, and it was equally important to know the kind which the society needed. The daily's thrust was that the society needed chemical engineers who were morally sensitive not only to protect the owner's but also to protect the society's interests which would include, in the terminology used in this chapter, the interest of all concerned, i.e., of the owner, customer, management, other businessman, and the environment.

The real problem is how to ensure that the manager is let to function the way he ought to without the risk or fear of being chucked out of his job. It may look the simplest to say that this can be done by making both the owner and the manager adequately morally sensitive. But that would be the hardest thing to do. It seems to me that the moral balance, or equilibrium, can be ensured only by the joint efforts of the community of owners, community of managing personnel, and the government with some sort of judicial supervision and control. However, the details of this suggestion cannot be worked out here.

That it is morally right to do business to earn one's livelihood is true but not in an unconditional sense. One's moral right to do a certain business would be determined by the moral status of the business concerned. Nobody can have any sort of right to earn his livelihood by doing a kind a business which is in itself vile or destructive of social harmony. For example, nobody can have the right to indulge in the business of providing accommodation for adulterous pairs to meet on the ground that he does it only to earn his three meals a day, or even on the ground that he does it to get some money to pay the mess bills of a group of poor blind students. This is because doing anything to encourage adultery is intrinsically (as well as extrinsically) evil. This is a matter of general ethics, and not just a regional one of business ethics, which business ethics cannot infringe. As Aristotle[10] says, adultery, — and therefore encouraging it, — is an intrinsic evil because it is evil no matter who does it, when he does it, where he does it, or for which purpose he does it. When Tulādhāra says that harmful things like alcoholic drinks are not to be sold in his shop, his indication is towards the moral permissibility of the actual nature of the business one chooses to do, implying that trading in a thing which is evil, or harmful to the society, cannot be a permissible business. One has the right to earn his livelihood by doing business but not by business of the latter variety.

A businessman sells or produces things which his customers buy because they need them, or find them useful. But sometimes he also makes things available for sale which they do not presently need, or want to have, but if they once use them, they are likely to develop a liking, or desire, for them. In course of time they may feel the need of those things, or begin to need them. There is a great scope of being ethical as well as being unethical here. A businessman may create needs in his customers for things which are harmful, as well as for things which are useful, for them. The producers and traders of low-fat edible oils have created in many needs for these oils which are useful for their health, while those who trade in *haśīśa* have created needs for things which are highly injurious. Business expands and economy develops by bringing in the market new products, and therefore it is necessary to do that. But if moral caution is not exercised, a lot of damage may be done to the customer's interests by the introduction of new goods. A businessman can say that by selling the goods he sells he fulfils the needs of his customer and thereby helps him to live well. But this he can say only if he is morally cautious about the kinds of goods he sells. A customer may say that the trader has to supply the good he wants, the good which fulfils a need of his, if he is willing to pay its price. The trader has no right to say which need of his is worth fulfilling, and which one is not. But nobody has the moral right to help a man fulfil a need of his if he knows that helping him to do that is going

10. Aristotle, *Nicomachean Ethics*, 1107: a 16.

to, or is likely to, cause him a great harm. Therefore, a trader is well within the bounds of business ethics if he refuses to supply such a thing, i.e., to help the customer to fulfil the alleged need by supplying him the good he wants to buy.

While responding to Jājali, Tulādhāra says that in doing his business he tries to avoid doing any harm or wrong to anybody, and when doing some harm to someone is unavoidable, he tries to do only the minimum. He seems to imply that the very nature of the practice of a business is such that sometimes the businessman has to harm some other person (or persons) without his (or their) deserving the harm, and in such a situation the best moral course is to do the minimum harm. Quite obviously it means that sometimes it is morally permissible, i.e., morally not wrong, for a businessman to unjustifiably harm another person. Since the context is the context of business, to say this would mean that if the interest, or logistic, of the business makes it unavoidable to harm someone without any moral justification, it is morally right to do that provided that the harm is reduced to the minimum. This sounds to be something like the theory of the dirty hands: Since you cannot avoid dirtying your hands if you are in a business, try to keep the dirt on the hands as thin as possible.

The *Mahābhārata* war itself may be said to be an illustration of the theory of dirty hands. The general lesson of the war, as conducted by Kṛṣṇa, seems to be that one cannot win a war, howsoever righteous his purpose in waging it, or fighting it, may be, unless he does certain things which are not morally permissible. He has only to exercise caution in keeping the number of impermissible, i.e., morally wrong, moves to the minimum. This may be Tulādhāra's point. The difficulty with accepting this point of view is that the concept of thin dirt, i.e., that of a minor impropriety, is not only vague, but it is almost impossoble to make it precise. Therefore, one businessman may consider a particular impropriety glaring which another one considers insignificant. Secondly, it is also possible that what a businessman considers a minor impropriety, a customer, or an employee of his, may consider glaring, and *vice versa*. In a Hindi movie, an employee of a restaurant, on the first day of his work, after serving food to a customer, notices that, the big container, from which he has served *dāl* to him, contains a dead cockroach. He rushes to his table and tells him not to eat the *dāl* becaue of the dead cockroach in the main container, since for him, the *dāl* has become uneatable. So is it for the customer who leaves the table. But for the owner of the restaurant the presence of one dead cockroach in a pot containing several litres of *dāl* is a very insignificant, or negligible, kind of uncleanliness. But the employee's informing the customer of this fact, for him, leading to the customer's leaving the restaurant without eating the food and without paying for it and thereby causing monetary loss to him, is a big lapse on the part of the employee. Thereby, he dismisses him without even paying for the day's work.

It is a common saying among businessmen that no business can be done without committing some immoralities, and these immoralities may be to the disadvantage of the managerial staff, the customer, some other businessman, or the environment. Since the owner owns the concern they must be, he may think, to his advantage if they are to have any effect on his interests. But the other concerned parties may not consider unquestionable, and it may not be unquestionable even on objective grounds, that the ownership of a concern entitles the owner's interests to override their interests if they have done nothing which justifies the overriding, or which has caused the situation necessitating the commission of the immoralities.

Perhaps the businessman is right in saying that some immoralities are unavoidable in business life, and perhaps Tulādhāra's advice to keep them to their minimum is the most realistic. But how to help reducing unavoidable wrongs to their minimum? The government of the country may take some steps provided those who man it have the maturity to decide the limit of morality/immorality in business practices and the moral will to get them implemented. Can the philosopher, or the moral philosopher, do anything in this matter? In fact, the level of morality in business, as in governance, depends largely on the level of morality in general public life, i.e., on the general level of morality of the people. Effective steps to keep the level of immoralities to the lowest in business can be taken only by the joint or cooperative efforts of the business community, the people who suffer their pinch, and the government which also includes the politicians because really they govern, or control the government. The philosopher can only highlight some relevant and important but not-bothered-about moral principles, if there are any, and state in clear, emphatic, terms, as a result of his analysis, some *mental habits, some thinking, or reactive, patterns, in business life* which encourage amorality, immorality, or anyone's propensity to harm someone else nonchalantly. Apart from this he cannot play, *as a philosopher*, any other big role in ameliorating business ethics.

Improprieties in business ethics are not because of the fact that existing ethical theories are inadequate. A businessman, or anybody, for that matter, does not need a theory, or a theorist, a Mill, or a Kant, or a social-moral leader, a Gandhi or a Jai Prakash, to tell him that selling, or trading in, harmful materials like *haśīśa*, underweighing goods which are being sold, giving false information about the prevailing market price of a commodity, infringing the terms of a contractual business agreement, etc., are morally wrong. We know, and so does the businessman, that they are wrong, without the help of any ethical theory. It cannot therefore be said that the philosopher's inability to give a clear-cut, simple, non-controversial, theory of the right and wrong, is, even to some extent, responsible for the prevalence of immoralities in business, or in any other sphere of soical or private life. Ethical theories are not unnecessary (intellectual) baggage, but they need not be invoked to help us decide in every case whether or not a certain move is morally permissible. Our moral common sense is all that we most often need to use in making moral decisions. Only in some tricky, not-often-encountered, or dilemmatic, cases an explicit appeal to an ethical theory is needed, and prevailing immoralities are very seldom due to such cases, or the results of our not getting the needed help from some theory or theories.

In some cases, particularly in big business, ignoring the principle of treating or respecting a person as a person, a wrong conception of happiness, a distorted, or disproportionately structured, picture of the good life, can be a promoter of immoralities. For example, if in one's picture of the good life, happiness, or social respectability cannot be had without combining success in business with political power, and political power cannot be had without making his hands dirty, some immoralities are bound to enter his business deals. It may also be the case that the political or governmental ethos of his country is such that a businessman, who has no link with politicians in power, does not get the respect or consideration he deserves, or does not succeed in his business. Then, it is the politics, or government, of the country which carries the can for at least some of the immoralities in big businesses. Political links do not matter much in small businesses. Perhaps this is the reason why Gandhi is against promoting big business houses and in favour of encouraging village centres of small businesses, or village industires. Behind his theory of village centres of business, or his concept of *svadeśī* (indigenous) lies his picture of the good life relevant to the practice of any business. His picture is very much like that of Tulādhāra. In such matters philosophy, or conceptual analysis, can play an important role. By (a) identifying the prevalent pictures of the good life in the sphere of business, (b) analysing their important components, (c) picking out these components which tend a businessman to adopt immoral practices, (d) discovering promoters of this tendency ensuing from the country's political and bureacratic practices, (e) locating factors in the code of conduct prevalent in business management which are likely to contribute to neglecting, or becoming indifferent to, general moral considerations, or considerations relevant to a particular business, etc., the philosopher can make clearly visible to the public eye how immoralities enter in business life and how they can be stopped from entering, or be made ineffective if they per chance enter anytime.

Philosophy, including applied ethics which is specifically concerned with business ethics, is a cognitive instrument (*jñāpaka kāraṇa* or *sādhana*) of moral improvement and not an actuating, or desired-effect-producing, instrument (*kāraka kāraṇa* or *sādhana*). It is not alone in having this limitation. Even the practitioner of the science of medicine, accepted by all to be a very useful and result-oriented science, is very much like the philosopher or applied ethicist, in having a similar limitation. A physician does his job creditably well if he correctly diagnoses his patient's disease and prescribes the right medicine as per the existing medical knowledge. We do not expect him to put the medicine into the patients's mouth. And, even if he tries to do that, the medicine would go into his stomach only if he wants to eat it. In the case of an unwilling patient the physician can only tell him the beneficial effects of eating the medicine on his health and the advantages of being healthy. So can do the philosopher *via* his analysis of the pictures of the good life prevalent in business circles and/or by depicting a better picture of the good (business) life. Both the applied ethicist and the physician work on the assumption that normally human beings want to regain their lost health, moral, or physical-mental, and that they normally would take at least some steps in this direction if they are told in clear and knowledgeable ways what these steps are. Nobody would say that it is an irrational assumption because it is not. Nor is it unrealistic because it does not suggest that all human beings want to become, or would try to become, when helped by them, absolutely free from all immoralities, or all diseases. It only suggests, or entertains, the hope that a good number of them would try to reduce their number, or effect, to the minimum. By working on a realistic assumption, neither applied ethics, nor the science of medicine, which is an applied science, would be looking down upon, or declaring unviable, the ideals of absolute freedom from all immoralities, or from all diseases.

Part III

The Background Conceptual Framework

10

Acknowledgement, Application, and Morally Justified Violation of a Moral Principle

IN the chapters of part I, in some way or the other, I have tried to locate some of the problems in applying some classical Indian ethical concepts or principles in determining what one should do or aim at, and in those of part II, in a little more general way, some of the issues involved in applying general ethical principles or concepts to determine whether or not one is performing in a morally upright way some specific social roles. In all of them a certain way of looking at the nature or function of applied ethics has been presupposed or left lurking in the background. It is time now to bring it to the forefront. This will be done in this chapter.

The primary purpose of a moral principle is to provide guidance in living a morally desirable life. This it can do only if it is empirically, and not only logically, possible to act in accordance with it. That is, it must be possible to apply, or implement, accordance with it. That is, it must be possible to apply, or implement, it in the world we live in. That would be the case only if (a) the world we live in is such that it does not, or can be transformed into one which would not, make its application impossible, (b) human nature is such that human beings acknowledge, or can be persuaded by the use of rational means to acknowledge, that it is a valid moral principle, (c) when they acknowledge it, they have the inclination which is, or can be made, again, by the use of rational means, strong enough, to motivate them to act in accordance with it, and (d) the concept, or concepts, involved in the structure of the principle are instantiable, i.e., they are such that generally it is not impossible to apply them to concrete cases. We assume that the conditions (a) to (d) are satisfied when we do applied ethics. Normally they are satisfied because, in most cases, we have no difficulty in applying a principle in a concrete situation. But sometimes we do find it difficult to apply it: We find it difficult to decide what is the best thing to do, or after deciding, difficult or impossible to do it. In such cases we have to be satisfied with doing what is good enough, or right enough, in that situation, though not definitely the best, or absolutely the right, thing to do. This means that in such a situation we do not completely follow the principle. What we actually do can be said to be a case of toning down, making an exception to, even violating, the principle concerned. And all this we do for a moral reason. That is, we violate the principle in a morally justified way: Since we cannot do the best, we have to be contented with having done what is good enough, and we have to because the world is what it is.

It is necessary, therefore, to discuss how ethics is related to the world. I shall do it by elaborating, in my own way, a remark made by Wittgenstein. The direction in which the elaboration takes us, or in which I make it go, may not be the direction in which Wittgenstein would like it to go. But that does not matter for the purpose of this essay.

"Ethics does not treat of the world", says Wittgenstein, Ethics must be a condition of the world, like logic".[1] Logic must be a condition of the world, as I take him to mean, in the sense that it determines what the world may or may not contain: the world can contain only that which is logically possible and cannot contain anything which is not. This does not mean that it contains, or must contain, all that is logically possible. It means that any *X* it contains, or may contain, must be logically possible.

But no sense can be given to the corresponding terms 'ethically possible' and 'ethically impossible'. Ethical principles do not determine the possibility or impossibility of anything they are relevant or applicable to; rather, they determine its desirability or undesirability. Of course, they are not relevant to anything and

1. *Notebooks*, 1914-16, p. 77e.

everything, but only to certain types of things, like individuals, their groups, their actions, motives, intentions, attitudes, plans and policies, projects and projections, etc. We can then speak of ethically desirable and undesirable things, that is, things which are in accordance with, or violative of, ethical principles. But we cannot say that ethics must be a condition of the world in the sense that the world must have only ethically desirable things. To say that would be flying in the face of facts because the world does contain at least a few ethical evils, that is, ethically undersirable things. However, we definitely can say that the world should contain ethically desirable things. It is (almost) a logical truth that a desirable world must contain ethically desirable things. Negatively speaking, if a world does not contain any ethically desriable thing, or contains lesser number of ethically desirable than ethically undesirable things, it would not be a desirable world, or would at the most be only a marginally desirable world.

To make ethical desirability a condition of the desirability of a world means that even if it is desirable in other, say, political, economic, etc., but not in ethical, respects, it would not be a desirable world. Ethical goodness is foundational to all other kinds of goodnesses in the sense that its presence in any one of them heightens the latter's natural or distinctive value, and its absence in the latter, or the latter's having been polluted with some ethical evil, does the contrary. No non-ethical goodness can sustain itself, or its dignity, unless it is accompanied, or fortified, with some kind of ethical goodness. A necessary component of our ethical concern is a concern, or care, for the welfare of others. In a world, whose inhabitants completely lack this concern, any non-ethical goodness, like economic, political, etc., it may have, if it can have any, would have only an anaemic existence.

The things which a world may contain can be classified into the following types: things which it ought to have, things which it ought not to have, things which it may or may not have, and things whose absence in it would not make it ethically poorer but whose presence in it would add some lustre to its ethical value. We can call the above four types of things obligatory, forbidden, permissible, and recommended. In an ideal ethical world the number of the forbiddens would be nil but all the other three types it can very well accommodate. In any actual world, all the four types of things exist. The normal way to improve its ethical quality is to minimise the number of forbiddens and increase that of the obligatory and the recommended. The permissibles are ethically indifferent, and therefore their status, that is, any plan or policy about encouraging or discouraging the existence of some one or ones of them, is determined, in any society by some other, non-ethical, considerations. For example, which direction a house should face is generally determined by considerations which may be climatic, spatial, situational, economic, etc., and seldom by any ethical consideration.

It is empirically possible for an actual world to have all of the four types of things, and it is a matter of fact that our world contains all of them. Here the analogy with logic breaks. No possible (therefore, actual) world can have what logic forbids or disallows, that is, what is logically impossible, and no world can miss or avoid to have what is logically obligatory for it to have, that is, what is logically necessary. Corresponding to the ethically permissible, we have the logically possible which may or may not be empirically possible. Nothing in logic corresponds to the ethically recommended. Logic allows, disallows, or requires, but does not do any of these things in a more or less manner. Therefore, there is no place in logic for anything which may be called the logically recommended, that is, something more logically possible than the merely logically possible and less logically required than the logically necessary. The concepts of logical possibility, impossibility and necessity do not admit of degrees. In the ethical context, on the contrary, we have the concept of being recommended which applies to a thing of which we cannot say that the desirable world ought to have, but only that it would be a good thing if it has it. Its importance becomes clearer if we contrast it with the permissible, the ethically neutral. It does not matter to the desirability of a world whether or not it has it, but it does matter to it if it has what it is recommended to have. Having it carries more credit than having the permissible, less credit than having the obligatory, and not having it carries no discredit, and definitely less discredit than not having the obligatory.

From granting to ethics the status of being a necesary condition of the desirable world, two very important lessons follow: One about the relation of ethical theory to the desirable world, which I would call the built-in applicability of the former to the latter, and the other about the relation of the ethically desirable to other kinds of desirables, which I would call the primacy of the ethical.

An ethical theory primarily aims at telling us what is ethically desirable and thereby what is ethically forbidden, permissible, or recommendable. If something is neither ethically desirable nor undesirable, neither obligatory nor forbidden, it is permissible. The connection of ethical theory with the desirable world, therefore, must be very close. It must be true of the latter, not in the sense of being accurately descriptive of it, because it 'does not treat of the world', but in the normative sense; it should tell us what is involved in being ethically desirable, or what makes a thing ethically desirable and distinguishes it from the undesirable, the permissible, and the recommended. Since ethical desirability is the condition of a desirable world, it occupies the place of primacy in the sense that any world, to be desirable in any way whatsoever, must first be ethically desirable. That is, to be desirable economically, politically, etc., it must first be ethically desirable: If something is not ethically desirable, it is not desirable economically, politically, etc. The converse of it is obviously not true because no other kind of desirability, economic, political, etc., can be said to be a condition of ethical desirability.

Some professional philosophers as well as non-philosophers complain (i) that present-day ethical theorising has become very technical and sophisticated and (ii) therefore cut off from the practical affairs of life, meaning thereby that it has become inapplicable to real life situations.

The first part of the complaint is true but there is no reason at all to grieve over it. Becoming technical and sophisticated is a sign of advancement and growth. Even a folk song to be sung well has to be sung in a technical and sophisticated manner.

The second part of the complaint is invalid because the technical sophistication of a theory does not make it inapplicable if it is not otherwise inapplicable. A general understanding of the broad aspects of an ethical theory is enough for applying it in normal situations. Only in a tricky situation one needs to take into account its technical, sophisticated, precisified, version. And, there may occur a problem in the case of which even an acknowledged possessor of ethical knowledge may fail to see how the relevant theory or theories are to be applied to yield a satisfactory solution. This would not necessarily imply that the theory or theories concerned are inapplicable. Rather, it may simply imply that the problem is unusually complicated and human intelligence finite on account of which the application of ethical knowledge has become so difficult. When Draupadī asks Bhīṣma to tell her whether *dharma* allows Yudhiṣṭhira, even after his having lost his freedom and therefore his agency, to have the moral right to put her, who is not a thing but his wife, on the stakes, his saying that, because the meaning of *dharma* is extremely subtle and deep, he does not know how to answer her question, very well illustrates this truth.[2]

But we are not always in a Bhīṣma-like situation. In the majority of cases we know how to apply the available ethical knowledge, or which part of it to apply. We do apply it and solve our ethical problems, which may sometimes require immediate action, and sometimes only taking a decision to act in a certain manner at some appropriate time in the immediate, or not too immediate, future. Solving an ethical problem either way involves applying an ethical principle or a point of view, to the situation concerned. More often than not the application takes place in a smooth, effortless, manner. Sometimes it is so smooth that we feel no pressure at all on our moral nerves.

An ethical theory has some sort of a built-in applicability. That it has to have it is not an ethical but a logical requirement. It is a requirement for its being an ethical theory. An ethical theory is one about what is worth doing, achieving, or cultivating; that is, about what sorts of actions we should do, what sorts of experiences or things we should try to have, and what sorts of character traits we should have or cultivate. It tells us in a systematic conceptually organised way what could be a moral duty, a value, or a virtue, which in fact, amounts to telling us what sort of life would be a good life from the moral point of view, a life we should live. It can be applied in more than one way, or on more than one level. I shall

2. *The Mahābhārata*, Vol. I, Dyūta Parva, (Gita Press), p. 898.

mention here only three such ways or levels: judgemental, decisional and persuasional. Take, for example, the consequentialist theory that an action is right if the majority of its consequences are more likely to be useful than harmful to personal and social well-being. We apply it in the judgemental way when we judge an action of an individual, or of a group, say, a political party or a university's syndicate, right or wrong on the basis of its actual or probable consequences. A theory is applied in the decisional way when an individual uses it to decide what he should do in a concrete situation. This he does when he is not sure which way he should go, and then seeks to take help from the ethical theory or theories he is acquainted with, or has already accepted.

The use or application of a theory, as I have said, is not always made in a conscious, effortful, manner. One does that only when the alternative he should choose is not obvious, or when he finds more than one course of action claiming execution. Almost every normal individual possesses some ethical knowledge, partly inherited from his cultural heritage and partly acquired through his own reflection on certain situations he had been directly or indirectly involved in. This ethical knowledge stands by him in most of the cases in which he has to take a moral decision. Only occasionally does he need to make an effort to apply an ethical theory (or principle), or to explore which ethical theory can be relevantly applied, to the then situation. He may then even have to decide with how much rigour or stringency the relevant theory is to be applied in order to have a fit between the situation and the theory, without either sacrificing the spirit of the latter or ignoring the distinctive demands made by the former.

It does not mean, however, that one would always abide by the theory or principle he considers relevant to his decision-making. A decision to act, or one which is acted upon, can be taken on more than one ground, and not only on a moral ground. The application of an ethical theory would give him only a moral ground for doing, or forbear doing, something, which may or may not be sufficient to motivate him to do, or avoid doing, the action concerned. Some other motive or motives may overshadow the moral consideration. But this does not mean that the theory concerned has not been applied or is inapplicable. The fact of the matter is that it has been applied but not acted upon in spite of its having clearly shown what the agent should have done. After considering whether or not he should get a certain booth captured, a candidate may find it morally impermissible on account of its likely consequences, but he may still go ahead with his plan of capturing it if his moral will or determination is weak, or is overpowered by his strong desire to win the election by hook or by crook.

A theory is used in the persuasional way when it is used by an individual, who is himself convinced of its viability, to convince another individual (or a group of individuals) to accept it and make his (its) behaviour conform to it wherever it is relevant. Here again it is not necessary that he succeeds in convincing his subject, or his subject acts accordingly even though he has become convinced of the merits of the theory. Jai Prakash Narayan was himself convinced of the theory that the electorate, which elects a certain individual to represent it on a public body, has the moral right to call him back, to de-elect him, even before his term has expired, if it finds that he has conspicuously failed in promoting the legitimate interests of the electorate which was his moral duty. He became a hyper-active moralist, in a laudatory sense, because, instead of limiting his moral conviction only to himself, he started a moral movement to convince the then Indian society of the moral necessity of de-electing some elected representatives: His was a moral move to change the then political and legal or constitutional ethos of Indian electoral practices or conventions, which was misconstrued as a political movement for destabilising the social or political order.

The three ways of being applicable are not completely independent of, or unrelated to, each other. The judgemental and decisional uses are almost identical, or very much the same. To judge that something should be done, as per the ethical theory one accepts, is to have a very good, or the best, reason for deciding to do it, or for doing it, if the judger is also the agent groping for the right decision. Similarly, and rather more obviously, to decide what to do, or not to do, in the light of the theory, is to judge that the theory approves, or disapproves, of doing it. The third one is also not unrelated to them. To try to persuade someone to *X* on the ground that *X*-ing is the moral thing he should do would be pointless, both logically and ethically, if their persuader himself does not judge it to be the moral thing, and is not prepared to do it though it is also his moral duty as much as it is of the person or persons he is trying to persuade. Such a move would signify the persuader's ethical hypocrisy as well as metaethical insensitivity to the logic of the ethical concepts involved in the game. Being aware of all this, though, I have mentioned them as three ways only to make the modes of an ethical theory's applicability clearer.

To apply a theory, or a principle, to a given situation is, in effect, to apply a concept, and every theory has a concept, or a set of concepts, which may be called its root concept or concepts. For example, the root concept of consequentialism is the concept of utility, or well-being, in terms of which it explicates other concepts. When, on consequentialist grounds, one judges that *X*-ing is right, or decides to *X* as the right thing to do, he applies the consequentialist notion of utility to *X*-ing. This for him is the correct notion of rightness because he has accepted consequentialism. To try to persuade someone to *X* on a moral ground is always to apply a moral concept to *X*-ing. It is obvious then that a theory can be applied if and only if it tells us clearly what are the conditions which *X*-ing should satisfy in order that its root concept, or concepts, can be applied to it.

Bhīṣma expresses his inability to answer Draupadī's question, already referred to, on the ground of *dharma*'s meaning being too subtle, and is not prepared even to openly condemn Duḥśāsana's attempt to derobe her. This inability of his can be interpreted to mean that the then theory of *dharma* does not, according to him, clearly specify the conditions whose satisfaction by an action would make it congruent with *dharma* (*dharmānukūla*). On the other hand, for Vidura and Draupadī it does and therefore makes amply clear that an action like Duḥśāsana's to derobe a woman like Draupadī is against *dharma*.

A theory would also become inapplicable if, though the criterion given by it is clear and precise, it is not possible to decide whether or not *X*-ing satisfies it. This seems to be the case with the divine command theory of, say, rightness. According to it one ought to *X* if and only if god has asked or commanded him to *X*. The notion of God's command is quite clear, or at least tolerably clear, but it seems impossible to know whether or not God has commanded one to *X*. When confronted with this difficulty, theological ethicists, by and large, appeal to some scripture or scriptures which, they claim, have been revealed by god. Apart from the problems of deciphering what exactly is the purport of a scriptural injunction, of two injunctions incongruous with each other, or of an injunction seemingly immoral, to say that one should always consult some age-old scripture to ascertain what he should do when he has to make a decision concerning a matter to which scriptural consultation is relevant, has a derogatory implication for god himself, namely, that god stopped thinking after revealing his commands in the scripture(s).

There is also another factor which makes an ethical theory inapplicable, unattractive, or forbidding. An ethical theory may be formulated, and generally it is, by a highly gifted individual, a versatile thinker, a savant, or a man of extraordinarily noble and elevated character. But it is meant for normal people who have normal abilities to do normal things but are also liable to commit some immoralities. Therefore, if a moral theory keeps moral norms so high that they become unreachable for the common man, prescribes principles he cannot emulate, or recommends actions he cannot perform, it is bound to be dissuasive. The common man may not dare to try to follow it, or apply it, to solve his moral problems. Moral norms, principles, criteria of rightness, etc., do not have to be so easy and soft that no effort is ever needed to live up to them. But living up to them must be possible not only in the logical but also in the empirical sense. That is, the human nature being what it is and the human world being what it is, it must be possible for a normal human being to desire living a good moral life and to actually live it, may be with more or less of his own trying, or procuring direct or indirect assistance from education, social surrounding, cultural heritage, etc.

In brief, what an ethical theory presents as the desirable in the ethical sense, as the desireworthy, must also be desire-able, that is, capable of being desired in the psychological sense. If it can be desired only by a set of extraordinarily gifted individuals, it can be used only by them in leading a good moral life. It would not then do what an ethical theory should. Ethical guidance, which it aims at giving, is needed more by ordinary than by extraordinary people. It was the realisation of this fact which inspired Buddha to present an ethical code he called *madhya mārga* (middle path). He realised that there was no point in laying out a road on which only the extremely sturdy could walk.

The human world and human nature are extremely complex and non-static. They keep raising, and therefore have to face, newer and newer ethical problems. These problems can be looked at in more than one way, and that is why different moral philosophers, looking at them from different points of view, have offered a number of theories and principles. But the theories and principles are not so different, or incongruous, as to make it impossible to decide which one to apply in which situation. Sometimes it may be difficult to make a choice of the relevant principle, but the demands of life almost always show the way if one has the will. On the theoretical level it may not be possible to say with full confidence which theory is the best, or which principle the most comprehensive. But in practical life the situation is not so bad. The situation one is in quite often forces, which is also a way to help, him to select a principle of action.

That an ethical consideration has the primacy, or an overriding authority, is clear from the fact that no non-moral consideration can take away, or curtail, for example, the moral rightness of an action, if the latter is morally right. On the other hand, a contrary moral consideration can cancel, or very greatly reduce, the non-moral rightness of an action, that is, a rightness grounded in some non-moral consideration.

The moral rightness of an action can be a very good ground, or, the best ground, for attributing to it some other kind of rightness, say, political rightness. But the *vice versa* is not, or need not be, true. All this is obvious from the common-sense fact that we consider it quite in order to call, for example, an action politically right, or prudentially right, because of its being morally right, but not the *vice versa*. This is true even of actions considered to be right on some religious consideration. It may be said that no action can, or should, be said to be right, from the religious point of view, if it is morally wrong. In fact, one of the methods quite frequently adopted by religious reformers to purify or improve the functioning of a religion is to suggest dropping or modifying those of its prescriptions or proscriptions which they consider morally wrong, unjustified, or insignificant.

But despite its overridingness, a moral principle is itself sometimes superseded, or rather over-powered, and in more than one way. This should not make on raise his eyebrows because to say that it is overriding is only to say that it has the authority, or moral right, to supersede a non-moral principle, and not that it has the power to do that. Some of the ways in which, or occasions on which, such a thing may happen are as follows:

(a) A particular moral principle, for example, that of truth-telling may be overridden by another one which is more comprehensive, or of higher authority, than the former. It has been shown in chapters 1 and 2 that sometimes it is preferable to tell a lie to telling the truth, for example when the life of an innocent person, is likely to be saved by telling the lie and endangered by telling the truth. When the chances of a moral principle's conflicting with another are likely to occur frequently we modify or tone down the one which we consider to be of a lower authority than the other. It is for some such reason, i.e., on account of valuing abstinence from harming an innocent person more than truth-telling that classical Indian thinkers prescribe that the truth be told, the pleasant truth be told, but not the unpleasant truth, nor even the pleasant untruth;[3] and not that 'truth ought to be always told'.

When one tells an untruth to save an innocent man's life, he would not be considered guilty of violating the spirit of the principle of truth-telling, because saving an innocent man's life would be considered a good moral ground for telling the untruth, or, a morally justified way of violating the moral principle of truth-telling. On the other hand, in such a situation, if he tells the truth and thereby helps the killer in killing the innocent man, we would say some such things as 'He followed the principle blindly', 'he is (in a bad sense) a moral fanatic', etc. What actually happens when we make a genuine exception is that we do not make an exception to the morality of the principle but to the scope of its application. This we

3. *The Manusmṛti*, 138, (Vaidika Dharmasastra Prakasana Samstha, Delhi) p. 65.

do on the ground that granting to it unlimited scope may sometimes sanction a move which is obviously immoral. But when an exception to a principle is made on a non-moral ground, for example, prudential, political, religious, etc., it would hurt the morality of the principle.

(b) There is another type of case in which there is no doubt in the agent's mind about the relevance or applicability of a moral principle, but still he does not put it into practice because of the weakness of his (moral) will. He knows very well what he ought to do, but does not do it, or does something else which he knows he ought not to. He may do the immorality in a huff, or because he is so overpowered by the desire to do it that he is not able to pay adequate attention to the immorality of what he is doing. To put it metaphorically, he is not able to smell the stink the immorality of the act emits. Or, he may not be in a huff, or overpowered by a contrary desire, and may even try to think out whether or not he should do the immorality. He does the immorality because the motivating power of the desire to do it is stronger than that of his moral will. It is this kind of immorality which Yudhiṣṭhira commits by telling the celebrated untruth about Aśvatthāmā's having been killed. He knows that he ought not to tell it, still he tells it on Kṛṣṇa's persuasion.

The reasoning which Kṛṣṇa offers to show that in the present situation it is morally justified to violate the general moral principle of truth-telling amounts to giving the following moral argument to Yudhiṣṭhira:

> (1) (a) You certainly want to win the battle and (b) your wanting to win it is morally right as (c) it is a righteous battle. (2) You can win only if Droṇa ceases to fight. (3) He will only if he is killed or himself decides to stop fighting. (4) He cannot be killed by anyone on your side. (5) He will himself decide to stop fighting only if he is made to believe that Aśvatthāmā, his son, has been killed. (6) He will believe that only if you announce that Aśvatthāmā has been killed. (7) Anouncing it is surely telling an untruth. But (8) telling an untruth to win a righteous battle is morally justified. (9) It is morally right to do what is morally justified. (10) Therefore, it is morally right for you

to tell the untruth that Aśvatthāmā has been killed.

This argument is formally valid. Therefore Yudhiṣṭhira can reject it only by rejecting any one of its premises. He cannot reject (1) (a), (2), (3), (4), (5), (6) and (7) because they are true factual statements, (1) (c), which is a moral judgement, because he himself has been holding it since he started preparing for the battle, (1) (b) because it follows from (1) (c), and (9) because it is a deontic truth. He can reject only (8) which is a moral judgement morally sanctioning the violation of the moral principle of truth-telling, but he does not, which may be due to (a) his accepting it as true, or to (b) the influence of Kṛṣṇa on him, or to (c) his strong desire to win and weak moral will. The context of the argument, in the *Mahābhārata* suggests that he does not because of (b) and (c). It is the only untruth Yudhiṣṭhira has told in his life and that too because of the persuasion, or pressure, of Kṛṣṇa, a hyper-commital, hyper-activist, Kṛṣṇa (*kṛṣṇavākya pracoditaḥ — Māhābhārata*, Vol IV, 3692:54).

An important feature of an immorality done by a morally weak-willed person is that the latter knows, or at least believes, that he has done something wrong. He may even repent a little later, or even in the very process of doing the wrong thing. And, when some suffering, or punishment, is inflicted on him on account of it, instead of grudging the infliction, he may feel relieved, or having atoned, because he would think that he deserved it. All this is true not only of a Yudhiṣṭhira but of a good number of ordinary mortals as well.

An immorality done by a weak-willed, akratic agent is no doubt an immorality, and examples of it, involving minor as well as major lapses, can be very easily located in every society. But they need not make us feel pessimistic. The agent's awareness or acknowledgement that he has failed to act according to his own moral principle, his feeling of self-repentence, may be used, along with some other devices, to strengthen his moral will and thereby to minimise immoralities attributable to weak will. A very common way to motivate a man to stop committing an immorality he is prone to, adopted by moral reformers, even parents when dealing with a wayward child, is to generate in him a feeling of shame for it, or to intensify the feeling if it is already there though in a feeble form.

(c) There is a third kind of infringement of a moral principle which the agent commits neither in a huff, nor in a state of mind in which his moral will has lost completely, or almost completely, its power to determine the nature of his actions. The agent commits it with full self-control, with a will fully operative. He may even commit the infringement in accordance with a well-thought-out plan for what he has done. This kind of immorality can be described more accurately as an expression of a strong immoral will than as one of a weak moral will. Its agent does not feel in any way ashamed of having done it, and may even feel proud of the prowess in doing it.

An immorality of this type is not the result of the agent's failing to apply, or misapplying, a moral principle, nor of his inability to apply one because of his being confronted with a moral conflict or dilemma. It is the result of his having bad, perverted, moral principles. The principles which well-meaning citizens of his society cherish he does not cherish, and the ones he cherishes are uncherishable, or unmaintainable. A perverted moral principle can be shown to be perverted by an argument and one may thereby hope to give a good reason to the holder of the former to stop acting in accordance with it and committing the immorality resulting therefrom. But this can be done only if there is at least some point of moral agreement between him and the latter. Moral argumentation works successfully only when both the sides have a common stock of principles, however small the latter's number may be, and not when they do not. It is to handle such cases that we have the machinery of the legal enforcement of morals. If a moral principle is converted into a juridical law, then it can be enforced on an offender of it, no matter whether or not he accepts it as a law. But if legal machinery itself becomes indolent, or corrupt, the situation becomes extremely frustrating for morally or legally sensitive citizens. It is not impossible then that they resort to the use of violence to stop immoralities. The latter may beget further violence. The result may then be complete social and moral chaos. That chaos leads to construction, or re-construction, may be a soothing belief, but the risk involved is too great to justify frequent use of violence.

The view that a moral consideration has built into it an overriding authority over any non-moral consideration can be held as a metaethical and also as an ethical position. One may assert it on the basis of a logical analysis of a moral judgement, or of some specific moral concepts, such as those of moral obligation, moral rightness, moral reason for doing something, being morally commendable or preferable, etc. But equally cogently he can offer it as a substantive ethical thesis. For example, he may say that the human nature and the human world being what they are, human well-being, or a desirable and meaningful existence for all, or at least for the majority of, human beings can be ensured only if moral considerations are considered as having the authority to override all other considerations. The thesis of overridingness simply means, as already explained, that if any time there is a conflict between a moral and a non-moral consideration, the former has the authority to override, or supersede, the latter.

There is something in the very logic of the word 'moral' that to have a moral reason for doing something is to have a conclusive, sufficient, reason for doing it, and this is not the case with other types of reasons. After admitting that there is a moral reason for *X*-ing one cannot ask for another reason for doing it, though even after admitting that there is some other kind of reason, say, prudential, political or religious, for it, he very well can. With a moral reason against *X*-ing and a non-moral reason for *X*-ing, if one chooses to *X*, he may be accused by the metaethicist of logical stupidity, meaning thereby that he is logically too dull to understand what is involved in the concept of moral reason, or too irrational to forbear doing that against doing which there exists a conclusive reason. The ethicist may, on the other hand, accuse him of moral stupidity which would mean that he is morally too insensitive to feel the pull of a moral reason, or too wicked to avoid doing what is morally wrong.

To accept the overriding thesis as a guiding principle of one's life is to become committed to lead a moral life. And if it becomes an operative principle in the life of a society, it would not only ensure social harmony and prosperity, but will work as an Occam's razor to cut off some socially irksome, or apparently insoluble, problems. For example, the best way to soften the rough edges of religious fundamentalism which erode social cohesiveness and peace, is as shown in chapter 6, to convince the fundamentalist that some of his doctrines go against moral common sense: Since it is morally right to treat men and women as equal, it is wrong to debar women from studying the Vedas, even if the Vedas say so; since all women, irrespective of their religious affiliation, are equal, it is morally wrong to debar some from some of their rights because they belong to this or that religion. Similarly, one can tell the political fundamentalist: Since it is morally wrong to prefer a less meritorious person to a more meritorious one, it is wrong to do that even if the two belong to two different castes or religions; when there is a moral reason to treat *A* and *B* alike, they ought to treated alike even if there is a political reason to treat them differently.

Even a metaethical view can have some practical application. This is true even of some very technical ones. For example, when a metaethicist says that no set of factual assertions can entail a moral judgement, even, though factual assertions are relevant to its acceptance or rejection, the obvious lesson is: Do not expect to give (or get) a rock-bottom argument to justify a moral judgement on the basis of a set consisting only of factual assertions. In the same way, from the view that when a person judges that something is morally right it only means that he likes it, one can draw the lesson: Be prepared, if you hold this view, to admit that the same move may be both morally right and morally wrong (because you may like and I may dislike it).

The above are, one may say, though connected with practice, mainly logical applications of some metaethical views. It may be true, but it cannot be an objection to what I have been trying to show. Moreover a metaethical view can also be used in a more earthly, substantive, manner to help one out of an agonising situation.

Suppose *B* unncessarily keeps rebuking and humiliating his neighbour *A*. *A* then decides to become completely indifferent to *B*, thinking there is no way to have any friendly relation with him. But on the New Year's Day he picks up courage, goes to his house and wishes him a happy new year. Instead of being softened, *B* again rebukes him. Now, instead of reacting to him, *A* starts blaming himself for having wished him, knowing fully well the kind of person he is. He blames himself for having shown weakness of the will by acting against his own best judgement that it is impossible to befriend *B*, against his own determination to be completely indifferent to him, etc., etc. He thus suffers intensely from a feeling of self-repentence, a feeling of guilt for having himself been responsible for his own humiliation. At this point he recollects the metaethical distinction between obligatory and recommended or supererogatory actions, and realises that what he has done is a supererogatory action for which he deserves moral merit, or admiration. He argues with himself as follows:

> I have gone out of the way to wish a happy new year to a man who hates me, I have responded to hatred by love and thereby have shown greatness. Therefore, if I have shown weakness of the will, I have shown it in having done something good and great which should make me feel elevated and happy, and not guilty and repentent.

He thus backs himself up and becomes his normal self, and he does all this by making use of a metaethical distinction.

It is true, however, that when philosophers speak of applying an ethical theory, they generally have in mind a normative ethical theory. That is why 'applied ethics' has become (almost) synonymous with 'applied normative ethics'. Mainly to correct this imbalance I have given examples of applying some metaethical ideas.

Applying an ethical, or a metaethical, theory is a voluntary action. Like any voluntary action it can be done with any sort of motive, ethical or unethical. To illustrate what I mean let me turn to the example of the two neighbours, *A* and *B*, already given.

Suppose *A* asks *C* if he should go to *B*'s house to wish him a happy new year. *C*, who knows the background very well, may do either one of the following:

(a) Himself believing in the ethical principle 'Love thy neighbour as thyself' and intending that *A* and *B* should also follow it, he may advise *A* to go to *B* and wish him a happy new year, his motivation being to get started the process of establishing the relation of good neighbourliness between the two. His motivation would then be ethical and, therefore, his application of the ethical principle, in his advice to *A*, would also be an ethical application of it.

(b) Suppose *A* returns rebuked and starts blaming himself for having gone to *B* and blaming *C* for having advised him to do so. *C* then may tell *A* that he has done nothing wrong, but something noble by returning love for hatred, by doing something supererogatory. Therefore, neither is he blameable for having wished him a happy new year, nor is *C* for having given him the advice. *C* would now be using the metaethical notion of a supererogatory, or ethically recommendable, action, with an ethical motivation.

(c) But *C* could have advised *A*, with an unethical motive, to do what he did, for example, with the motive of getting him humiliated by *B* and thereby arousing in him intense hatred, which was so far non-existent, for B, hoping that then each one would try to physically assault the other. The way Vālmīki depicts Kaikeyī's pressurising Daśaratha to keep his blanket promise of fulfilling two of her wishes, whatever they may be, gives a good ground to the reader to assume that she uses the principle of promise-keeping, a venerated one of classical Indian ethics and of Raghukula (Daśaratha's ancestors), with blatantly unethical motives of getting her son, who was not the rightful claimant to the throne, enthroned, and getting her step son, Rāma, who was, exiled. Some of the Purāṇas depict Yudhiṣṭhira — and this can be supported by reading in between the lines of the *Mahābhārata*'s account — as having used the ethical principle 'A mother's instruction ought to be obeyed by her children' unethically in getting Draupadī wedded to all the five brothers including himself.

(d) *C* may as well use the metaethical notion of the supererogatory to dissuade *A* from going to *B* with the unethical motive of keeping alive the existing hostility between *A* and *B*. He may tell *A* that his wishing *B* a happy new year would certainly be a good gesture. But it would be a supererogatory action, an action he is not obligated, or morally required, to do to a man so hostile to him. He would not, therefore, be doing anything wrong in not wishing him. And, why to do something morally not required, but only recommended, to a person like *B*?

Our comprehension of the act of applying an ethical principle, whether with an ethical or unethical motive, would definitely become richer if it is imbued with a proper understanding of at least some of the important levels on which one's commitment to the ethical principle or principles he applies, or is required to apply, to a certain case, could be operative. Whenever he sincerely holds an ethical principle, he has a sense of commitment to uphold the dignity of the principle in whichever way he thinks appropriate. His complete lack of commitment to the principle, or principles, he says he holds, would make him a hypocrite.

Sense of commitment admits of levels or degress. One who has no ethical principle at all, and therefore no sense of commitment to any, would be the hypothetical, completely amoral, person. I call him a hypothetical being because I do not think it is empirically possible for any human being to be completely amoral, that is, completely indifferent to all moral principles he is aware of. The hypocrite is not without any moral principle. His is the interesting case of a person whose real principles are different from those which he publicly declares to be his.

Assuming that every normal person has some ethical principle or principles and that to have one is to have a sense of commitment to it, I will discuss what seem to me the three important levels on which the latter may be operative. I shall call them (a) sub-committal, (b) committal and (c) hyper-committal.

(a) The sub-committal person has some principles and is committed to them like any other normal person. But in certain cases, for some reason or reasons, private or public, he suspends, subdues, or makes inoperative, his sense of commitment to some of them. His sub-committal attitude does not, however, make him morally neutral.

Moral neutrality is by and large an untenable notion. If to be morally neutral means to be neutral to both morality and immorality, that is, to take a neutral stand between two issues one of which is morally right and the other morally wrong, then it is not to be morally neutral. One cannot be neutral to immorality without

4. *The Mahābhārata*, Vol IV, Droṇabadha Parva, (Gita Press) pp. 3692-3.

becoming immoral. To be neutral, in the natural way, should mean to have no leaning towards either one of the two sides, to be unwilling to approve or disapprove of either one of them. But not to approve of the moral, as well as not to disapprove of the immoral, is to be immoral, and therefore to cease to be (morally) neutral. To be neutral between the moral and the immoral is like keeping one's mouth tight-lipped in a congregation one is attending and is supposed to participate in when a controversy is going on between two persons of whom one is pleading the cause of justice and the other opposing it tooth and nail. The tight-lipped neutral and the open-mouthed champion of injustice are, Manu rightly says, equally contemptible from the moral point of view.[5]

If on the other hand, the morally neutral is said to be one who, of two morally right issues, does not favour either one more, or less, than the other, then he is not morally neutral. He is, in fact, one who approves of both the issues, and therefore is not really neutral, or indifferent, to either one of them. If we still want to call him neutral, we can do that in an attenuated sense, meaning thereby that he does not mind which one of the two issues is acted upon. For example, of the two proposals, one to found a free primary school for the children of the poor citizens of an area and the other to found a charitable hospital for the same people, one may say he is neutral to them, simply to indicate that he equally approves of both of them and not that he is equally indifferent to both them.

One may be neutral to all religions in the sense that he is neither in favour of, nor against, anyone's following, or not following, any one of them, and may himself not follow any one of them. This is so because it is possible to be completely non-religious or areligious, but not to be completely non-moral or amoral.

5. सभा वा न प्रवेष्टव्यं वा समंजसम् ।
अब्रुवन्वि ब्रवन्वाापि नरो भवति किल्विवी ।। १३।।

One should either not attend the congregation, or if he attends, he should speak what is congruent with justice. The silent, as well as the apeaker against justice, deserves to be condemned.

The Manusmṛti, p. 121, (Vaidika Dharmasastra Prakasana Samstha, Delhi). See also the *Mahābhārata*, Vol. I, Dyūta Parva, p. 904, (Gita Press) for a similar remark by Vidura.

The sub-committal individual may suspend his commitment to a moral principle for more than one reason.

(i) For example, he would do it in a morally justified way when he does it because he thinks its application to the present case conflicts with another principle to which also he feels committed. Gautama asks his son Cirākārī to kill his mother because he believes that she is guilty of having committed adultery with Indra. Cirākārī is committed to the principle 'To obey his father's commands is a son's sublime duty.' But he finds it difficult to implement it because its implementation would come into conflict with another principle, 'It is also a son's duty to protect his mother', to which also he is equally committed.[6] He suspends his commitment to the former and keeps thinking how to solve the dilemma. His dilemma is ultimately dissolved by his father who withdraws his order when he realises that his wife is not really to blame because Indra, by appearing before her in the garb of Gautama himself, made her believe that he was her husband. She offered her body to him under the false impression that she was offering it to her husband.

(ii) One may also suspend his commitment to a principle, even though there is no conflict between it and another principle, if he is not sure of the case in hand being the right case for the principle to be applied to. Gautama would have suspended his commitment to the principle 'A woman ought to be beheaded if she commits adultery', had he been unsure of his wife's being a clear case of adulterous beha-

6. पितुराज्ञा परो धर्मः स्वधर्मो मातृरक्षणम् ।
अस्वतन्त्रं च पुत्त्वं किं तु मां नानुपीडयेत् ।। ११।।
स्त्रियं हत्वा मातरं च को हि जातु सुखी भवेत् ।
पितरं चाप्यवज्ञाय कः प्रतिष्ठामवाप्नुयात् ।। १२।।

It is the son's highest duty to obey his father's order and to protect his mother. He is never independent, but always under the control of his parents. Therefore, what should I do to avoid the anguish resulting out of non-performance of duty? Which son can ever be happy after killing a woman, and that too his mother? Who can remain dignified even after flouting his father's order?

The Mahābhārata, Vol. V, Śānti Parva, (Gita Press) ii-12, p. 5107.

viour. As mentioned above, after realising that it is not, he withdraws his order to kill her, repents for having given it, pardons her, and thanks Cirākārī for having taken so much time, as was his wont, in deciding what to do.

(iii) There is also a third way of being sub-committal. I shall call it the strategic way. To reply to a moral question, to suggest a solution to a moral problem, is to apply a moral principle. Its application in the proper way may yield a reply going against the self-interest of the replier, and its misapplication or non-application a reply going against his dignity as a morally respected person. When put in such a situation, if one suspends his commitment to the principle involved, or concerned, and becomes non-committal, saying that he cannot reply this way or that way, or that he does not know the reply, I will call him a strategic sub-committal person.

Bhīṣma's response to Draupadī may be described as strategic. He is a man committed to *dharma*, to leading a *dhārmic* life. Being well-versed in the Dharmaśāstras (sacred literature), he is expected to know what is, and what is not, in accordance with *dharma*. That he knows all this and a lot more he himself owns and demonstrates when, lying down on his death-bed of arrows, he teaches to Yudhiṣṭhira, on his and Kṛṣṇa's request, all kinds of moralities, private, public and political. Kṛṣṇa, who, as per the tradition, never errs, calls him the great knower (*mahāprājña*) and the great repository of *dharma* (*dharmamayonidhiḥ*).[8] It is very unlikely that such a

7. *The Mahābhārata*, pp. 5109-11.

8. संहारश्चैव भूतानां धर्मस्य च फलोदयः ।
विदितस्ते महाप्राज्ञ त्वं हि धर्ममयो निधिः ।। १९ ।।

The Mahābhārata, Vol. V, Chapter 50, p. 4549. (Kṛṣṇa says to Bhīṣma:)

The great savant, because you are the great repository of *dharma*, you know all such things as when are living beings destroyed, what is the result of *dharma*, when does that arise.

See pp. 4548-50 for Kṛṣṇa's high regards for Bhīṣma's erudition, purity of life, and moral wisdom, excelled by no one he knows of. The largest part of volume V is devoted to recording Bhīṣma's replies to various types of *dhārmic* questions asked by Yudhiṣṭhira.

Bhīṣma really found the meaning of *dharma* so subtle or deep that he could not use it to answer Draupadī's question. Therefore, it would not be unfair or incorrect to interpret his expression of inability to give the reply, which is the same thing as the suspension of his commitment to *dharma*, as strategic. This needs some elaboration which I will give right now.

To say that the meaning of *dharma* is too subtle that it is sometimes not clear whether or not something is in accordance with it is to make a metaethical claim. In modern terminology it means that the necessary and sufficient conditions for the application of the concept of *dharma* are not definitively and exhaustively stateable. Therefore, there may be occasions when we cannot categorically say whether or not something is *dhārmic*. But Draupadī's case is not an ordinary, humdrum, or trivial, one: A woman has been put on the stakes as if she were a chattel, and lost, by a husband who has already lost his free agency, and that woman is being derobed in public. If the existing concept of *dharma* is not usable or applicable to this case, if it does not give to an expert applier of it like Bhīṣma, a good moral ground to condemn the act of derobing, it is an unviable, incompetent, concept. What is needed, therefore, is to make it usable by properly analysing and precisifying it. It is such occasions which necessitate the analysis and precisification of concepts. Bhīṣma should have proceeded to do that because he is not only a scholar but also a repository of *dharma*. But he does not do any such thing: He simply uses the metaethical claim about its extraordinary subtlety as a reason for not replying to Draupadī's question whether or not, as per *dharma*, she has been lost by Yudhiṣṭhira to the Kauravas.

One may say, as has been shown earlier, that he uses the metaethical claim as a device, or strategy, to circumvent his responsibility to reply. It is not implausible to call it his strategy because both the affirmative and the negative answers to the question are likely to be embarrassing for him: Suppose he says it is *adhārmic* for Yudhiṣṭhira to have put her on the stakes because he has already lost his freedom, or because a wife is not her husband's chattel or property, or because Yudhiṣṭhira is not the sole owner of her, and therefore the attempt to derobe her is *adhārmic*; or, that the derobing attempt is intrinsically so abominable that in itself it is *adhārmic*, whatever may be Yudhiṣṭhira's own status, or claim on her. He knows he would then anger Duryodhana which he does not obviously want to. On the other hand, he also knows that, if he says that all this is *dhārmic*, he would lose the respect people have for his moral stature. Therefore, he uses the metaethical defect of the concept of *dharma* to justify his silence, which is very much similar to that of Manu's silent man in a court of justice where injustice is being manoeuvred by some vocal members of the court. Vidura minces no words in saying things which justify the appropriateness of this analogy.[9]

Some of the things which Bhīṣma actually says in this regard are really revealing. He not only reminds her of his earlier statement about the hyper-subtlety of the concept of *dharma* and his consequential inability to answer her question, but even tries to pass the buck to Yudhiṣṭhira. He tells her that, being an expert in *dhārmic* matters, Yudhiṣṭhira alone can give the correct answer.[10]

9. यो हि प्रश्नं विब्रूयाद धर्मदर्शी सभागत: ।
अनृते चा फलावाप्तिस्तस्या: सोऽअर्धं समश्नुते ।। ६३।।

The knower of *dharma* who goes to attend a congregation but does not answer the question asked, shares half of the (demeritorious) consequence of telling an untruth.

— *The Mahābhārata*, Vol. I, Sabhā Parva, p. 904, Gita Press.

10. उक्तवानस्मि कल्याणि धर्मस्य परमा गति: ।
लोके न शक्यते ज्ञातुमपि विज्ञैर्महात्मभि: ।। १४।।
न विवेक्तुं च ते प्रश्नमिमं शक्नोमि निश्चयात् ।
सूक्ष्मत्वाद् गहनत्वाच्च कार्यस्यास्य च गौरवात् ।। १६।।
युधिष्ठिरस्तु प्रश्नेऽस्मिन प्रमाणमिति मे मति: ।
अजितां वा जितां वेति स्वयं व्याहर्तुमर्हति ।। २१।।

Blessed Draupadī, I have already told you that the way *dharma* works is very subtle. Even expert saints in the world cannot accurately know it. →

This is an ethical, and not a metaethical, device as is the earlier one, since it is an advice to refer the matter to a moral authority. But it is not as innocent or flawless as it may seem to be. According to the then acceptation the grandnephew (Yudhiṣṭhira) is not a higher moral authority than the granduncle (Bhīṣma), and this is not unknown to the latter. Even history supports it, as is testified by the former's taking, after the war is over, his final moral lessons from the latter. These devices by Bhīṣma must have made morality wail more helplessly than even Draupadī herself. Kṛṣṇa does save Draupadī from being derobed, but not morality. Morality does get derobed, and that is the greatest tragedy, or at least one of the greatest tragedies, of the *Mahābhārata*.

(b) The committal attitude is the normal man's attitude towards his moral ideas, principles, or theories. If he holds a moral principle, for example, the principle of truth-telling, whenever telling the truth is relevant or required, he feels committed to follow or use it in one or more than one of the three modes, judgemental, decisional and persuasional, discussed earlier, as per the demand of the situation he is in. All this he may not, of course, do when he is afflicted with a conflict between this principle and some other principle, or some opposing desire, or with akrasia. When dealing with someone else, the committal person does try to persuade him to follow the principle he holds and considers it appropriate for him to follow. But he goes only up to a certain point, and then leaves the latter to decide according to his own judgement and moral common sense.

A very good example of the committal attitude is Vidura's. Whatever his own moral understanding convinces him to be right or wrong, he tries to abide by it, expresses his judgements fearlessly, frankly, and honestly, and tries to persuade the relevant persons to

→ I cannot give a definite and correct solution of this question of yours because of the nature of *dharma* being extremely subtle and deep and the question of deciding what is and what is not *dhārmic* being extremely important.

In my opinion, Yudhiṣṭhira alone, whose knowledge of *dharma* is perfect, is the most authoritative person to answer this question. He himself should say whether or not you have been lost in the game of dice.

The Mahābhārata, Vol. I, Sabhā Parva, p. 907, Gita press.

act according to the principles he thinks they ought to. This he does even with Duryodhana and Dhr̥tarāṣṭra in whose moral integrity he does not have much faith. He is the only person who openly pleads for immediately stopping Duḥśāsana from trying to derobe Draupadī, as it is, according to him, an immoral act. But he too proceeds only up to the point of pleading, persuading, and arguing, and stops there even when his efforts are not met with success. He complains and cajoles, frets and fumes, but does nothing beyond that.

Vidura represents the ideal type of a normal committal, or moral, person. To say this does not mean or imply that every normal moral person always does, or would do, whatever Vidura does. Vidura is not a strategist like Bhīṣma. What the latter calls the hyper-subtlety of the notion of *dharma* does not bother him, nor does it deter him from unambiguously declaring that the derobing attempt is immoral. It may even he said that the notion of *dharma* is not for him so subtle, as it is for Bhīṣma on his own confession, that it becomes unusable in the present case. That is why he finds no hurdle, conceptual or normative, in calling the act *adhārmic*. He categorically says, addressing all the great men assembled there, that because of their not answering Draupadī's question, who is crying like an unprotected woman, *dharma* itself is being injured here.[11]

(c) The hyper-committal individual is a hyper-active moralist. His commitment to his moral principles, to his way of looking at what is and what is not morally desirable, that is, to his moral perspective, is so great that he is not merely satisfied with trying to convince someone of its worth, and leaving it to him to act according to his own best judgement. His mode of thinking is something like this: I am convinced on irrefutable grounds that any A ought to X in any situation S. Since A is in S, he ought to X. Therefore, I ought to convice him that he ought to X and see that he actually X-es. If I do not try to convince him that he ought to X and see that he does,

11. द्रौपदी प्रश्नमुक्तैवं रोरवीति हत्यनाथवत् ।
न च विब्रूत तं प्रश्नं सभ्या धमोऽन्त पीडत्यते ।। ५९।।

After putting her question to you Draupadī is crying like a woman who has none to support her. But you are not answering it. Therefore, *dharma* suffers in this congregation.

— *The Mahābhārata*, Vol. I, Dyūta Parva, pp. 904-6.

I would be failing in my duty: Since *X*-ing ought to be done by *A* and I know that it ought to be, it is my duty to see that he does what he ought to. If I do not make him *X*, he would be failing in his duty, I in mine, and I would be doubly guilty because I would also, to some extent, be responsible for his failure. On the other hand, if I make him overcome his unwillingness to *X* and make him *X*, he would be doing his duty, I mine, and I would have the additional moral satisfaction or credit of having made, or helped, him perform his duty, of having guided him in leading a moral life.

The hyper-committal moralist does not make a distinction between persuading and pressurising, between what W.D. Falk calls, guiding and goading. He does not see any conceptual gap between 'ought' and 'must'. He finds it not only natural but perfectly in order to glide down from 'ought' to 'must': Since I am convinced that *A* ought to *X*, I ought to see that *A X*-es; since I ought to see that he *X*-es, I must; since *A* ought to *X*, he must.

Hyper-activism in the application of moral norms or principles does not generally succeed. Kṛṣṇa's hyper-activism succeeds with Yudhiṣṭhira, as has been shown in his making the latter tell the untruth, because of the latter's desire to win and Kṛṣṇa's influence on him. But when he tries to make the unwilling Arjuna willing to fight, he has not only to reply to a number of moral objections raised by Arjuna against fighting, but also to show his cosmic form to silence him, as shown in chapter 2. To see that form he starts trembling (*bhayena ca pravyathitam mano me*) and requests Kṛṣṇa to pardon him for his audacity in raising objections to his asking him to fight.[12]

A human being cannot use Kṛṣṇa's method of applying his ethical views to convince any one to do or make him do what he thinks the latter ought to do. The human way of applying ethics consists in making one rationally convinced that a certain thing is morally right and that doing it is not only obligatory bcause of its being what it in itself is, but also because doing it, the ethical, is, on the whole, in the best interest of all concerned, including him. It is

12. *The Gītā*, chapter. XI: 9-16.

See this book, chapter 2, for an examination of Kṛṣṇa's replies to Arjuna's objections.

different from indoctrination because it works by appealing to his rationality, to his rational will which is not different from his moral will, the will to do that for which there exists a good moral reason. This would be the same thing as convincing him of the primacy of the ethical. It cannot be done in the manner of a hyper-committal hyper-activist because hyper-activism quite often arouses resistance from the other side and therefore may become counter-productive. Applied ethics has to be consequentialist in the sense that any method of applying an ethical principle, or norm, is to be judged utilitarianly, i.e., by the results it produces, or is likely to produce. These results must generate, or strengthen, if they are already there, good moral habits of mind in the individuals on whom, or for whose moral education, the exercise of applying ethics has been done, or is being done.

Bibliography of Author's Writings

Books

Karma Causation and Retributive Morality, ICPR, New Delhi, 1989.

Problem of Ends and Means in Private and Public Morality (ed.), IIAS, Shimla, 1989.

Rules of Language, Poona University, Pune, 1989.

Aesthetics, Morality and Jivanmukti: Evaluation of an Indian Perspective, Karnataka University, Dharwad, 1992.

An Outline of Philosophy (Hindi), Shukla Book Depot, Patna, New Edition, 1996.

Dharmakirti's Theory of Inference (Forthcoming).

Articles

"On Wittgenstein's Transcendental Ethics", *Journal of Indian Council of Philosophical Research,* Vol. XII/1-1, 1989.

"Professor Devaraja on the Emergence of Facts", *Indian Philosophical Quarterly*, Vol. XVI/4, 1989.

"A Response to Professor Devaraja's Reply", *Indian Philosophical Quarterly*, Vol. XVII/1, 1990.

"Bounds of Thinking", *Prajña*, Vol. XI, 1990, Utkal University, Bhubaneswar.

"Aurobindo on Reality as Value", *Journal of Indian Council of Philosophical Research*, Vol. IX/1, 1991.

"Ability, Obligation, and Option", *Freedom, Dharma and Rights*, ed. by Grighton Peden and Yeager Hudson, The Edwin Millen Press, Lewiston, 1993.

"Murty's Critique of Revelation: A Pleasure-Tripper's Overview", *The Philosophy of K. Satchidananda Murty*, ed. by S. Bhattacharya, ICPR, New Delhi, 1994.

"The Theory of Purusarthas: A Proforma of Human Values", *Studies on the Purusarthas*, ed. by P.K. Mohapatra, D.S.A. in Philosophy, Utkal University, 1994.

"The Paradox of Obligation", *Journal of Indian Council of Philosophical Research*, Vol. XI/2, 1994.

"Philosophy, Education and the Quality of Life", *Indian Philosophical Quarterly,* Vol. XXI/2, 1994.

"Reactive Attitudes, Rationality and Determinism", *The Philosophy of P.F. Strawson*, ed. by P.K. Sen and R.R. Verma, ICPR, New Delhi, 1994.

"Morality to Override Religion: Working out a Lead from Svami Vivekananda", *Indian Philosophical Quarterly*, Vol. XXII/4, 1995.

"Must Self-Consciousness be Non-Referential?", *Journal of Indian Council of Philosophical Research*, Vol. XV/1, 1997.

"Applying Ethics: Modes, Motives and Levels of Commitment", *Journal of Indian Council of Philosophical Research*, Vol. XIV/2, 1997.

"Philosophical Enquiry and Concepts", (Hindi), *Parāmarśa*, Vol. 19/3, 1998.

"Language, Philosophy of Language and Linguistics", (Hindi), *ibid.*, Vol. 19/4, 1998.

"D.P. Chattopadhyaya's Picture of the Interdisciplinary", *Philosophy of D.P. Chattopadhyaya*, (Centre for Studies in Civilisation, 1998).

"Formal Logic and Autonomy of Ethics" (Forthcoming).

"Man and Man's God: A Timeless Dialogue II" (Forthcoming).

[*Note*: For works published before 1989, see the bibliography included in *Karma Causation and Retributive Morality*.]